Biology
of
Man
in
History

Edited by
Robert Forster
and
Orest Ranum

Translated by
Elborg Forster
and
Patricia M. Ranum

Biology
of Man
in History

Selections from the

Annales
Économies, Sociétés, Civilisations

The Johns Hopkins University Press
Baltimore and London

The Johns Hopkins University Press, Baltimore, Maryland 21218
The Johns Hopkins University Press Ltd., London

Library of Congress Catalog Card Number 74-24382
ISBN 0-8018-1690-4 (clothbound)
ISBN 0-8018-1691-2 (paperbound)

Library of Congress Cataloging in Publication data
will be found on the last printed page of this book.

lw
4-20-81

Contents

Introduction

In the first issue of the *Annales* in 1929 Lucien Febvre denounced isolated research whether pursued by historians or sociologists, anthropologists or economists. The articles of the *Annales* were intended to break down the "high walls" that kept each of the separate disciplines of the social sciences apart like autarchic tariff barriers. The *combat* against isolation is to be won "not by articles about method, not by means of theoretical disquisitions, but by means of examples, by means of achieved results."[1] Under the joint editorship of Lucien Febvre and Marc Bloch the *Annales* became one of the boldest and imaginative journals of historical sociology in the Western world.

The intellectual aims of the *Annales* from their beginning about fifty years ago have been threefold: (1) a comparative and interdisciplinary approach to history that attempts to "mine" the social sciences in order to fashion a "social history" in the widest sense of the term, (2) an effort to embrace the whole of human activity in a given society (*histoire totale*), and (3) a conscious rejection of narrative history and classical biography in favor of problem-oriented history. The editors of the *Annales* never tire of such phrases as "social structure"—a static slice of society from top to bottom—and the "*longue durée*"—the long-run development of one hundred to two hundred years. The "event" is held in disrepute.

Since World War II the *Annales* have increasingly emphasized quantitative history, especially as applied to demography, meteorology, price history, economic growth and income distribution. The number of charts, graphs, tables, and maps in the journal reflects this penchant for quantification as well as an increasing interest in the collection and manipulation of data by use of the computer. Even more recent has been the emphasis on the history of popular attitudes and values (*mentalités*) which has brought the *Annales* even closer to cultural anthropology, biology, psychology, and linguistics without loosening their long-standing

[1]Quoted by F. Braudel in the *Journal of Modern History*, Dec. 1972, p. 462.

ties with human geography, economics, and sociology. Without question, the *Annales* have been a path-breaker in social history (or historical sociology with which it merges), discovering new perspectives and interrelationships (*rapports*) through a very resourceful employment of new "tools" and approaches. Occasionally, to be sure, the imagination and boldness of approach fail to convince, for the *Annalistes*, as Febvre said, must prove their new hypotheses by empiric evidence. Not every *Annaliste* can attain the high standards of scholarship set by Marc Bloch, Lucien Febvre, Fernand Braudel, and more recently by Pierre Goubert and Emmanuel LeRoy Ladurie. Fortunately, a long archival tradition rescues most French scholars from the dangers of airy speculation, and as a group, the *Annalistes* remain, in the words of J. H. Hexter, "the most productive and lively school of historians practicing their art today."[2]

* * *

With this volume The Johns Hopkins University Press inaugurates an annual publication of "Selections from the *Annales*." Each collection of articles is considered by the editors worthy of translation for a wider audience among English-speaking readers and they are arranged thematically. This collection entitled "Biology of Man in History" includes eight articles chosen by the editors as examples of the *Annalistes* at work. "Biology of Man" simply designates such basic physical aspects of the existence of ordinary human beings as sex, hunger, and disease. Taken together, the eight articles reflect the characteristics of the *Annales* outlined above—the interdisciplinary approach, "total history," problem orientation, quantification, and the history of attitudes and values, grounded in the scholarly craftsmanship we have come to expect from the "school."

The eight articles are presented in four categories by subject matter. The first two by Evelyne Patlagean and Jean-Louis Flandrin, on marriage and birth control, are principally studies in changing attitudes. Patlagean demonstrates how cultural imperatives—especially a generalized religious asceticism—shaped a whole society's attitudes toward family limitation in the early Byzantine Empire. Flandrin examines a large sample of penitentials and synodal statutes in the medieval West from the sixth to the sixteenth centuries, arguing that Church theologians slowly came to

---

[2]J. H. Hexter, "Fernand Braudel and the Monde Braudellien . . . ," *The Journal of Modern History*, Dec. 1972, p. 529. For an excellent summary of the purposes of the "*Annales* school," see Emmanuel Le Roy Ladurie, *Le Territoire de l'Historien* (Paris, 1973), pt. 1 and passim. For a harsh and somewhat gratuitous criticism of the *Annales*, see J. H. Plumb in the *New York Times Book Review*, Dec. 31, 1972.

regard birth control as acceptable (or least "sinful") in sexual relations outside of marriage, and that "before the massive introduction of contraception into marriage, the apprenticeship of these measures was learned in 'sin.'"

The second two articles deal with disease. The first, by J.-N. Biraben and J. LeGoff, describes a number of aspects of the Great Justinian Plague of the sixth century: its origins, medical characteristics, incidence, and its temporal and geographical course in fifteen successive waves from about A.D. 540 to 770 from Antioch to Marseille. The authors also suggest some of the political, social, and psychological consequences of this series of plagues, but their main purpose is to explore its medical characteristics and magnitude. Jean-Pierre Peter's article on disease at the end of the eighteenth century uses the survey reports of the Paris *Societé Royale de Médecine* to examine the countless eighteenth-century diseases and to construct a meaningful medical vocabulary. But even more, Peter recreates the "world" of the rural sick, depicting the anguished and groping response of family, community, and country doctor to the ever-present threat of disease, epidemic, and death. In Peter's own words, it is part of a "crucible of incoherent forces, of upside-down logic, an unregulated universe." In addition to the special characteristics we have ascribed to the *Annales*, Peter's article contains a bonus to his readers in a pulsating, evocative prose, reflecting what he calls "a fantastic adventure."

The third group of articles treats diet and famine. Eliyahu Ashtor investigates a wealth of Near Eastern literature, from Syrian physicians' prescriptions to Egyptian cookbooks, from Western travel accounts to Arab chronicles, stretching from the ninth to the fifteenth century. He examines the tastes and eating habits as well as the components of diet by social class, making explicit comparisons with comparable social groups in the contemporary Medieval West. Ashtor is able to evaluate nutritive levels based on Near Eastern workers' wages, demonstrating among other things a major rise in the nutritional standard of living among the laboring classes in the century after the Black Death (1348–49). Emmanuel LeRoy Ladurie focuses more narrowly on the physical effects of food scarcity on female fertility. Using twentieth-century medical reports, particularly from Germany during both world wars, LeRoy Ladurie explains—by projection—the low birth rate that accompanied the famines of the sixteenth and seventeenth centuries, not by psychological shock, lassitude, or artificial birth control, but by the purely biological response of amenorrhoea or temporary female sterility.

The last two articles are really "proposals for research," each advancing a new "tool" to help explore a broader field of historical inquiry. Zbigniew Zabinski constructs an index of the purchasing power

of wage earners by evaluating in silver the minimum nutritional requirements of a workingman in sixteenth-century Europe. Zabinski is thereby
able to measure living standards (in food at least) over time and space in
a much more reliable and meaningful manner than economic historians
have done in the past. The article by Michèle Bordeaux on geographic
hematology is the boldest and most controversial in the collection.
Bordeaux attempts to correlate certain ethnic groups, identifiable by
blood types, with certain practices of customary private law. The author
is extremely cautious in her hypotheses, disclaiming that sero-
anthropology is a "miraculous key" to the origins of legal institutions.
Still, her proposal to join hematology, geography, legal history, and
local folklore is another reminder of the imaginative reach of the *Annales*
school.

R. Forster
O. Ranum
Baltimore, June 1974

Biology
of
Man
in
History

1
Birth Control in the Early Byzantine Empire

Evelyne Patlagean

The demographic decline during late Antiquity has long been an academic truism. The idea originated on the basis of Western or Balkan experiences and above all was colored by the pessimistic conception of the *Untergang*.[1] But beginning with the fourth century this theory leaves too many unexplained or incongruous facts, which for some time now have not been questioned by historians of the West[2] or the East,[3] where the situations, problems, and chronology differ. This essay will deal with the Byzantine Empire, that is to say with the regions surrounded by the sea on the west, the imperial frontier on the east, Thrace on the north, and the desert which connects Egypt to Palestine on the south.

A historical study of population fluctuations between the end of the third and the beginning of the seventh century is obviously impossible, at least when compared with the demographic history that has been obtained from European data after the fourteenth century. Yet the history of the Byzantine transition from Antiquity to the Middle Ages, which occurred during this period, must include a demographic dimension, not

Annales: E.S.C., Nov.–Dec. 1969, pp. 1353–69. Translated by Patricia M. Ranum.
[1] See, for example, *Histoire du Bas-Empire* (Paris, 1959), pp. 2–7, a French translation by Palanque of E. Stein's *Geschichte des spätrömischen Reiches . . .* , 2 vols. (Vienna, 1928–49); and F. Lot, *Le fin du monde antique et les débuts du Moyen Age*, rev. ed. (Paris, 1951), pp. 75–83.
[2] For example, S. Mazzarino, *Aspetti sociali del quarto secolo* (Rome, 1951).
[3] P. Charanis, "Observations on the Demography of the Byzantine Empire," *Proceedings of the Thirteenth International Congress of Byzantine Studies, 1966* (Oxford, 1967), pp. 445–63.

only because the population decline is regularly cited (or, to be more exact, postulated) as a decisive factor in the changed economic and social structure,[4] but also because the relationship between population and society is perhaps clearer when the social organization is relatively simple, as is the social organization we are studying here. The historian who has no statistics and, to tell the truth, none of the normal evidence at his disposal must try to find a different path to a demographic study and must even modify the kinds of questions asked. One of these modifications concerns the study of fertility, that is the relationship between the number of births and the total population.[5] As one might suspect, there are few or no statistics available for births. A total of a few dozen families from the provincial bourgeoisie—completed families, from which we must presume in a majority of cases that no members have been omitted—can be accumulated by searching through literary sources, and especially by deciphering funeral inscriptions, in which, however, the ages are not indicated and from which, in addition, married daughters are almost always omitted. Derisory though they may be, the statistics derived from this evidence are of inestimable value, for they are the only test for the descriptions of behavior with which literary sources abound. But ultimately, in such a situation, literary sources, so necessary for any inquiry into fertility, assume a preponderant position. Such is the case for Byzantine society and other past or present societies without statistics.[6] Therefore we must specify under what conditions and to what extent the history of behavior can serve demographic history.

For two reasons we have chosen to study the various negative attitudes whose common result is the limitation of fertility. First, the importance placed upon these attitudes in literary sources has helped strengthen the doctrine concerning the demographic foundations of the *Untergang*. Second, the voluntary birth control procedures available to Christian Antiquity have recently been examined by J. T. Noonan, Jr., and by Keith Hopkins.[7] Despite the merit of these studies, we must question their perspective, which is arbitrarily restricted and, therefore, historically deceptive. Indeed, the two works share the same point of departure: the projection into the past of a contemporary cultural problem, which in the case of both authors is discussed, explained, and to that extent legitimate.

[4]See A. E. R. Boak, *Manpower Shortage and the Fall of the Roman Empire* (Ann Arbor, Mich., 1955).

[5]See L. Henry, *Manuel de démographie historique* (Geneva-Paris, 1967), p. 78.

[6]See E. Naraghi, *L'étude des populations dans les pays à statistique incomplète* (Paris-The Hague, 1960).

[7]John T. Noonan, Jr., *Contraception, a History of Its Treatment by the Catholic Theologians and Canonists* (Cambridge, Mass., 1966); part of our references to the Church Fathers have been borrowed from Noonan.

Both authors also focus their attention principally upon conception. While the degree of detail is not always equal, each author shows that the medical tradition transmitted from Greece to Rome involved at times not only total confusion between contraceptive and abortive measures, but also frequent recourse to ineffectual procedures, even purely magical ones.[8] They stress that the different forms of birth control were used in illicit and venial relationships, and that the simplicity of infanticide would have recommended it as a method for the common people. Hopkins, who was more curious about social history, observes that every reference to birth control has disappeared from the same medical treatises during the Christian era. He sees in this silence the proof of a hostility not only toward voluntary birth control but toward the enlightened and liberal civilization of the Early Empire, which would have conferred advantages upon women. Noonan, on the other hand, visibly wanted to supply the historical record needed for the contemporary Catholic debate over contraception. He therefore wrote a book which is chiefly devoted to a study of the historical origins of these ideas—a remarkable study, by the way—and which likewise only considers the question of contraception in terms of the procedures, efficacious or not, used to prevent births. His history is one of ecclesiastical decisions and their imperial ratification, rather than one of actual behavior in society. Noonan concludes only that it is difficult to measure the actual spread of voluntary birth control practices. His very approach is indicative of the reticence about birth, conjugal relations, and marriage which prevents the Church from taking special interest in this problem, although it did speak out clearly against abortion, which it likened to murder, and against infanticide.[9] He conjectures that the fourth-century Church would have gone much further in this direction had it not been urgently concerned with setting its teachings clearly apart from those of the dualist heresies, which radically condemned procreation because they judged the created world to be evil and condemnable.

Noonan's and Hopkins' information, which is incomplete on several points, must be organized in a different fashion if it is to assume its correct place in a complete historical perspective. Indeed, under the heading of voluntary birth control, demographic history should include not only measures aimed at preventing conception, but also abortion and

---

[8]K. Hopkins, "Contraception in the Roman Empire," *Comparative Studies in Society and History* 8 (1965–66): 124–51.

[9]We must mention here the useful collection of texts made by F. Dölger, "Das Lebensrecht des ungeborenen Kindes und die Fruchtabtreibung in der Bewertung der heidnischen u. christlichen Antike," *Antike u. Christentum* 4 (1934): 1–61. Concerning penal repression beginning with Septimus Severus, see T. Mommsen, *Römisches Strafrecht* (Leipzig, 1899; reprint ed., 1955), pp. 636–37.

infanticide, as well as abstinence from any intercourse which might result in conception. The individual's choice among these different steps is dictated by cultural motivations, in the narrow sense of the term, and by economic and social conditions. The combination of these two factors accounts for the social scope of any single attitude toward birth control. Those who adopt none of these measures are characterized by the absence of voluntary birth control. Voluntary birth control, its justifications, and its techniques must therefore be seen as a part of the behavior concerning procreation and marriage, and this behavior itself must be viewed as a part of the social and cultural whole of the Byzantine Empire during this first period of its existence. Here we are giving the word "society" its modern meaning, and we must try to discover whether such behavior varied according to social levels. The word "culture" must be interpreted in its broad sense, as a congeries of steps—some of which are technical and others mental—which form a society's specific tools for acting, that is to say the sort of organic relationship which exists between possible methods of birth control and the mental attitudes toward these procedures and everything related to them. Thus, the social problem crops up again in other terms, since the question arises whether in this matter differentiated cultural levels correspond to social levels. But there is still more. Voluntary birth control—itself dependent upon cultural and social factors, as we have just said—must also be seen in relation to the economic and social conditions which objectively limited fertility on the different levels of Byzantine society of this period. Moreover, the distinction between what one wants and what one submits to is not always evident, and therein lies the difficulty and perhaps the interest of this problem in demographic history.

We therefore propose to study the control of fertility rather than the control of births, and to discover "why" before we describe the methods used—in other words, to specify first the immediate reasons for limiting fertility, which were often expressed by the contemporaries themselves. These reasons are a reflection of the cultural continuity of dying Antiquity, and of the religious trend which was becoming evident in the official church of the Byzantine Empire and in the heretical groups which held a dualist vision of the world. They also result from the social function and the economic conditions of marriage itself.

I

In the Greek cities of the Levant in the fourth century, Christian preaching was the expression of a brief but brilliant cultural equilibrium between the classical tradition and evangelical innovation. Both inspired the major ideas presented to the public concerning marriage and procreation; both vied with one another in giving these ideas a profoundly negative tone. This tone was even more marked among heretics coming from the Gnostic and Manichean tendencies. Such positions permit us to sense that voluntary birth control might well have included measures other than the contraceptive or abortive attempts which one might be tempted to associate with it. Obviously it is essential to verify whether the culture depicted by the authors whose works we today have at our disposal was that of the society as a whole; but we shall ask that question later.

The Stoic inheritance in Christian preaching about this subject has been successfully unraveled by Noonan. Preachers owed to Stoicism the idea of the perfected world, the idea that one must not hinder nature, including procreative activity. From their predecessors these preachers borrowed the theme of the afflictions which befall the woman, wife, and mother, especially as a result of marriage and the family. Even though a girl's docility toward the partner chosen by her parents, the husband's despotism and infidelity, the pain of childbirth, and the anxiety felt over children are commonplace themes, they are repeated too frequently, and too many details refer to the experiences of well-to-do families of the time, for us to brush aside these passages as mere literature.[10] Moreover, to an ancient society which apparently had become wholeheartedly Christian, the New Testament proposed maxims which had been inspired by the expectation of an imminent end of the world, for example: "They that have wives be as though they had none" (1 Cor. 7:29-31). The end result of all this was a doctrine concerning the place of procreation in the world plan and the theological and moral significance of marriage. Preachers and monastic authors of hagiographies expressed the orthodox version, while the heretical version, despite a few direct expressions, can chiefly be discerned through the attacks of polemicists and through a hagiography whose message is partially veiled.

First of all, Christian writers of the fourth century considered that it was no longer necessary to procreate as it had been since the beginning of human history. Basil of Caesarea cites the words of Paul which were quoted above; and to the person who might raise as an objection the

[10]Gregory of Nyssa, *Traité de la Virginité*, trans. and comp. M. Aubineau, in *Sources Chrétiennes* (Paris, 1966), vol. 119, chap. 3; John Chrysostom, *La Virginité*, ed. H. Musurillo, ibid., vol. 125, chap. 57; John Chrysostom, *A Théodore*, ed. and trans. J. Dumortier, ibid., vol. 117, letter 5; Eusebius of Emesa, *Corpus christianorum*, Series Latina (Turnholtum, 1971), vol. 101, homily 4, para. 4 ff, and homily 7, para. 16; see D. Amand de Mendieta, "La Virginité chez Eusèbe d'Emèse et l'ascètisme familial dans la première moitié du IVᵉ siècle," *Revue d'Histoire Ecclésiastique* 50 (1955): 777–820. For the antecedents of the theme, see Aubineau's Introduction to *Sources Chrétiennes*.

Biblical command "Be fruitful and multiply," he replies in advance, "I laugh at the person who does not discern the circumstances surrounding these commands."[11] The people felt they were living in a world which henceforth was complete, had reached its term, and was ripe for its temporal end and eternal salvation, as this statement from the pen of Basil of Ancyra indicates: "The whole Earth formerly void of inhabitants from then on became peopled, and Our Lord, knowing that in every region the ears of wheat of mankind are already numerous and loaded with descendants, deems that the time has come to harvest these sheaves," that is to say, the author explains, "through virginity to carry into another life the seeds of our life."[12] Preaching in favor of virginity, John Chrysostom, in one burst of words, links the beginning and the end of the world: "Everything will disappear, they say, cities and houses, fields and crafts, animals and plants"; but all this happened after the Fall, and virginity, by interrupting carnal birth, will put an end to the human condition which issued from such a birth.[13] There are numerous other expressions, some more striking than others, of this sort of eschatological anticipation, the first sign of which was the end of propagation.

Procreation is not, therefore, the sole or sufficient justification for marriage. The most elevated, most desirable state is virginity, free from the anguishes of the carnal life and devoted to a spiritual felicity which was lauded in the literature of the day.[14] Marriage, instituted after the Fall, preserves from sin those ordinary beings who could not endure asceticism,[15] on the condition, however, that it not degenerate into licentiousness which, although licit, would nonetheless be sinful.[16] Therein lies the true justification for marriage, and not in the henceforth superfluous multiplication of human beings. This principle leads to a special distinction between marriage and procreation. John Chrysostom uses sterile unions (e.g., the long sterility of Abraham) to separate the conjugal oath, which continued to play its moral role, from procreation, which was sent from above to accomplish the command "Be fruitful and multiply."[17] But this distinction in no way resulted in the practice of birth

---

[11]St. Basil of Caesarea, *Lettres*, ed. Y. Courtonne (Paris, 1957–66), vol. 2, letter 160 (circa 373).

[12]Basil of Ancyra, *De vera virginitatis integritate*, in *Patrologiae graecae*, ed. Migne (Paris, 1857–1903), vol. 30, col. 777, para. 54 (hereafter cited as *PG*).

[13]John Chrysostom, *La Virginité*, chap. 14, para. 1.

[14]See T. Camelot, "Les traités *De Virginitate* au IV siècle," *Mystique et Continence, Etudes Carmélitaines* 31 (1952): 273–92.

[15]Gregory of Nyssa, *Virginité*, chap. 12, para. 4; John Chrysostom, *La Virginité*, chap. 19; *In illud: Propter fornicationes uxorem*, chap. 1, para. 3, in *PG*, vol. 51, col. 213.

[16]Gregory of Nyssa, *Virginité*, chap. 8, lines 30–40, chap. 9, lines 1–2; John Chrysostom, *La Virginité*, chap. 34.

[17]John Chrysostom, *La Virginité*, chap. 15, para. 1; and *In illud* (see note 15, above).

control, one of the possible alternatives. The concept of marital relations and of births was too restrictive to permit this. In a certain manner births provide a way to measure marital relations. Numerous births are possible proof of condemnable excess. The sole means of birth control compatible with such premises is the breaking off of conjugal relations, by continence or even by physical separation, on condition, we shall see, that these steps be based upon mutual agreement. Gregory of Nyssa cites as an example Isaac, who engendered a single son and who then devoted himself to an inner life, which was symbolized by physical blindness.[18] In hagiographic stories intended to serve as examples, couples separated after having had two children, a son and a daughter.[19]

Using the same premises as a point of departure, heretical thought carried abstinence to the extreme, since it categorically condemned any union and any birth as a surrender of principles to the created world, which it considered profoundly evil, and as an increase in the amount of corrupted matter.[20] However, the distinction between heretical and orthodox teachings is sometimes so subtle that it is no longer pertinent for social history. Even contemporaries confessed that virginity and conjugal continence are identical behaviors which had been given separate connotations only because of theological considerations. We can sense how troubling the resemblance must have been when we read the exhortation addressed to newly married couples in the apocryphal *Acts* of the apostle Thomas, which was included among the sacred texts of the dualist sects:

. . . Know that as soon as ye preserve yourselves from this filthy intercourse, ye become pure temples, and are saved from afflictions manifest and hidden, and from the heavy care of children, to whom not one of these blemishes and hurts cometh nigh; and ye shall be without care and without grief and without sorrow; and ye shall be hoping [for the time] when ye shall see the true wedding feast; and ye shall be in it praisers [of God], and shall be numbered with those who enter into the bridal chamber.[21]

However, the heretical doctrine against marriage also had unique characteristics which were viewed as an open threat to the entire social order.

---

[18]Gregory of Nyssa, *Virginité*, chap. 7, line 3.

[19]*Apophtegmata Patrum: Carion*, para. 2, in *PG*, vol. 65, cols. 250–51; "Histoire d'Athanasia et Andronikos," Bibliothèque nationale, Paris, Fonds Coislin, 126, fols. 317–19. See note 72, below, for the personal testimony of Nilus of Ancyra, father of two boys.

[20]See H. C. Puech, *Le Manichéisme* (Paris, 1949); G. Blond, "L'hérésie encratite vers la fin du IVᵉ siècle," *Recherches de Science Religieuse*, 1944, pp. 157–210; and "Encratisme," *Dictionnaire de Spiritualité*, vol. IV, part 1 (1960): 628–42; J. Gribomont, "Le monachisme en Asie Mineure au IVᵉ siècle: de Gangres au messalianisme," *Studia Patristica* 2 (1957): 400–415.

[21]A. F. J. Klijn, *The Acts of Thomas* (Leiden, 1962), p. 71.

But in order to understand them, we must now move to the field of social behavior.

II

First, we must describe marriage in Byzantine society beginning with the fourth century. Marriage itself revealed a social differentiation of motives and attitudes and, despite the difficulties and hesitations within the judicial statutes, the social evolution of the institution is clear. As in any traditional society, the society of the Roman Empire was built upon the family and the cohabitation of couples. On this point we must not take too seriously the few texts relative to the most wretched slaves or to the rich old bachelors of the capital, or even the frequency of aristocratic divorce at certain periods. Byzantine society inherited two sorts of unions, which were distinguished from one another by the presence or absence of notarial documents, that is to say, of possessions. The Christian benediction in marriage rites, known to be a private gesture from the beginning of the fourth century, would not become a sanction with universally indispensable and sufficient civil consequences before the beginning of the eighth century.[22] This would come as the solution to the contradictory efforts of the legislator, who during this entire period attempted to confer an equally constraining validity upon every union, while at the same time maintaining the distinct forms established for the various social categories on the basis of rank and possessions. Only unequal unions created difficulties, unions in which the poor woman and her children had to be protected from the arbitrary behavior of the rich man, who might have sent them from his home whenever he pleased.[23] We shall not go into the details of the judicial development[24] and shall stress only one point which is important for our study: the marital association of rich or merely well-to-do persons was based on the possession and administration of a fortune, and that of the poor upon the carrying out of a daily activity

[22]E. Herman, "De benedictione nuptiali quid statuerit jus byzantinum sive ecclesiasticum sive civile," *Orientalia Christiana periodica* 4 (1938): 189–234.

[23]K. E. Zachariä von Lingenthal (ed.), *Corpus juris civilis, Novellae constitutiones Imp. Iustiani*, Novella 74, A. 538, c. 5, and Novella 53, A. 537, c. 6 (which uses the traditional numbering). (Hereafter cited as *Nov. Just.*) See the concordance, 2: 431–32. See also H. J. Wolff, "The Background of the Post-Classical Legislation on Illegitimacy," *Seminar* 3 (1945): 21–45.

[24]See especially P. Meyer, *Das römische Konkubinat* (Leipzig, 1895); P. Bonfante, "Nota sulla riforma giustinianea del concubinato," *Studi S. Perozzi* (Palermo, 1925), pp. 283–86; R. Orestano, *La struttura giuridica del matrimonio romano dal diritto classico al diritto giustinianeo* (Milan, 1951), vol. 1 (the only one published); and J. Gaudemet, *L'Eglise dans l'Empire romain* (Paris, 1959), pp. 515–56.

which if interrupted would make the association itself impossible to maintain. None expressed it more succinctly than Justinian, in a *novella* which outlined with great precision the social level of the different forms of marriage:

. . . as for the poor persons, obscure soldiers still in the services, and peasants, they can with impunity unite without acts and live in cohabitation; their children will be legitimate, heirs to the paternal modesty in occupations and to the ignorance associated with the army or the fields.[25]

This is a different world from that of the ascetic renunciation of marital relations, a world in which one senses that any birth control methods must have been adopted for harsh and down-to-earth reasons. Indeed, the history of behavior, which we can now begin to discuss, will show us the forms taken by social differentiation in this respect.

Let us begin with an easy task and consider first of all the various steps by which a household could avoid paying the consequences of conjugal cohabitation, that is, the increased propagation and support of children. As Hopkins thought, these methods were essentially restricted to the lower classes or even the poorest social group. This is especially clear in the case of the simplest measure—infanticide, and its delayed form, exposing the child along the public road.[26] But we must also take into account other methods used by the poor couple to rid itself of offspring it could not feed which placed the child in such a situation that, even if it survived, it could not look forward to a normal family life. In such cases, the fertility of the following generation would be affected. By the fourth century, the sale of very young children by parents who had no other possessions was the usual and final expedient of the poor. Children were sold into slavery.[27] The repercussions of this procedure are especially clear in a sixth-century document, the *novella* of 535, which observed—while forbidding the practice—that peasant families from the regions near Constantinople were selling to the pimps of the capital their daughters, some of whom were not yet ten years old.[28] This was perhaps an escape valve for excessive economic pressure—or perhaps for a scarcity of

[25]*Nov. Just.*, 74, A. 538, c. 4.

[26]On the relationship between law and customs and infanticide, exposing infants, and selling children, nothing can be added to Mommsen's *Römisches Strafrecht*, pp. 617–20.

[27]Laws of different dates collected in P. Krueger (ed.), *Corpus juris civilis, Codex, Codices Justiniani* (Berlin, 1877) (hereafter cited as *CJ*): *CJ*, IV, 43 (*De patribus qui filios distraxerunt*); and *CJ*, VIII, 51 (*De infantibus expositis liberis et servis, et de his qui sanguinolentos emptos vel nutriendos acceperunt*). See Basil of Caesarea, *Homilia in illud Lucae, Destruam*, para. 4, in *PG*, vol. 31, col. 265.

[28]*Nov. Just.*, 14, A. 535.

potential marriage partners—in the rural areas, but it also meant a decrease in the fertility of the succeeding generation. This precious text might suggest many such possibilities to us were it not an isolated document. We do know that, during the same period, the Church was taking in and keeping as its own abandoned children found in the streets.[29] This might also be considered as part of the general trend.

The premature termination of pregnancies does not appear in Graeco-Christian literature among the accusations made against the great ladies of Antioch or Constantinople, and no preacher echoes Juvenal. On the other hand, a familiarity with contraceptive measures, notably abortive potions, was credited to women living in an irregular situation, to prostitutes or at the least to solitary women.[30] Later, the Byzantine canonists Johannes Zonaras and Theodorus Balsamon would also attribute the use of such potions to women who wished to hide a sin from their parents or from their masters.[31] A reference to this is found in the *Secret History* of Procopius of Caesarea, in a narrative devoted to the youth of the future empress Theodora.[32] In addition, the penitential attributed to John the Faster[33] recommended making a special effort to question widows and nuns—once again single women—on this subject. Of course these instructions were issued through a desire to weigh the seriousness of sins according to the individual. Though these instructions were not absolute, they are no less interesting. At any event, the methods used seem to have been sufficiently effective for us to consider contraception a reality, although the methods are not always precisely explained. We have the letters of Basil the Great, bishop of Caesarea, who notes that abortion generally involved the death of the patient, but he is the only one to make this observation.[34] In his arguments condemning the practice, he rejects

[29] *Nov. Just.*, 153, A. 541, based upon the report of a priest from Thessalonica.
[30] Canons of the Council of Ancyra, 21, dated 314, Rhallis-Potli, *Syntagma Kanonon* (Athens, 1852–59), 3: 63.
[31] Rhallis-Potli, 4: 96; and 2: 519.
[32] Procopius, *The Anecdota or Secret History*, trans. H. B. Dewing (London: Cambridge, Mass., 1954), 9: 19.
[33] See the translation edited by Dom J. Morin, "Commentarius Historicus de disciplina in administratione sacramenti poenitentiae . . . ," *Antiqui Poenitentiales* (Paris, 1651), p. 84. Edited and unedited translations are listed in V. Grumel, *Régestes des Actes du Patriarcat de Constantinople* (Constantinople, 1932), vol. 1, *Les Actes des Patriarches*, pt. 1, *Les Régestes de 381 à 715*, no.** 270. The alleged author was patriarch of the capital between 582 and 595, but the series of canons circulating under his name are in part based upon an older text, probably related to the canons of Basil of Caesarea and containing, in addition, elaborations posterior to John the Faster, almost certainly written between the end of the eighth and the beginning of the tenth century. See H. G. Beck, *Kirche und theologische Literatur im byzantinischen Reich* (Munich, 1959), p. 424.
[34] Basil of Caesarea, *Lettres*, vol. 2, letter 188, para. 2 (circa 374).

the usual distinction about whether or not the child has assumed human form.[35] The distinction is noted in the *Secret History*, however, which reports that Theodora succeeded in terminating her pregnancies before this moment had arrived, and that the single time she failed and allowed that moment to pass, she subsequently gave birth to her sole descendant.[36] The penitential attributed to John the Faster contributes important information concerning the methods used, belying the hypothesis that there was confusion in the minds of the common people between contraceptive and abortive measures. Indeed, the author, referring to his experience as a confessor, observes that women know both how to prevent conception and how to terminate a pregnancy. He refers to the use of potions, some of which were said to make one permanently sterile, while others had a monthly abortive effect, and still others could terminate a confirmed pregnancy. It can be said in summary that concrete methods of birth control were sought in accordance with the dictates of personal finances. Though we cannot form a sure hypothesis, birth control techniques and the economic motivations behind them seem to belong to specific social groups characterized by precarious relationships and the difficulty of making a living, while women raised in stable and financially comfortable families, shut off from the world as they were, were not mentioned in this connection. We therefore must agree with Hopkins' conclusion, but only on condition that limits be placed on the degree of influence these voluntary contraceptive measures may have had on demography.

In order to appreciate fully the factors which characteristically limited the fertility of the poor, we must recall what has been said above concerning their marital situation. The poor family was an unstable one, because it was totally bound to the specific economic activity by which it made its living. As a result, broken marriages, separations, even flights were characteristic. As early as the fourth century, Libanius defined the dishonest poor man of Antioch as a man who had neither wife nor child and who was not of that city.[37] Pitiful bands of lepers upon whom Gregory of Nyssa exhorted the faithful to have compassion;[38] vagabonds without shelter or home town who had to be expelled from Constantinople by a magistrate especially created by Justinian;[39] Isaurian laborers

[35]See Dölger, *Das Lebensrecht.*

[36]Procopius, *The Anecdota*, 17: 16.

[37]Libanius, *Orationes*, ed. Foerster (Leipzig, 1903–22), vol. 3, p. 300, oration 41, para. 11.

[38]Gregory of Nyssa, *De Pauperibus Amandis Orationes*, ed. A. van Heck (Leiden, 1964), vol. 2, passim.

[39]*Nov. Just.*, 80, A. 539.

who came alone or in groups to work on monastic constructions in northern Syria;[40] Thracian peasants who had fled because creditors had seized their land after two successive crop failures[41]—such were the multitudes of wandering individuals who give us an indication of the conditions of family life.

The poor family, therefore, appears to have had a number of specific characteristics in regard to voluntary or forced birth control. Having said this, we shall see that the whole of Byzantine society at the end of Antiquity was marked by a considerable movement to avoid marriage. Christian preaching thus seems to be supported by fact. But the historian must not be satisfied with these initial appearances. He must determine to what degree this preaching might have been a determining factor or, on the contrary, whether it was itself influenced by the demographic and social situation in which it developed. The basis for an answer can be found by examining the different ways by which marriage was avoided during the period between the fourth and seventh centuries. Several of these ways were experimented with during the fourth century, but Byzantine society would later tend to eliminate them in favor of a single choice: the cloister. Formulated by the end of the fourth century, this alternative would have its full demographic and social effect at the end of the fifth and the beginning of the sixth century, and would then remain indelibly written into the Byzantine social structure, although the phenomenon would be noticeably transformed during the last decades of the sixth century.

The most radical and most subversive experiment was made by the vast heretical movement which shook the Byzantine world in the fourth century and whose theological premises we have referred to above.[42] Rooted in third-century Gnosticism, which was contemporary with Manicheanism, this heretical movement had not died completely, since from it sprang the vigorous Paulician movement and perhaps, on the borders of the Empire, that of the Bulgarian Bogomils. This experiment took place in a remarkably stable territory: Phrygia, Pamphylia, and the Armenian region; in the fourth century it cropped up in those provinces speaking the Syriac language—Mesopotamia and Osrhoene—from whence it spread across northern Syria. The behavior of groups and individuals, which interests us here, is known through all-too-rare doctrinal treatises, conciliar interdicts, orthodox polemics, a very curious

---

[40] P. Van den Ven, *Vie de Saint Syméon Stylite le jeune* (Brussels, 1962), vol. 2, passim.
[41] *Nov. Just.*, 32, A. 535.
[42] See note 20, above.

body of hagiography in which the heretical model can be discerned under a surface of false orthodoxy, and funeral inscriptions in Phrygia and Pamphylia. After reading this evidence, the import of the heretical refusal to marry becomes clear: it was nothing less than a total refusal to follow any of the rules upon which society was built.

Men of that day conceived of the world as a well-defined hierarchy of antagonisms which regulated society, the Church, and nature. Nature was clearly identified with social and religious rules which gave it form. The dualist heretics destroyed this edifice by reversing or negating these essential antagonisms and by making their position manifest to the public through ostentatious behavior contrary to everyday proprieties, such as social relations and the rules of the Church. A listing of this inverted behavior—which we cannot include here—would in a sense recreate for us the entire social picture. Now, the distinction between the sexes may be considered the basis of the human condition. Their relationship affects the three orders mentioned above. On the level of nature, it is evident in the specific appearance of each sex, their separation in daily life, and sexual attraction. The social and religious hierarchies are affirmed by the words of St. Paul, "The head of the woman is the man."[43] as exemplified in the hierarchy involving husband and wife. In this, heretical practice found a favorite theme. Indeed, in about 340 the Church Fathers of the Synod of Gangra, on the borders of Armenia, listed a series of heretical disorders which it condemned, and pointed out that women often shaved off their hair, which indicated their social position, and wore men's garments.[44] In a similar context, such unusual scenes as those in which Symeon of Emesa impassibly entered a women's bath or gamboled among prostitutes[45] was not interpreted as an ascetic victory but as a scandalous affront to the natural order. In his treatise on heresies composed circa 374–76, Epiphanius of Salamis pointed out with disgust the indifference shown by the heretical bands who would rest helter-skelter wherever their wandering led them.[46] The logical consequence of these activities was that the entire social and religious organization of relationships between the sexes was overthrown. Wives ran off or

---

[43] *I Cor.* 11: 3.

[44] P. Lauchert (ed.), *Die Kanones der wichtigsten altkirchlichen Concilien nebst den Apostolischen Kanones* (Freiburg–Leipzig, 1896), p. 80 (hereafter cited as Council of Gangres). See the complaint about taking women as spiritual guides for the group (Timotheus Constantinopolitans Presbyter, *De Receptione Haereticorum*, para. 18, in *PG*, vol. 86, col. 46–51).

[45] Leontios von Neapolis, *Das Leben des Hl. Narren Symeon*, ed. L. Rydén (Uppsala, 1963), pp. 149, 155.

[46] Epiphanius, *Panarion*, ed. K. Holl, *Griechische Christliche Schriftsteller* (1915–33) 80 (Messalianer), 3, 3–6.

committed adultery, married priests were disavowed, and priests refused
to say prayers in the homes of married couples;[47] monastic isolation was
infringed upon.[48] Conciliar condemnations and polemical refutations
combined complaints about licentious disorders with complaints about
worthless chastity. Let us, however, stress at the outset that this movement cannot be attributed to any particular social group. For complex
reasons which we shall not go into here, the adherents of the movement
refused to play the social role which they had been assigned. Some
rejected servitude, others work, others wealth and the distribution of
alms.[49] In fact, the style and details given about the deceased in the
heretical inscriptions of Asia Minor indicate that the movement was
prevalent among the cultivated provincial bourgeoisie.[50]

To what degree did the movement contribute to birth control? This is
an appropriate point at which to make a cautious study of the available
texts. Titus of Bostra and his contemporary, Epiphanius, accused the
heretics of pursuing pleasures which remained sterile. The former was
making a general allusion to contraceptive and abortive practices.[51] The
latter dwelled on frightful descriptions of scenes which had a collective
and ritual nature and which, moreover—as he naively confessed—he
hoped would make the reader shudder.[52] We must admit that our
information on the whole is too scanty and the psychological basis for the
heresy too intangible for us to find the pages useful, for we do not know
whether the authors indicate a behavior which would be extremist under
any circumstances, or even whether they were borrowing a part of their
calumnies from the repertory of heresiology which was already well
developed at this date. Likewise, it is very difficult to judge the influence
of sects of this type through the vehement denunciations made by
Epiphanius concerning their spread across Syria and especially into

[47]Council of Gangres, pp. 79–80.
[48]Council held under Iesuiahb I, in 585, c. 9 ("*Liber Graduum*," ed. M. Kmosko,
Patrologia Syriaca [Paris, 1916], vol. 3, XV 13 and XIX 15).
[49]Council of Gangres, passim; Epiphanius, *Panarion*, 47, 80, passim.
[50]Scattered inscriptions in the *Monumentae Asiae Minoris Antiquae*, especially in vol. 1
(1928), vol. 7 (1956), and vol. 8 (1962). One should consult the collection arranged by W. M.
Calder, "The Epigraphy of the Anatolian Heresies," *Anatolian Studies presented to Sir
W. M. Ramsay* (Manchester, 1923), pp. 59–91; and A. Wilhelm, "Griechische Grabinschriften aus Kleinasien," *Sitzungberichte der Preussischen Akademie der Wissenschaften,
Philosophisch-historische Klasse* (1932), pp. 792–865.
[51]Titus of Bostra, *Adversus Manichaeas*, bk. 2, chap. 33, in *PG*, vol. 18, col. 1198; in an
analogous development, Augustine accused the "Manichees" of making use of women's
sterile periods to separate conjugal relations from procreation, and he considers that wives
by doing this lowered themselves to the level of prostitutes. Augustine, *De Moribus
Manichaeorum*, bk. 2, chap. 18, *Patrologiae latinae*, ed. Migne (Paris, 1844–1903), vol. 32,
cols. 1372–73 (hereafter cited as *PL*).
[52]Epiphanius, *Panarion*, 26, 4.

monastic circles. This brings us to the real historical problem: by whom and to what degree were the heretical ideas on marriage and procreation followed?

In the mountainous provinces of Asia Minor, heresy was lived daily. Epigraphy offers proof of the practice of voluntary celibacy[53] and also of continence observed within marriage; yet conjugal society was not as a result subjected to a scandalous destruction which was dangerous for the social order. The priest of Dinek Saray in Isauria found moving words for the wife who behaved as a sister to her ascetic husband.[54] On the other hand, a Phrygian couple which belonged to the "holy and pure Church"[55] had a daughter; they had no additional children, however, and we do not know whether to credit this fact to conversion to a heretical sect, efficacious contraception, or a break in conjugal relations after one child, as in the exemplary life of the Lady Matrona.[56] A collection of heretical homilies from the fourth century, the *Liber Graduum*, written in the Syriac language, is the only one from this period to mention a hierarchy of two levels, the Perfect and the Just, the former alone abstaining from marriage, as they did from work and from the distribution of alms.[57] At Emesa, on the other hand, in an urban setting in which heresy had gained a footing but in which the various influences mingled, the preacher Eusebius rejoiced to see how many individuals abstained from marriage and how many couples, without separating, gave up marital relations periodically or permanently.[58] What role does heresy play in these attitudes? Eusebius of Emesa, whose own orthodoxy sometimes has rather suspect overtones, went into details on this point. The image he painted was undoubtedly more common and more significant than that of the groups whose ostentatious behavior Epiphanius described. Strict observance of the heretical doctrine, which aimed at frustrating nature and destroying the conjugal hierarchy along with all other hierarchies, was undoubtedly a lesser factor than was private choice (sometimes brought on by necessity) inspired by a negative attitude which seemed to permeate the entire culture of the period. Thus limited in its effects, the heresy did not introduce a discordant note into the culture; it indicated its most radical tendency.

[53]Calder, "Epigraphy," example no. 5 (p. 81), two spiritual sisters; no. 9 (p. 87), a woman who lived in continence (ἐνχπατευσαμένη) cf. the name of the sect of the Encratites); no. 11 (p. 90), a eunuch priest.
[54]Wilhelm, "Griechische Grabinschriften," pp. 792–809.
[55]Calder, "Epigraphy," example no. 6; *Monumentae Asiae Minoris Antiquae*, 7: 92.
[56]"Vita Matronae higumenae," *Acta Sanctorum Novembris* (Brussels, 1910), 3: 790–813, c. 2.
[57]*Liber Graduum*, XV 13, XIX 15.
[58]Eusebius of Emesa, *Corpus christianorum*, homily 7, para. 9.

III

Upholding conjugal society, whose facade remained even though it had been destroyed from within, characterized another movement of the fourth century—that of spiritual marriages which, although not heretical, nonetheless drew the anathemas of the preachers. Present in the Christian world between the third and the sixth centuries,[59] it is known to us in its Byzantine form through the fourth-century homilies, notably the two works of John Chrysostom.[60] It is plausible that the funeral inscriptions of Asia Minor in which unmarried persons called themselves brothers and sisters sometimes also refer to such marriages. Such situations are not incompatible with heresy.[61]

Here again, it is hopeless to attempt to recreate the day-to-day reality of such unions. John Chrysostom ridiculed them for often sinking to the level of ordinary marriages, with all their consequences. However, he stressed that many of them remained sterile, although he refused to consider them necessarily virtuous, since sterility was also enjoyed by prostitutes. Moreover, he indicated that such marriages were present on all social levels, and that the social role of the partners was in no respect modified by the absence of sexual relations. The rich made the most of their wealth and sometimes even increased it; the poor went about their work. Spiritual marriages died out after the end of the fourth century, probably doomed by the progress of monasticism. This leads us to two observations. First, the cultural motivation of birth control through abstinence seems to be a very primordial or at least an independent motivation, since this motivation is associated with economic considerations which in any event differed according to the various social levels. Second, the conjugal relationship as a social component was not replaced. Indeed, monasticism's innovation would consist in proposing forms of association and organization which would be entirely free from conjugality and which would nevertheless have the capacity to carry out the various social roles.

The spread of monastic life styles was preceded by experiments which already showed a proclivity for celibacy and which took place either before or after marriage. The social group involved is rather clearly indicated. This unwillingness to marry seems to have occurred frequently in the comfortable urban milieu of the fourth century. The economic

---

[59] H. Achelis, *Virgines Subintroductae. Ein Beitrag zum VII Kap. des I Korinthierbriefs* (Leipzig, 1902).

[60] John Chrysostom, *Les cohabitations suspectes. Comment observer la virginité*, ed. and trans. J. Dumortier (Paris, 1955).

[61] *Monumentae Asiae Minoris Antiquae*, 1: 228, 303; 7: 96.

motivation, although different for sons and daughters, is obvious. The marriage date of sons would be delayed, and John Chrysostom reproached families for thus sacrificing their sons' morality for personal ends.[62] On the other hand, celibacy for girls was decided upon at an early date and in a definitive fashion. Indeed, Basil of Caesarea admitted that a goodly number of young girls were consecrated to virginity solely to provide funds for their brothers' marriages.[63] Unmarried girls were not lacking in the milieu of the curiae of Antioch, in which pagans and Christians rubbed elbows.[64] Eusebius of Emesa asserted, in his previously cited discourses, that the father made the decision and that the ascetic generally continued to live with her parents. The cultural motivation was not, however, absent. On the contrary, it would be decisive in comfortable and rich circles, where possessions and social role did not necessarily require marriage. Indeed, the social function of the rich person in Byzantine society—and we plan to prove this elsewhere—consisted of graciously redistributing the possessions which accumulated in one's hands and of thus continually making sure that the circulation of wealth did not become blocked. The ancient Greek concept of the "euergetes," or benefactor, went hand in hand with Christian charity. Now, if the bad example was that of the rich girl who used her freedom for immoral purposes,[65] the good example was that of the donatrix who could give even more freely since no family obligations weighed upon her fortune. Gregory of Nyssa described thusly his sister Macrina, who remained unmarried after the death of her fiancé and stayed with their widowed mother.[66] Charity also played a role in separation after marriage, which remained orthodox provided it was based upon mutual consent. We find examples in hagiography. For instance, we have the story of Athanasia and Andronikos, a married couple which spent its nights carrying out tasks for organizations of charitable men and women to which each belonged; they eventually separated in order to go into the desert following the deaths of their two children.[67] The famous *Life* of Melania the Younger, a Greek biography of an important Roman matron and saint of the fifth century, tells us that she and her husband gave up sexual relations after the deaths of their two children—a daughter whom they

---

[62]John Chrysostom, *In Epistolam I ad Thessalonicenses*, chap. 4, homily 5, in *PG*, vol. 62, col. 426.

[63]Basil of Caesarea, *Lettres*, vol. 2, letter 188, 18 (circa 374).

[64]See P. Petit, *Libanios et la vie municipale à Antioche au IVe siècle apres J.-C.* (Paris, 1955), pp. 328–29.

[65]John Chrysostom, *Les cohabitations suspectes, Comment observer la virginité*, vol. 1.

[66]Gregory of Nyssa, *Vita Macrinae*, ed. V. Woods Callahan, in *Gregorii Nysseni Opera*, ed. W. Jaeger (Leiden, 1952), vol. 8, pt. 1, pp. 374–414.

[67]See note 19, above.

had consecrated to virginity at birth, and an infant son.[68] They distributed their immense fortune to charitable works, completing in one fell swoop the task which should have occupied their entire life. The Syriac history of the widow Sosiana[69] provides the same example. Orthodox asceticism thus allowed people to avoid the grave sin of refusing to carry out their social function, a sin for which, as we have seen, the heretics were specifically blamed.

These stories reveal the echo of the negative ideas concerning procreation, whose theoretical foundations we have discussed above. These ideas seem to have exerted as much influence upon consciences in society—at least judging from literary texts—as did a desire or a need to rely upon children. The birth of a son was obviously required. It was expected by Melania's husband and by the husband of Paula, St. Jerome's illustrious Roman penitent.[70] Sterility was a disgrace.[71] But praise for large families as such is found neither in sermons, to be sure, nor in the eulogies of funeral inscriptions. On the contrary, the concept of having children is restrictive and underemphasized. When Nilus of Ancyra separated from his wife after having had two sons by her, he justified his decision in these terms:

I thought that this was enough for the continuation of the race, and for care in my old age. I judged that any being endowed with reason should not enjoy pleasure to the point of satiety, nor exploit the impunity given by the law to the point of abusing nature, but ought on the contrary to stop promptly, after having given himself to the care of One who founded marriage for the increase of the race and who certainly did not institute it as a reward for our infirmity. I am doing this to make sure that—once my virile power has flown, in years to come, and desire has been extinguished by the spontaneous calming of old age—my vowing myself to chastity will not be attributed to the necessity of age rather than to the generous ambition of choice.[72]

The liberation of the body, especially among women, therefore appears to have been associated with chastity—at least in these examples from actual lives—and not solely with birth control, to which it would be anachronistic and deceptive to attach too much importance here. For example,

[68] *Vie de sainte Mélanie*, ed. D. Gorce, in *Sources Chrétiennes*, vol. 90 (Paris, 1962), paras. 1–6.

[69] John of Ephesus, *Lives of the Eastern Saints*, trans. E. W. Brooks, *Patrologie orientale*, vol. 19 (1925), chap. 55, pp. 191–96.

[70] St. Jerome, *Epistola CVIII*, para. 4, in *PL*, vol. 22, col. 880.

[71] John Chrysostom, *In Annam*, sermon 1, para. 4, in *PG*, vol. 54, col. 639; and all the developments referred to in note 10, above.

[72] Nilus of Ancyra, *Narratio II*, in *PG*, vol. 79, col. 601.

Melania the Younger begged her husband, Pinian, to accept shared chastity or that of his wife alone, and her biographer has her say:

See, all my possessions are at your disposal, so that, once you have become their master, you may use them as you wish. Simply give my body freedom, so that I may present it unsullied, like my soul, to Christ on that awesome day.[73]

Pinian compromised, agreeing to give up marital relations when they had had two children who could inherit their possessions.

Those in comfortable or rich circles, therefore, were offered a certain amount of choice in fulfilling their social function (which was to distribute their wealth). Once their possessions had been dispersed, however, and this social function had been completed, a monastic function was the sole role open to them. This role remained available to them after a physical separation based on mutual consent. The Church and the law alike authorized it, and it was undoubtedly an action at least as prevalent as actual divorce.[74] Among the poor classes, the problem was a different one, as we have seen. For girls and widows without sufficient resources, solitude was not as easy as the spiritual marriage so criticized by the Church; and wives were sometimes not left alone by choice but as a result of that dislocation common to the poor family, which we have already discussed. At an early date the Church attempted to incorporate virgins and widows into religious orders, that is to say, into stable groups in which permanent positions gave them the right to regular assistance.[75] The canonical age of widows was, however, fixed at sixty. Younger women were not considered reliable enough, and the *Apostolic Constitutions* proposed that they simply be granted aid which would dispense them from having to remarry owing to economic need.[76] Beyond that, the Church had available only canonical punishments for those who entered into second and even third marriages. This development permits us to assume that remarriages must have been numerous and necessary.[77] The case of virgins was handled in a similar fashion. Basil asked that the practice of dedicating little girls to virginity be stopped, unless the girl had

---

[73] *Vie de sainte Mélanie*, vol. 90, para. 1.

[74] Basil of Caesarea, *Regulae fusius tractae, Interrogatio XII*, in *PG*, vol. 31, col. 948; *Nov. Just.*, 22, A. 536, c. 5; and *Nov. Just.*, 117, A. 542, c. 10, the latter being devoted to the matter of divorce.

[75] H. Leclercq, "Veuvage," "Veuve," *Dictionnaire d'Archéologie Chrétienne et de Liturgie*, vol. 15, pt. 2, pp. 3007–26; "Monachisme," ibid., vol. 11, pt. 2, pp. 1774–1947.

[76] *Constitutiones Apostolorum*, in *Didascalia et Constitutiones Apostolorum*, ed. F. X. Funk (Paderborn, 1905), 3: 1, 2. See Basil of Caesarea, *Lettres*, letter 188, 24 (circa 374).

[77] J. Dauvillier and C. de Clercq, *Le Mariage en droit canonique oriental* (Paris, 1936), pp. 195–200.

made the decision of her own accord; such a procedure would help eliminate situations where girls would break their vows when they reached adulthood.[78]

IV

The formative stage of monasticism which we have just described was generally restricted to urban circles and to women. But we know that, beginning with the fourth century, the movement which was to take women and especially men far from the villages and cities and out into the solitudes of the desert or the mountains was already developing in the Byzantine Empire.[79] Ascetic withdrawal assumed two different forms: the retreat of the hermit into solitude and that of the monk into the monastic community—both known by the end of the third century, although the former actually influenced social history before the latter. The solitary hermit earned a living by making matting, baskets, and pots, sometimes aided by a disciple; he would occasionally encounter distant neighbors and travelers in search of edification; he would go to sell his products in the village market and would periodically join with other hermits for religious celebrations. He remained the veritable ascetic model of the fourth century, as shown in travel accounts about the Egyptian or Palestinian deserts.[80] Yet, no matter how strongly we might suppose the eremitical stream to run, no matter how diverse its social recruitment might appear, it can only be seen as a vast assortment of individuals, a tally of fugitives.

Efforts to create a collective organization were scarcely evident in the Levant before the second half of the fourth century, and even then they were small-scale experiments, in Cappadocia and in Palestine. Monasticism only assumed social and demographic significance with the development of the great, productive communities during the fifth century, in the regions where the soil and the roads were favorable for the influx and installation of hundreds, even thousands of men, coming from nearby,

[78] Basil of Caesarea, *Lettres*, letter 188, 18 (circa 374).

[79] The histories of early monasticism almost completely ignore the economic and demographic problems and center upon the spiritual commentary. The essential facts are presented in a few pages in Leclercq's article, "Monachisme," cited in note 75, above; in J. Daniélou and H. Marrou, *Nouvelle Histoire de l'Eglise*, vol. 1, *Des Origines à S. Grégoire le Grand* (Paris, 1963), pp. 310–318; and also in A. Vööbus, *History of Asceticism in the Syrian Orient, a Contribution to the History of Culture in the Near East* (Louvain, 1958–60).

[80] *Histoire des Moines d'Egypte*, drawn up circa 400; Palladios' *Histoire Lausiaque*, circa 419–20; and John Cassin's *De Institutes* and *Collationes*, circa 420. See Daniélou and Marrou, *Nouvelle Histoire de l'Eglise*. All these works indicate the situation at the end of the fourth century.

adjoining, and even distant regions. The points of concentration are well known: the olive-growing regions around Bethlehem,[81] the limestone outcroppings behind Antioch,[82] and the main routes to the Sinai,[83] to name some.

Then only did Byzantine society possess a totally efficient organization, exclusive of marriage and the family, yet one in which the very simple roles of normal society were to be found. The rich man gave his gold or his land to increase the monastery's capabilities; the man born poor or the one who had willingly become poor would go there to work. But we must stress here the overall importance of a cultural factor which was at work especially among the rich: it was because their culture impelled them in a certain measure to turn away from marriage and procreation that they were able to supply monasteries with the means to support the contingent which came there to live—a masculine contingent, by definition, for female communities could not carry on the same activities and doubtlessly were less important for that reason.

The demographic siphoning off of the current generation and, as a result, of future generations—a process which was set in motion in childhood or on the eve of a marriage, as hagiographic tales indicate—henceforth had available a means whose success can be seen by the early fifth century in a decline in individual ways of avoiding marriage. The impetus of monasticism's vast building program slowed on the whole during the last decades of the sixth century. It appears that the calamities which were ravaging the Empire after 530—of which the plague was only the worst—occurred at the very moment when the monastic siphon had been functioning over enough generations for the effects on population to have already accrued. The consequences of this juncture are therefore measureable.

Such at least is the demographic conclusion which we propose here. But the social structure was nevertheless permanently modified. The family and groups of families no longer played an irreplaceable role.

V

To summarize, we have attempted to show that birth control at the beginning of the Byzantine era not only included contraceptive measures,

---

[81]V. Corbo, *Gli Scavi di Kh. Siyar el-Ghanam (Campo dei Pastori) e i monasteri dei dintorni* (Jerusalem, 1955).

[82]G. Tchalenko, *Villages antiques de la Syrie du Nord. Le Massif du Bélus à l'époque romaine*, 3 vols. (Paris, 1953–58).

[83]See M. Avi-Yonah, "The Economics of Byzantine Palestine," *Israel Exploration Journal* 8 (1958): 39–51.

but pure and simple abstinence as well. Abstinence was observed on such a wide scale and in such a variety of forms that it became a pertinent element in demographic and social history. However, we have not resolved the question which we asked at the beginning concerning the relationship between cultural attitudes and the initial demographic crisis. And so we do not want to overestimate the scope of our conclusions. We believe that the families which are known through epigraphy, and the evidence of construction activity found in the soil, indicate that men were not lacking, at least until the accumulated calamities of the sixth century. Would men on the contrary have been too numerous had the social structure not been modified by the trend described above? Were men really scarce after 550? Those are chapters in a demographic history which are still to be written.[84]

---

[84]We are sketching this out in a book now in press, *Pauvreté économique et pauvreté sociale à Byzance, IVe-VIIe siècles*, Civilisations et Sociétés (Ecole pratique des hautes études, VIe section).

2
Contraception, Marriage, and Sexual Relations in the Christian West

Jean-Louis Flandrin

An understanding of demographic behavior implies a knowledge of the behavior patterns of the populations being studied. From this statement one proceeds immediately—too immediately—to the idea that in a Christian society, such as that of the medieval or modern West, the prescriptions of the religious law are decisive. True, one cannot neglect them; but they are not everything. Church doctrine has never been passively accepted by an entire population; it does not build upon virgin consciences. Each social milieu adapts doctrine to its own needs, its customs, its traditional beliefs.

I suspect that no one questions this on the level of generalities; but when making a detailed study, it is often easier to proceed as if unaware. Thus the inquiry into behavior must focus on the diffusion of Church doctrine, on the one hand, and on the dilemma of the "good Christian or the sinner," on the other. Of course, it is extremely difficult to know what each social group does with that doctrine, to what degree it accepts it, refuses it, or transforms it. To stimulate new research, we must at least stress our ignorance and not conceal it.

With regard to contraception, which is my concern here, I will not attempt to study the examples provided by one specific group, as this introduction seems to imply. The thesis presented here may be too general, considering the limited sociological scope of my documentation

Annales: E.S.C., Nov.–Dec. 1969, pp. 1370–90. Translated by Patricia M. Ranum.

and its chronological dispersion. Indeed, this study does not result from painstaking research; I am simply trying to show the inadequacy of the ideas which have until now been accepted and to stimulate new research.

Let us recall briefly the generally accepted ideas. The most radical thesis was that of "unthinkableness"—so brilliantly defended by Philippe Ariès[1]—which asserted that, until a recent date, contraception was unthinkable in the Christian West and that love, sexual intercourse, and procreation formed an integral whole. Because this notion was largely grounded upon the silence of medieval theologians, it was rapidly proved invalid. Father Riquet soon found fault with it on the basis of the vices denounced in the penitentials of the early Middle Ages.[2] Most recently, an American scholar, John Noonan, has shown the importance of medieval condemnations against contraception in its many forms.[3] It is henceforth difficult to maintain that no one thought of separating sexual intercourse and procreation, and that all those theological debates, all the work of the preachers and confessors, were concerned with a problem which did not exist in the practices of the day. Noonan believes that this sin was committed by married couples as well as extramaritally. But were these contraceptive measures used on a scale appreciable at the statistical level on which demographers function?

Demographers have long accepted the existence of efficacious contraceptive techniques in medieval society. However, they have considered them as limited to the milieu of prostitution, and for the rest of the society they have held fast to the idea of a "natural fecundity." This is a misleading concept, and people have begun to question it. If the majority of demographic historians have kept a cautious and ambiguous silence concerning the fertility of extramarital sexual relations,[4] others have not hesitated to determine the frequency of such relationships on the basis of

[1]Philippe Ariès, *Histoire des populations françaises et de leurs attitudes devant la vie depuis le XVIIIe siècle* (Paris, 1948).

[2]See the article by Father Riquet in *Population*, Oct.–Dec. 1949; and Philippe Ariès' reply in *Population*, July–Sept. 1953. Both are available in English in O. and P. Ranum (eds.), *Popular Attitudes toward Birth Control in Pre-Industrial France and England* (New York, 1972).

[3]John T. Noonan, Jr., *Contraception, a History of its Treatment by the Catholic Theologians and Canonists* (Cambridge, Mass., 1966).

[4]Among the articles and works by the team at the Institut national d'études démographiques (I.N.E.D.), directed by Louis Henry, see in particular the collective work, chiefly by Hélène Bergues, *La prévention des naissances dans la famille* (Paris, 1960). It includes a guarded paragraph by Louis Henry on "Relations sexuelles en dehors du mariage," pp. 368–69. Guarded, but ambiguous, since one finds: "This frequency can only be arrived at indirectly through illegitimate conceptions . . . ; thus anything having to do with prostitution and adultery is eliminated. . . ." This implies that other sorts of illicit relations are discernible via the number of illegitimate births.

the number of illegitimate births.[5] I shall discuss this rash position in the second part of this article.

First, however, I will concentrate on denouncing the immediacy of the relationship between the behavior of medieval Christians regarding contraception and the doctrine of the Church as formulated by the theologians of the period. Indeed, it is clear that many Christians acquainted with this doctrine not only did not follow it but did not accept it. That is, on this point they conformed to a moral ideal which was not that of the Church of their day.

How else can we interpret the well-known testimony of Monseigneur Bouvier, bishop of Le Mans, concerning the Catholic couples in his diocese in 1842?

Almost all young couples do not wish to have a large family and nevertheless are morally incapable of abstaining from the marriage act. Questioned by their confessors on the way in which they exercised their marital rights, *they generally appear to be extremely shocked* and, once warned, do not abstain from the conjugal act, nor can they be won over to an indefinite multiplication of the species . . .

. . . All willingly agree that infidelity toward one's spouse and willful abortion are very grave sins. And only with great difficulty can some of them be persuaded that they are obliged, under pain of mortal sin, either to observe perfect chastity in their marriage or else to run the risk of engendering a numerous posterity.[6]

Must the discrepancy between the behavior which these young Catholic couples considered appropriate and that which the Church was

[5]See, for example, Emmanuel Le Roy Ladurie, *Les paysans du Languedoc* (Paris, 1966). Speaking of the very long period of sexual inhibition "which the young experience before marriage," he explains in note 4 of vol. 1, p. 644: "This period of inhibition, much longer and more rigorous than in our contemporary culture, exists as a result of a combination of factors (which the work of Goubert, 1960, and for Languedoc, those of Godechot and Moncassin, 1964, have elucidated): a) the absence or the very minor importance of contraception before 1730 in Languedoc as in the Beauvaisis; b) the very low percentage of premarital conceptions and of illegitimate births in general (0.5% in Languedoc during the entire eighteenth century). If premarital sexual relations were really frequent, they would, as a result of ignorance of contraception, have resulted in a very large number of illegitimate births. That is not the case."

Indeed, in his thesis on *Beauvais et le Beauvaisis* (Paris, 1960), Pierre Goubert wrote, after having observed that illegitimate births never exceeded 1 percent of the total births in a village, and having said that unmarried mothers went to the city to be delivered: "One trend merits being stressed: the very great respect for the religious law which forbade extramarital conception." This formulation appears to me an excellent one, since it refers to conceptions and not to sexual relations. But one must admit that the unprepared reader risks missing this nuance.

[6]Quoted in full by Hélène Bergues, *Prévention des naissances*, pp. 229–30. Concerning this evidence, see also Noonan, *Contraception*, pp. 401–2.

trying to impose upon them be attributed to the influence of openly anti-Christian models in a society which no longer had any religion but the religion of the State? Perhaps in part. But there seems to be more to it than than. To support this, interesting evidence can be found from the eighteenth century, that is, before the Revolution had freed conjugal morality from ecclesiastical surveillance. Father Féline wrote in his *Catéchisme des gens mariés* (1782):

> The majority of husbands imagine that everything is permitted them and do not think of seeking advice. They cannot be persuaded that a confessor has the right to enter into the discussion of these sorts of questions. They appear scandalized if one happens to bring up the subject in the confessional. Women, through bashfulness, modesty, shame, dare not declare their anxiety. They wait for the confessor to speak to them about it first. It is not rare to find [women] who, after several years of marriage and an infinite number of transgressions, reply coldly to a confessor who has the charity to question them concerning conjugal chastity, that they never confessed the sins for which they are being reproached because their previous confessors had never asked about them.[7]

Admittedly, this evidence is less explicit than the preceding text. And it does not throw into relief the sincerity of the married couples in their error. But is it not essentially aimed at contraception in marriage? And whence the arrogance of the sinners if not from a feeling that they are in the right?

As early as 1748, moreover, St. Alphonsus Liguori, hostile to Jansenist practices, discouraged confessors from inquiring about the sins of married persons. For if the sinner did not confess on his own, it meant he was unaware that he was sinning. If the confessor destroyed this good faith and did not succeed in making him give up his sin, he transformed an unwitting sin into a mortal one.[8] What really is the theory of "good faith," if not the awareness that other models of behavior existed among Catholic peoples than those formulated by the theologians?

We know that theologians, under the blanket concept of the "sin against nature," included all sexual acts which do not result in the insemination of the woman, and that they considered this "sin against nature" as the greatest of sexual faults, even more serious than incest or the rape of a nun. Noonan does not hesitate to consider this ranking within the hierarchy of sins as the principal means by which contraceptive practices were discouraged.[9] But to accept this means also to accept

---

[7]See Bergues, *Prévention des naissances*, pp. 227–29.

[8]See Noonan, *Contraception*, pp. 375–79.

[9]See Noonan, *Contraception*. At the beginning of chap. 9, "Sanctions," Noonan writes: "By stamping contraceptive behavior as mortal sin, the theologians of the high Middle Ages,

without debate the theory that different social groups understood this expression in the same manner as the theologians, and that, like the theologians, they considered the acts it designates to be the worst sexual transgressions.

Must we therefore conclude that sincerity while sinning is a new phenomenon, characteristic of the eighteenth and even the nineteenth century? And must we say that during preceding periods a sin could be unwittingly committed solely because Church doctrine had not been sufficiently diffused? I do not think so. On the contrary, I believe that—with the exception of a few devout circles—the status given by theologians to the concept of the "crime against nature" was never fully accepted.

Indeed, the purpose of this concept seems to me to be twofold. On the one hand—and Noonan placed too little stress on this—it is polemical: it is a question of persuading those accustomed to practicing sterile acts that these acts are a form of sodomy, condemned by St. Paul on the basis of Old Testament texts and considered by him as contrary to nature. This procedure is an ordinary one and had already been used to group all sorts of fornication under the sixth commandment, concerning adultery. On the other hand, it is explanatory and rationalizing: the evil of these acts lies in their very opposition to the law of nature. I therefore interpret this position as being the antithesis of an interdict; and I doubt whether it succeeded in becoming a part of the moral conscience of the Christian masses in the Middle Ages.

Though I have not studied local customs and folklore, let us at least see whether the law includes this concept of a crime against nature. It is well known that judicial procedure sent sodomites to be burned at the stake

---

in agreement with the penitentials and the Fathers, maintained the most serious and most universal deterrent to contraceptive usage by a conscientious Christian. . . . To the extent that the Christian people were informed of the sinful character of the act, and to the extent that they were devoutly seeking their salvation, the branding of contraception as mortal sin must have been the most powerful sanction against its practice" (p. 258). And further on: "The theologians and canonists proclaimed that nonprocreative marital intercourse, including coitus interruptus, was a form of the sin against nature. Peter Cantor, John Gerson, Bernardine, and Antoninus assimilated such intercourse to the even uglier category of sodomy. . . . In the ranking of sins of lechery, the sin against nature was said by *Adulterii malum* to be worse than incest. Gratian's ordering was maintained by the standard works of theology. In Thomas' *Summa theologica*, the sin against nature, including the sin in marriage, is the greatest of sexual vices, being worse than fornication, seduction, rape, incest, or sacrilege . . ." (pp. 260–61).

"This kind of ranking contributed to a social attitude: these descriptions functioned as epithets as well as analyses. To the best of their linguistic ability, the medieval scholastics sought to label contraception as an affront to decency, life, and nature. The man who engaged in contraceptive behavior had not only to ignore the spiritual consequences, but to defy the social ideals of his community" (p. 261).

and condemned to death all those guilty of bestiality; but though it was very strict about incest and adultery, there was no concern at all with other unnatural acts.

In principle, canon law shows more concern. It sets forth three penalties for husbands guilty of deceiving nature: denial of the conjugal bed, separation or divorce "*a toro*," and annulment of the marriage. But research in judicial archives would be required to find out whether these penalties were really applied before the nineteenth century, and at this point no one seems ready to confirm this. Even if they were applied, they would have been aimed at contraception within a marriage and not extramaritally.

While those involved in extramarital relationships were not punishable under canon law, they could still be chastized through the confessional, which had the authority to exert pressure on those committing unnatural acts by demanding greater penance than for other sexual sins.

During the early Middle Ages, the penance imposed for such sins is known to us through the penitentials. Noonan, who studied twenty of them dating from the sixth through ninth centuries, shows us that all penitentials, save one, were concerned with one or several contraceptive measures. Not only "poisons creating sterility"—apparently connected with the crime of sorcery—but two sorts of unnatural intercourse[10] were considered grave sins by all those mentioning them. Many authors imposed for these sins a penance equal to that for homicide; and all considered them more serious than aborting a fetus of less than forty days. This severity—as Noonan has clearly observed—suggests that these contraceptive measures were attacked in their own right and not in order to protect a potential human life. The penance for these sins points out the order of their magnitude: from three to fifteen years of fasting.

In the case of onanism, the penance was slightly less—two to ten years—but the order of magnitude of the penance was identical. And, in the only two works which mention it explicitly,[11] it was included in the same article as that dealing with contraceptive and abortive potions and was punished with the same severity. This information had eluded Noonan's predecessors, and it is of marked interest. I note, however, that this practice is only referred to in two articles which are in every way identical, and that no penitential mentions it alone. It is thus difficult to measure its real status at the time.

[10]These unnatural acts were oral intercourse—"*seminem in ore*"—and anal intercourse—"*a tergo*"—the first of which is encountered in five, and the other in nine of the eighteen penitentials. (See Noonan, *Contraception*, pp. 162 and 164.)

[11]The Saint-Hubert (chap. 57) and the Mersebourg B (chap. 13) are two eighth-century Frankish penitentials. They describe this act as "the spilling of seed in coitus with a woman, as the sons of Judah did to Tamar." (See Noonan, *Contraception*, pp. 161–62.)

This is all the more true since a number of articles in the several penitentials I have read appear to contradict the works just mentioned in terms of the severity of the sin. It is first of all evident that solitary practices—which are also crimes against nature, according to later theologians—were viewed with great indulgence, even when they were committed by clerics, thereby profaning a church; the penance was from seven days up to fifty in the case of a bishop within a church.[12] It is thus a matter of minor sins, much less serious, for example, than sexual intercourse between married people during Lent,[13] than rape (punished by a year of penance),[14] and even less so than simple fornication.[15] But there is more: one wonders whether contraception was not encouraged in illicit relationships since the punishment was increased if the relationship was fertile, while on the contrary it decreased when the couple succeeded in sullying itself without a true copulation.[16] Hélène Bergues, who has pored over a similar text, has learned from it that scandal was penalized as well as the sin itself.[17] Agreed. But did this not implicitly orient the sinner toward measures which would avoid scandal?

Finally, a study of penitentials dating from the sixth through eleventh centuries reveals that the unitary concept of the "crime against nature," as later theologians would define it, was not current and that in any event certain acts later included under that heading were viewed with indulgence. Coitus interruptus, or onanism, the chief means of contraception in the modern period, still attracted little attention. Is this because it was

[12]See Migne's *Patrologia latina*, vol. 99, col. 1971–72: "*De fundendo semen.* Clericus si semen fuderit non tangendo, septem dies poeniteat. Si tangit cum manu, viginti dies. Si diaconus, triginta dies. Si presbyter hebdomadas quatuor.

"Presbyter si semen fuderit per cogitationem, septem dies poeniteat. Monachus similiter.

"Qui voluntarie semen fudit in ecclesia, si clericus est, quatuordecim; si monachus aut diachonus, triginta dies; si presbyter, quadraginta; episcopus, quinquaginta dies poeniteat."

[13]Ibid., vol. 99, col. 966. "Coinquinatus es cum uxore tua in quadragesima. Si hoc fecisti, annum unum poenitere debes, aut viginti sex solidos in eleemosynam dare. Si per ebrietatem evenit, quadraginta dies poeniteas."

[14]Ibid., vol. 99, col. 970. "*De fornicatione.* . . . Adolescens si cum virgine peccaverit, annum poeniteat. Si seme et fortuito casu, levigetur ei poenitentia et tantum usque ad annum plenum poeniteat."

[15]Ibid. "Si infra triginta annos adolescens fornicationem faciat, tres quadragesimes et legitimas ferias."

[16]Ibid. "Laicus maculans se cum ancilla Dei, duos annos poeniteat. Si genuerit ex ea filium, annos tres poeniteat. Si sine conjugio est, tres quadragesimas et legitimas ferias." The expression "sully oneself" (*maculans se*) is ambiguous. But if the third case is compared to the first, it appears evident that in the latter it is a question of intercourse. And it is sterile intercourse, as in the second case.

[17]See Bergues, *Prévention des naissances*, p. 209, in which the author comments upon a similar passage from the Cummean II penitential, anterior to the collection edited by Migne. "If a lay person corrupts a virgin devoted to God and loses his reputation and if he has a child of her, let this man do penance for three years . . . If, however, there is no child, but nevertheless he corrupts the virgin, he shall do penance for one year."

rarely practiced, as the heavy penance prescribed by two penitentials would lead one to believe? Or is it, on the contrary, that in illicit relations it was deemed less guilty than complete and fertile copulation? In the present state of research, it is impossible to draw a conclusion on this point.

After the eleventh century, the confessor was much freer to choose the penance he would impose upon the sinner, and as a result it is more difficult for us to gain a concrete idea of the importance given to different sins. Yet we would be wrong to believe that the confessors were totally free and to imagine that the historian has no freedom at all. A certain number of sins was indeed reserved for absolution by the bishop, and the parish priest could not therefore pardon them. It is clear that this more-difficult-to-obtain absolution made those mortal sins thus set apart appear more serious in the eyes of the Christian population. And, according to whether or not a sin was reserved, the historian has the right to consider the resulting interdict as more or less serious. Now, we possess a great number of medieval and modern synodal statutes, and these statutes rarely fail to include a list of sins reserved for the bishop of the diocese. We therefore have in them a means of measuring the weight, the stability, and the variability of religious interdicts, across space and time.

It is not my aim here to analyze these documents in a chronological or comparative manner. I will limit myself to an arbitrary sampling of seventeen lists of reserved cases—all French—lists which stretch from the thirteenth to the seventeenth century.[18]

First let us examine the list of reserved cases in the diocese of Cambrai (1300–1310). It has the merit of indicating for us the sins reserved for the bishop, those which he could delegate to the penitentiaries-general sent out into the deaneries, and those which he turned over to the parish priests and vicars. Sins against nature are found in all three groups:

—*reserved for the bishop*: sins against nature by a man over twenty years of age.

—*reserved for the penitentiaries*: sins against nature perpetrated by women of any age and by men of less than twenty; "manual pollution" at any age.

—*jurisdiction of the parish priest*: "disordered copulation with women"; the sin of "voluptuousness" or autoeroticism [*mollicies*]; sins against nature during childhood, for boys up to the age of fourteen and for girls to the age of twenty-five.

[18]Synodal statutes of the dioceses of Meaux (1245), Cambrai (1300–1310), Nantes (1387), Albi (1230, 1553, and 1695), Malines (1570), Besançon (1571), Reims (1585–1621 and 1677), Amiens (1411, 1454, and 1677), Agen (1666–73), Sens (1658); and, from the *Somme des Péchés* of Benedicti (1584), the list of cases reserved for the archbishop of Lyon and that of those reserved for the bishop of Paris.

By comparing these sins, we can deduce that those sins called simply
"sins against nature" are in all probability homosexual acts. They were
less serious for girls than for boys, and this appears to me to agree with
what is known of judicial practice. We must still determine the meaning of
the word "*mollicies*," since "manual pollution at any age" is referred to
elsewhere.[19] As for "disordered copulation with women," this may mean
simple fornication, which is not included elsewhere; it may also denote
any intercourse which obviously renders conception impossible and other
forms of intercourse deemed nonconformist solely on the grounds of
position. Let me stress that disordered copulation, like autoeroticism, fell
under the jurisdiction of the parish priest, while incest, when it involved a
close relative, was within the bishop's jurisdiction and, when the relationship was more distant, that of the penitentiary; sexual relations with nuns
were considered a form of serious incest and were under the bishop's
jurisdiction; adultery fell under the jurisdiction of the penitentiary, and
rape under that of the parish priest.

In the sixteen other lists, the cases reserved for the bishop are not
indicated. It is therefore not easy to dispell the ambiguity of the expression "sin against nature." But it is noteworthy that one of the sins against
nature is condemned with unusual constancy; that is sodomy, which is
explicitly mentioned ten times. Of these ten lists, only one uses the
concept of "sin against nature," and its scope is restricted: "sodomy and
any other even more grave sin against nature."[20] Six others include
bestiality with sodomy.[21] In addition, no other sin against nature is
specifically mentioned, with the exception of the autoerotic acts or
mollicies cited by the most severe of our synodal statutes.[22]

Why is this equivocal sin of autoeroticism mentioned only once, and
then on the strictest list? Why do they never openly refer to contraceptive

[19]The word "*mollicies*" which, in Antiquity, meant passive homosexuality, by the
thirteenth century had taken on the meaning of "solitary practices," or masturbation. Before
the nubile age, these practices did not involve seminal emissions and were considered to be
less grave. Moreover, voluntary ejaculation was not always manual: it could result from
"cogitation and delectation," from "locution or conversations with women or men," from
"reading immodest books" and "other means," as Benedicti specified in the sixteenth
century. Finally, "manual pollution" is not necessarily solitary, and when it is not, the sin is
more grave. This is the sole distinction which the bishop of Cambrai makes between
autoerotic acts, or *mollicies*, and "manual pollution."

[20]List of cases reserved for the bishop of Amiens in 1677.

[21]As in the diocese of Cambrai—if one accepts my interpretation—three synodal statutes
fail to mention bestiality among those sins reserved for the bishop: they are those of the
dioceses of Malines (1570), Besançon (1571), and Amiens (1411).

[22]That of the diocese of Nantes (1387). I call it more strict because it is the only one to
maintain an old Biblical interdict about conjugal relations during menstruation. In addition,
it mentions adultery, incest—both natural and spiritual—and the sins of the flesh "*cum
masculis, cum brutis, cum sanctimonialibus.*" Its evocation of autoeroticism is instructive:
"de peccato molliciei quod omme adulterum superat." This detail appears to weaken my

intercourse with women? Why never to masturbation? Is it out of discretion? But the ten lists which mention sodomy seem to show little concern for discretion and yet make no further references to it. Is this because these practices were not very widespread? But who will insist, on the basis of that principle, that masturbation was less widespread than sodomy or bestiality? After examining all these questions in light of what we have learned from the statutes of Cambrai, I tend to think that only sodomy and bestiality are hidden behind the expressions "sin against nature" and "sins against nature"; all other acts which the theologians included under that blanket concept were undoubtedly sins within the jurisdiction of the parish priest.

In the improbable event that these other acts are also designated by the expressions in question, we would be obliged to note that they were, at the maximum, reserved for the bishop in only seven of the seventeen lists studied, while incest is explicitly listed all seventeen times, adultery nine, and rape eight. In short, a study of the lists of reserved cases confirms what we have learned from judicial practice: the great crimes were sodomy, bestiality, incest, and adultery, and not the sin against nature as such, and less still masturbation or coitus interruptus. The numerous attestations of theologians to the contrary are polemical and rationalizing. They are not as revealing of social pressure and the reality of the interdicts as are the lists of reserved cases or judicial practice.

* * *

Now let us see whether contraception is forbidden with equal rigor within marriage and without.

Noonan, in his study of the penitentials, observes that, when they punished women for using contraceptive drugs, they were more indulgent toward the poor woman overburdened with children than toward the lewd one who tried to hide her sin.[23] Are we to conclude from this that

---

thesis. In reality it confirms the fact that this classification is not self-evident, since there is no need to say that much about homosexuality, bestiality, and sacrilege.

[23]Bede, in determining the penance imposed for abortion, wrote in his penitential: "It makes a big difference if a poor little woman [*paupercula*] does it on account of the difficulty of feeding or whether a fornicator does it to conceal her crime" (4.12). "The same rule," writes Noonan, "was followed for abortion by Pseudo-Theodore (6.4). The economic reasons which would prompt infanticide or abortion would seem to operate with equal force to stimulate recourse to contraception." (See Noonan, *Contraception*, p. 160.)

Burchard, in the eleventh century, is the first to assert this: "Have you done what some women are accustomed to do when they fornicate and wish to kill their offspring, act with their *maleficia* and their herbs so that they kill or cut out the embryo, or, if they have not yet conceived, contrive that they do not conceive? If you have done so, or consented to this, or

contraception as we define it was a more serious offense outside marriage than within? I do not think so. For the use of contraceptive drugs is an act which is distinct from intercourse itself; it is not a sin of lechery but a crime involving infanticide and sorcery.[24] Thus one can consider poverty and numerous children as an attenuating circumstance. But here I am talking of the sin against nature, that is, the sexual act which is of its own nature sterile. Now, we have seen that—with the exception of sodomy and bestiality—the penitentials were more strict about illicit sexual acts resulting in the conception of bastards than about those which were sterile. It seems to me that the penitentials were implicitly pushing people toward extramarital contraception.

Established between the twelfth and thirteenth centuries, Church law devoted three canons to contraception.[25] The canon "*Si aliquis*," borrowed from the penitentials, likens the use of "sterilizing poisons"[26] to homicide, while the two others—"*Aliquando*" and "*Si conditiones*"—attack contraception as contrary to marriage.[27] Now we have already said

---

taught it, you must do penance for ten years on legal feriae. But an ancient determination removed such from the Church till the end of their lives. For as often as she impeded a conception, so many homicides was a woman guilty of. But it makes a big difference whether she is a poor little woman and acted on account of the difficulty of feeding, or whether she acted to conceal a crime of fornication" (*Decretum* 19, in Migne's *Patrologia latina*, vol. 140, col. 972, as quoted in Noonan, *Contraception*, p. 160).

[24]Since Antiquity, and on into the eighteenth century, contraceptive drugs were generally cited along with abortive measures, poisons, love potions, and all sorts of magic or *maleficium*. On the other hand, the questions of infanticide, abortion, and contraception by sorcery are often handled together, while contraceptive intercourse is treated with the sins of lechery. Before the thirteenth century, the only examples likening these two sorts of sins to one another is to be found, if I am not mistaken, in these two Frankish penitentials of the eighth century which deal with the sin of Onan.

[25]By "Church law" I mean Gratian's *Decretum* (1140) and the *Decretals* begun by St. Raymond of Pennafort in 1230. To these can be added the *Sentences* (1154–57) of Peter Lombard, which have the same authority for theologians as the *Decretum* and the *Decretals* for canonists.

[26]Here is Noonan's translation of this canon: "*He who practices magic or gives sterilizing poisons is a murderer.* If someone (*Si aliquis*) to satisfy his lust or in deliberate hatred does something to a man or woman so that no children be born of him or her, or gives them to drink, so that he cannot generate or she conceive, let it be held as homicide" (Noonan, *Contraception*, p. 168). But none of the great canonists or theologians applies this categorical rule to self-sterilization.

[27]The canon "*Aliquando*" is taken verbatim from the "Marriage and Concupiscence" of St. Augustine. "Sometimes (*Aliquando*) this lecherous cruelty or cruel lechery reaches a point at which even sterilizing poisons (*sterilitatis venena*) are used, and, if the latter do not work, [they] extinguish and destroy the fetus in the womb in some manner, preferring that their progeny die before being born. Assuredly, if the husband and wife are both like that, they are not married, and if they have been like that since the beginning of their life together, they are not joined in marriage but in seduction. If they are not both like this, I dare say that either the woman is a sort of whore to her husband, or else he is an adulterer with his own wife."

that the only canonical punishments for any heterosexual copulation which was intrinsically contraceptive were aimed at a search for sterility in marriage, and not extramaritally. The stricter the enforcement of these canons, the clearer it becomes that contraception was considered an extramarital practice.

This is not surprising. These two canons, which came more or less directly from St. Augustine,[28] have to do with the question of sexual behavior in which, from the second to the nineteenth century, the doctors of the Church became totally engrossed.[29] Any attempt at carnal pleasure was condemned: the conjugal act was considered more than a carnal encounter; it was deemed an act of procreation desired by God and by nature. Indeed, St. Augustine, to return to him, believed that sexual pleasure was inevitably corrupted by lust and saw the procreative act as the necessary legitimation of the conjugal act. Even when St. Thomas Aquinas rehabilitated the notion of pleasure resulting from the marriage act, he firmly maintained that pleasure in the act should be condemned as an end.

Now, the characteristic end of any extramarital intercourse is the search for pleasure for its own sake. Arguing against concubinage, St. Thomas wrote: "Whoever, therefore, uses copulation for the delight which is in it, not referring the intention to the end intended by nature, acts against nature."[30] Elsewhere, he shows that any act of lechery is a mortal sin because it is not done for procreation and the rearing of offspring.[31] "The human seed," he wrote, "in which man is in potentiality, is ordered for the life of man. . . . And therefore disorder in the emission

---

This text was included by Gratian in his decree, "*Si aliquis*" having been superceded.

"*Si aliquis*" was taken up once more by St. Raymond, who included it in the *Decretals*; he also included the canon "*Si conditiones*," which is a corollary, drawn up through his efforts, of the Augustinian canon. "If conditions (*Si conditiones*) are placed upon the substance of the marriage—for example, if one says to the other, 'I will contract marriage with you if you avoid children,' or 'until I find someone more worthy in honor or in riches,' or 'if you turn to adultery for money'—the marriage contract, however privileged it may be, is nullified; although other conditions, base and impossible though they may be, must be held as invalid by reason of the privilege of marriage."

That is to say that the majority of conditions in the marriage must be considered null, for marriage is not conditional. But when these conditions are contrary to one of the basic grounds for the marriage—*proles, sacramentum* and *fides*, to list them in the order of the canon—these conditions are diriment; the marriage is invalid. In particular, to refuse procreation is to refuse the marriage.

[28]"*Aliquando*" came directly, "*Si conditiones*" indirectly.

[29]See the whole of Noonan's *Contraception*, and especially chaps. 3 and 4.

[30]St. Thomas Aquinas, *On the Sentences*, 4.33.1.3, quoted by Noonan, *Contraception*, pp. 241–42.

[31]St. Thomas Aquinas, *De Malo*, 15.2, obj. 14, analyzed by Noonan, *Contraception*, p. 243.

of seed concerns the life of man in potentiality."[32] This attack against potential life makes the sin of lechery a mortal one.

For St. Thomas the lecherous act not only injures the potential individual child in the squandered seed, but the human species in general, whose preservation is thus threatened.[33] "The seed, although superfluous for the conservation of the individual, is yet necessary to the propagation of the species. . . . Hence . . . it is also required that it be emitted to be of use in generation, to which coitus is ordained." And he concludes, "The disordered emission of seed is contrary to the good of nature, which is the conservation of the species."[34]

This argument is not aimed at contraception per se, but at fornication. For St. Thomas, any extramarital intercourse, be it biologically fertile or sterile, is a disorder in the emission of semen, an injury done to the human species, and consequently to nature and to God. By the very fact that it is sought outside marriage, its aim is pleasure and it perverts the order of nature. On St. Thomas' level of reasoning, contraception seems to add nothing to the sin of fornication, except, I imagine, a more concerted scorn for the laws of nature.

This disorder in the emission of semen can also occur within a marriage, and all theologians called the married couple's attention to this fact. Some considered the search for pleasure in marriage to be a mortal sin:[35] others a venial sin.[36] But all recalled St. Jerome's warning that the man who displays too much ardor while making love to his wife is an adulterer. Let us pause at the statement which Benedicti gave in 1584 concerning this warning:

The husband who, transported by immoderate love, has intercourse with his wife so *ardently* in order to satisfy his passion that even had she not been his wife, he would have wished to have commerce with her, is committing a sin. And St. Jerome seems to confirm this when he cites the words of Sixtus Pythagorician, who said that the man who shows himself to be an *uncontrollable lover* of his wife, rather than her *husband*, is an adulterer. And yet this is not to say that since the man has his wife's body at his bidding, he should take advantage of her as he

---

[32]St. Thomas Aquinas, *De Malo*, 15.2, quoted by Noonan, *Contraception*, p. 244.

[33]See Noonan, *Contraception*, pp. 244–45.

[34]St. Thomas Aquinas, *De Malo*, 3.122, quoted by Noonan, *Contraception*, pp. 244–45.

[35]These are, for example, St. Raymond (*Summa*, 4.2.8) and Monaldus (*Summa*, fol. 136 r°) in the twelfth century; St. Bernardine of Siena (*Seraphic Sermons*, 19.3) in the fifteenth: as well as the unknown summist used by Chaucer in his "Parson's Tale" (authors quoted by Noonan, *Contraception*, p. 250).

[36]Noonan (*Contraception*, p. 250) quotes, for example, Alexander of Hales, St. Thomas Aquinas, St. Bonaventure, William of Rennes, Durand of Saint-Pourçain, Peter de Palude, John Gerson, and St. Antoninus of Florence.

pleases, for the proverb says, "One can get drunk on one's own wine." Which means that a man must not use his wife as a *whore*, nor the wife behave toward her husband as with a *lover*: for this holy sacrament of marriage must be treated with all honesty and reverence. Note this, you other married couples who make of your bed your god.[37]

Ariès and Noonan have already wondered about what might comprise that "immoderate love" denounced by theologians and preachers. St. Thomas, St. Bonaventura, Gerson, and St. Bernardine of Siena take it to mean preferring sexual union with one's wife over union with God. Chaucer is also apparently criticizing this idolatry in his "Parson's Tale," leading Ariès to conclude that it is rather a question of amorous passion than of sexual depravity. Noonan observes that every mortal sin can be defined as a preference for a temporal end over the eternal union with God, and that unless this interpretation is understood to be particularly aimed at courtly love, it is inadequate.

Other theologians[38]—and Benedicti appears to agree—reproach the husband for having "commerce with his wife as if she were not his wife." Trying to arrive at a concrete meaning, Noonan conceives of only one solution: "Using one's wife as a whore" means preventing conception.

By its surprising parallel of the two words "lover" and "whore," Benedicti's statement permits us to move ahead in our thinking. By granting them the same value, he negates the dichotomy reached by Noonan and Ariès, both imprisoned in too contemporary a vision of things. Indeed, neither "lover" nor "whore" have the meaning and value which we give them today. The meaning of lover at that time was not very far from the current meaning, to the degree that, today as in the sixteenth century, the lover is animated by an emotion more limited than love for his neighbor. But the intent of the word in this text is completely different from today's meaning; contemporary Western civilization has given it a positive meaning,[39] and the Church today has accepted roughly the same

[37]Benedicti, *La Somme des péchez* . . . (Paris, 1601), bk. 2, chap. 9, "De l'excès des gens mariez" [On the excesses of married persons], no. 59, Bibliothèque nationale: D. 6502.

[38]Noonan (*Contraception*, p. 251) cites, for example, William of Auxerre, Alexander of Hales, St. Bonaventure, Astesanus, Durand of Saint-Pourçain, St. Antoninus of Florence. Albert the Great and St. Thomas Aquinas liken overly ardent love to "using one's wife as a whore," as Benedicti does here.

[39]See my article "Sentiments et civilisations," *Annales: E.S.C.*, Sept.–Oct. 1965, especially pp. 952–57. Concerning the Church's attitude toward love, many interesting things are found in Noonan, *Contraception*, especially pp. 324–25 (but there is a great deal more to be said about the late sixteenth century) and above all pp. 491–504. On the other hand, the author's comments about the Church's attitude toward love in the Middle Ages (pp. 254–57) did not seem very convincing to me.

connotation. Yet in the sixteenth century love was an extremely controversial subject and, on the whole, Christian morality denied its existence. The lover, in the Christian vision of that period, was a paramour, a wencher, a lecher, though at the same time he was what we today call a lover.

On the other hand, the word "whore," so abundantly used in that period, had the pejorative meaning which it still has today, but for reasons different from ours. We and our sixteenth-century ancestors both apply it to prostitutes; but we reproach them for playing the game out of love for money, while they reproached them for devoting their life to it. At that time, therefore, the word was properly applied to any woman who sought carnal relations out of passion or for pleasure; the honest woman was supposed to seek them only for the good of the marriage, in conformity to the duties of her position—we might almost say "from professional conscientiousness." This is a paradoxical about-face in the social values hidden behind a single word.

In short, the behavior of married persons is systematically contrasted with that of lovers; the former are connected with procreation, the latter with the search for sterile pleasure. Similarly, the "natural" manner of intercourse is contrasted with unusual ones, which are called unnatural and are suspected of being sterile.

Indeed, the positions of sexual intercourse are a traditional subject for theological discussions. "Unnatural" positions have never been condemned on the basis of a personalist view of marriage, in which the individual is supreme, but in the name of the age-old marriage rite,[40] which has at its foundation certain notions regarding the relationship

[40]For all theologians there is, indeed, a single, natural position for intercourse. All the interrogations of confessors on this matter begin with the question or statement, "You know the natural position. . . ." The thing is so obvious that almost no one ever says why that position is natural, except when they are attacking those which are not. We are faced with a custom whose origin must be sought in prehistoric times; it is connected, I imagine, with the ritual gesture of the plowman, although no text permits me to support this supposition. In any case, it seems clear to me that marital intercourse is a ritual, a fertility rite. Indeed, Thomas Sanchez, more explicit than most other casuists, begins his chapter by an explanation: "We must first of all establish what is the natural manner of intercourse as far as position is concerned. As for the latter, the man must lie on top and the woman on her back beneath. Because this manner is more appropriate for the effusion of the male seed, for its reception into the female vessel and its retention. . . ." Sanchez' genius lies in explaining everything promptly. However, when it comes to condemning unnatural positions, the question of pure ritual does not escape him: "It is an abuse of the sacrament of marriage, and it is evident that it is a perversion of the usage and also of the ritual . . . and that it is a sacrilege worthy of hell" (De Sancto matrimonii sacramento [Antwerp, 1607] bk. 9, dispute 16, q. 1).

between a man and woman[41] that exclude the idea of excessive pleasure,[42] and which shows concern for procreation.[43] When theologians have tolerated certain of these forms of intercourse—as they frequently did in the sixteenth century—it is on the condition that they have been shown to

[41]The position which theologians call "*retro*" and which Brantôme calls "*more canino*" had been denounced from the early Middle Ages on as lowering man to the level of the animal. Here it is not a question of intercourse between two partners, but of the honor of the human species. On this subject Sanchez wrote: ". . . Since nature has ordained this method for animals, the man who develops a taste for it becomes like them." However, the position "*mulier super virum*" appears more serious, and Sanchez attacks it much more vigorously:

"4) This method is absolutely contrary to the order of nature since it stands in the way of the man's ejaculation and the retention of the seed within the female vessel. Also, not only the position, but the condition of the persons is important. Indeed, it is natural for the man to act and for the woman to be passive; and if the man is beneath, he becomes submissive by the very fact of this position, and the woman being above is active; and who cannot see how much nature herself abhors this mutation?

"5) Because in scholastic history (ca. 31 *super Genesium ex Metodio*) it is said that the cause of the Flood was that women, carried away by madness, used men improperly, the latter being beneath and the former above. . . . St. Paul said to the Romans: 'Their women did change the natural use into that which is against nature,' and he places this sin among the deadly ones."

[42]The association of these unusual positions with the condemnation of overly ardent loves is invariable. Though excerpts from theological treatises make this apparent only rarely, many proofs are to be found. Among the lay writers, for example, Brantôme returns to the subject on several occasions, fascinated as he seems to be by "Aretino's positions": "In addition these husbands, which is worse, teach their wives, in their own bed, a thousand lascivious things, a thousand whorish acts, a thousand tricks, convolutions, new ways, and practice upon them those heinous positions of Aretino; so that from one glowing ember in their body a hundred are engendered, and they are thus turned into whores" (Brantôme, *Dames galantes*, ed. Maurice Rat [Paris, 1960] p. 26). And further on, in a more scholastic manner: "All these forms and postures are odious to God, so that St. Jerome said, 'Whoever shows himself rather an immoderate lover of his wife than a husband is an adulterer and is sinning.'"

Of course theologians also refer to this search for excessive pleasure. For example, Peter de Palude in his *On the Sentences* (d. 31, q. 3, art. 2, 5°) wrote: "Some say . . . that the man who knows his wife in an unaccustomed manner, even within the natural vessel, sins mortally, if this is done in a search for increased voluptuousness."

[43]Theologians were not unanimous in condemning these unusual positions, and the essence of the discussion was based on their fertile or sterile nature. These positions were called "unnatural" because they are contrary to the ritual of intercourse ordained by nature, because certain ones pervert human nature by modeling man after the animal, because others invert the nature of the male and the female, and finally because they are suspected of being sterile and are therefore contrary to the nature of marriage—unless the inverse is true, that is to say that voluptuous relations are deemed contrary to the nature of marriage and are therefore suspected of being sterile. The direction of this causal relationship is of little importance: what counts is the grouping of these characteristics under the general concept of sin against nature. Moreover, sterile couples were often suspected of having deserved this divine punishment for their lecherous practices. It would be nearly impossible for them to have been deprived of descendants, said the English preacher Bromyard in the fourteenth century, if they had sought the end intended by God: therefore they sought lust or riches in marriage. (See *Summa*, "Matrimonium," 8.10, quoted by Noonan, *Contraception*, pp. 268–69.)

be fertile,[44] and that they be used through necessity,[45] and not for pleasure. We might well wonder what impact this new example of theological rationalization had upon the faithful. In any event, a layman like Brantôme, who cannot easily be accused of excessive prudishness, mentions this opinion with obvious reticence:

> Other learned doctors say that whatever form is used is good, but that "*semen ejaculetur in matricem mulieris, et quomodocumque uxor cognoscatur, si vir ejaculetur semen in matricem, non est peccatum mortale.*"
>
> These disputes are to be found in the *Summa Benedicti*, the work of a learned Franciscan who has written very well about every sin and has shown that he had seen and read a great deal. Whoever reads this passage will find there a great number of abuses which husbands commit upon their wives. He also says that "*quando mulier est ita pinguis ut non possit aliter coire*" in any other position, that in such a case "*non est peccatum mortale, modo vir ejaculetur semen in vas naturale.*" Others say that it would be better for husbands to abstain from intercourse with their pregnant wife, as do the animals, than to sully their marriage by such outrages.[46]

Now, did he consider these "outrages" to be inadmissible in an extramarital relationship? This does not seem to have been the case, for he speaks lightly of those "positions of Aretino" in an extramarital context,[47] only

[44]The position *mulier super virum* is even justified in the name of the absorptive nature of the uterus. Such a justification, to tell the truth, is rare.

[45]The most frequent case is that of the pregnant woman who was afraid of harming her fruit by having normal relations with her husband. There are also many references to husbands who were too obese to have normal relations.

[46]Brantôme, *Dames galantes*, p. 32. The entire discussion of this question, beginning on p. 25, is very instructive. On several occasions Brantôme refers to the Scriptures, to the Church Fathers, and to the doctors of theology. Perhaps the intention of the discussion—to show that husbands are the chief persons responsible for the dissipation of their wives—weakens the value of his testimony. I do not, however, believe that the entire cause for the author's indignation can be found in this context of a speech for the defense.

[47]In an extramarital context, this, for example, is what he says: ". . . He bought from a goldsmith a very beautiful cup in silver gilt, a masterpiece and great speciality which was the best executed, engraved, and hallmarked which one could possibly find, on which were engraved nicely and subtly several of Aretino's positions showing a man and a woman . . . and above . . . several showing various manners of cohabiting between beasts" (Brantôme, *Dames galantes*, pp. 27–28). "When this prince entertained courtly ladies and maidens . . . his wine stewards never failed . . . to offer them a drink from it; . . . some remained astonished and did not know what to say; others remained ashamed and color rose to their cheeks; none of them said to her companions, 'What is engraved on that [cup]? I think those are filthy pictures. I will not drink from it any more. I would have to be very thirsty before taking another drink from it.' . . . and therefore, some closed their eyes while drinking, others, more shameless, did not. Those who had heard about the tricks of the trade, both women and maids, began to stifle their laughter; others burst out laughing. . . . Some said, 'Those are very lovely grotesques'; others, 'What pleasant mummeries'; and others said, 'What pretty pictures.'. . .

becoming indignant when he contemplates them within a marriage. Though he is rather insensitive to the rationalizations of the theologians, he appears to have fully accepted the contrast between matrimonial and amorous behavior which had marked the Christian doctrine of sexuality since the second century.

Doubtlessly the antinomy between pleasure and procreation inherited from classical morality[48] and carried on by ecclesiastical culture did not succeed in imposing itself completely. Brantôme himself reveals the existence of contrasting views;[49] and medical literature, nourished by other classical traditions, confirms this.[50] But in the same sentence Brantôme implies that this association of extraordinary pleasure with procreation is abnormal; and the medical profession, imitating theologians, expressed its suspicions that "overly ardent" love was sterile. Thus, despite the existence of an opposing viewpoint among some laymen, and despite the medical profession's Aristotelian mistrust of excess in general—an attitude which may be discerned in actual medical practice—it

---

"In short, there were a hundred thousand sorts of jests, and small talk on the subject. . . . It was very pleasant banter and something to see and hear; but above all, to my mind, the best was to contemplate these innocent maidens or those who feigned to be so. . . . Finally they became so used to [the cup] that they no longer felt any scruples about drinking from it; and others did even better and made use of such visions in proper time and place; and, even more, some debauched themselves in order to try it out: for every clever person wants to try everything.

"Those are the fine results of this beautiful and much talked of goblet. . . . In this cup the wine did not laugh at the people, but the people at the wine: for some drank while laughing and others drank while experiencing ecstasy . . ." (pp. 27–30).

This account, therefore, has nothing at all in common with the consistently indignant, serious, and moralizing tone which he adopts when speaking of such intercourse in marriage.

[48]See Noonan, *Contraception*, passim, but especially p. 46–75.

[49]For example, when he writes: "Nevertheless there are some women who say that they conceive better while in monstrous, supernatural, and strange postures than in natural and usual ones, espeially since they take more pleasure in them and, as the poet says, when they do it *"more canino,"* which is odious" (Brantôme, *Dames galantes*, p. 31).

[50]Here, for example, is what Jacques Dubois, called Sylvius, wrote in his *"De mensibus mulierum et hominis generatione* . . .*"* (Basel, 1556): '*Coitus inanis.* Praeter hos etiam coitus coitui succedens, et coactus alterutrius, vel utriusque concubitus, ut in his qui inviti, et sine amore juguntur, inanis est, ac sterilis: ut voluntarius et jucundus, est foecundus, nisi amor nimis ardens adsit."

For a contemporary French translation, see Guillaume Chrestien, *Le livre de la génération de l'homme* (Paris, 1559), p. 39, which paraphrased reads: In addition, there is also coitus following upon coitus, and coitus in which one person is compelled by the other: and either copulation—like that of those who are bored and are married and united without their will and without love—is vain and sterile, just as that which is voluntary, agreeable, and pleasant is fertile, unless there has been an overly ardent passion.

Is this a matter of a traditional association of pleasure with fertility, or is it the realization by physicians of the day that interpersonal attraction is necessary in marriage? This question deserves further research in other texts.

appears that the antinomy between pleasure and procreation was widely accepted by those outside ecclesiastical circles.

Pleasure, sterility, whims contrary to the order of nature—this is the associative context of extramartial sexual relations. But do we find texts which, speaking explicitly of contraception, make a distinction between married persons and fornicators?

First, in order not to mislead the reader who is unfamiliar with the moral and theological literature of the past, let us point out that all authors dealing with the subject unequivocally condemned contraceptive intercourse, and that this condemnation made no exception for intercourse occurring extramaritally.

Nevertheless, when discussing the conjugal versus nonconjugal context of these relations, they condemned contraception with special vehemence when it occurred within marriage. For example, John Gerson, writing at the beginning of the fifteenth century, notes briefly: "And this sin is more grievous the further one strays from the natural law: be it outside marriage or—*which is even worse*—within marriage. . . ."[51] And several sixteenth-century theologians insisted upon the fact that unnatural intercourse is more serious when committed by husband and wife than by two persons not united in marriage. In the latter case, the crime against the potential life is compounded by that of fornication or adultery, if one of the sinners is married. But when they are husband and wife, it is a double adultery. Thus Cajetan, Soto, Azor, and Sanchez, all important theologians, prescribe that the confession should state the aggravating circumstance "that the sin was committed with one's own spouse."[52]

Writing during the same period, Brantôme expresses a notion indicating that this judgment was accepted by laymen who were not particularly devout. Concerning married persons, he says:

. . . of the thousand cohabitations which the husband may have with his wife during the year, it is possible, as I say, that she may not become pregnant once . . . from whence comes the erroneous belief of some unbelievers that

---

[51]J. Gerson, *Instruction pour les curés* (1575), chap. 6, f. 17.

[52]When he justifies this ruling (see *De sancto matrimonii sacramento*, bk. 9, dispute 18, no. 5), Sanchez does not mention sacrilege and on the contrary appears to think that sin is less great when committed with the sinner's own wife than with the wife of another. However, in the chapter devoted to "unnatural positions," he accused these positions of being "an abuse of the sacrament of marriage," a "perversion of the usage and ritual," and of thus being "a sacrilege worthy of hell." (See *ibid., bk. 9, d. 16, q. 1*). Though Azor, in *Institutionum moralium* (Rome, 1600), vol. 3, bk. 3, chap. 20, q. 5, no. 5, does not explicitly refer to sacrilege, he specifies that there is a "special, malicious insult committed upon one's own wife, because she has been taken advantage of, and the wife has the right to a divorce," that is to say, to obtain a physical separation.

marriage was not so much instituted for procreation as for pleasure: which is a wrong belief and an incorrect way of talking, for, although a woman does not become pregnant every time one takes her, it is owing to some will of God, to us unfathomable, and He wishes to punish husband and wife, all the more so since the greatest blessing which God can send us in a marriage is a good progeny, and not through concubinage.

Then, immediately after this, he discusses the practice of coitus interruptus, and presents it as a part of the framework of adultery:

. . . there are a number of women who take great pleasure in having children by their lovers, and others not; the latter are unwilling to let anything be released within them, as much to avoid palming off upon their husbands children which are not really theirs, as to appear to be doing their husbands no wrong and not be cuckolding them since the dew does not enter them, no more or no less than a weak and upset stomach can be blamed when indigestible morsels are ingested, put into the mouth, chewed, and then thrown up.

Likewise, after the name "cuckoo" borne by those April birds which are thus called because they lay eggs in the nests of others, men are by contrast called cuckolds when others come and lay eggs in their nest, which in this case is their wife, which is the same as saying that they discharge their seed and make children for them.

That is how some women think they are doing their husbands no wrong by taking in [a man] and enjoying him until sated, without receiving his seed; thus they are suitably conscientious. . . .[53]

It is true that Brantôme does not unequivocally condone these ladies; but he obligingly develops their casuistic arguments; and nowhere does he become indignant at what is, in the eyes of the theologians, an unnatural practice. Not only will I conclude on the basis of this passage that coitus interruptus was practiced in courtly circles in the second half of the sixteenth century—this has already been pointed out[54]—but also that it seems to have been practiced extramaritally for moral reasons. For the argument—made with a touch of humor and paradox—is a moral one: "palming off children upon their husbands" was, in the mentality of that century, the principal crime of an adulterous woman, and contraception avoided committing it.

How could a Christian civilization have given birth to such a morality? How could such an argument have been openly developed? I believe I

[53]Brantôme, *Dames galantes*, pp. 38–39.
[54]See Bergues, *Prévention des naissances*, p. 143. Commenting on this text from Brantôme, Bergues correctly concludes that within the bourgeoisie and the nobility "coitus interruptus remained the most commonly used method and that it was not so rare when the partners were not married." But she fails to pursue the matter further and appears to have forgotten it in the remainder of the book.

have already made the answers clear: coitus interruptus was not considered as abominable a practice as sodomy or bestiality; it was surely less severely punished than incest or adultery; and since all extramarital sexual relations are normally sought for pleasure—and not for procreation—rendering them sterile did not increase the sinfulness.

It is true that this argument is not specifically found in the works of any theologians or casuists. That is doubtlessly because in plainly authorizing extramarital contraception one would in practice have encouraged sexual disorders.[55] Nevertheless, while speaking of simple fornication, the great Sanchez went so far as explicitly to uphold, with extreme prudence, an opinion concerning adultery akin to that described by Brantôme.

In fornicatory coitus, after the woman has emitted her seed[56] or the risk of emitting it has become inevitable,[57] is the man permitted to withdraw before his own semination? Certain learned men think . . . that this is not permitted and that on the contrary he is obliged to expel his seed . . . and they say that there is no possible doubt, because after a woman has ejaculated, the man is obliged to expel his seed in order to avoid a greater evil and complete the act for a nonlibidinous purpose, and thus this semination is not strictly fornicatory, but only materially so: so that for this reason it is not intrinsically evil. And this opinion is credible.

But it is much more credible not only that the man is not obliged to ejaculate then, but that in expelling his seed he becomes guilty of a new fault, and that this fault must be revealed in the confessional, unless it was not discerned during intercourse. Because in a licit act, nothing is illicit, and for that one must seminate; but there is something intrinsically evil in an illicit act which cannot be rendered honest in any eventuality.

And that does not prevent one from being obliged to choose the lesser of the two evils. Certainly, this nonsemination is in itself unnatural, and as a result more

[55]Noonan mentions extrinsic motives for maintaining traditional Church doctrine in the seventeenth century. (See *Contraception*, pp. 353–58 and 367–72). And we know the place they occupy in the recent encyclical *Humanae vitae*. However, Noonan does not mention Sanchez' text on coitus interruptus during fornication and does not appear to have seen the contrast on this point between marital and extramarital relations.

[56]Sanchez believed, in accordance with Galen's theory, that the woman like the man emits seed and that conception is born of a mixture of these two seeds. The fact that one member of the couple emits seed without allowing the other the time to do so would therefore constitute a contraceptive act.

[57]There has been some question about the basis of Galen's theory, and about whether the female seed was believed to be expelled at the beginning of intercourse or at the moment of orgasm. If one must choose, several reasons impel me to prefer the second interpretation. Moreover, Sanchez devoted a long and interesting discussion to learning whether—when the man abandons his wife before the moment at which she is supposed to emit her seed—that constitutes a grave sin. This is an interesting track to follow in order to learn about carnal union in different periods, and it should be followed. In the text which I have quoted, when Sanchez wrote "or when the risk of expelling it has become inevitable," it seems to me that he was implicitly drawing a parallel between the beginning of ejaculation in the man and of the orgasm in the woman.

wrong than fornication. But fornication is absolutely and simply worse, since it is so intrinsically wrong that it is never permitted.[58] Now, nonsemination is not so bad and unnatural that it is not permitted for a very compelling reason, as we have proved in the previous paragraph.[59] This is what will be acknowledged here: that is to say, *in order that fornicatory intercourse not be consummated to the serious disadvantage of raising the child. And the fornicator will not be accused of error if, in withdrawing from the woman, he ejaculates involuntarily outside the vessel.* Because the involuntary pollution resulting from a just cause is necessary and absolutely innocent. Likewise exempt from guilt is the fornicating woman who, acting from repentance over the crime she has committed, moves her body away so as not to receive the male seed and not consummate the fornication which had begun. And the man will not be considered in error if he spills his seed outside. Because that is not his intention and she is doing a licit thing in tearing herself away from a crime which has already been begun.[60]

These arguments were just what was needed to assuage the consciences of the ladies portrayed by Brantôme. As for the pious motives which must justify the withdrawal, is not the anguish being felt a form of regret over the illicit act? Is not sin pushed away at the very same moment as the temptress? And why is the embrace broken, if not for fear of causing harm to a potential child or its mother?

But what is the authority behind this text? Let us stress that Sanchez is not a negligible author nor one whose orthodoxy is suspect. And in this century of Jesuits he was the Society of Jesus's greatest specialist in marriage; many of his contemporaries considered him a walking encyclopedia and viewed him as a saint—which Alphonsus Liguori would have the good fortune to become in the eighteenth century.

Nevertheless, he had many enemies during the seventeenth century. Bayle, Jurieu, and the Protestants all held him in horror; Jansenist or rigorist theologians denounced him as lax; and Pierre de l'Estoile even tells how his book, which "had sold . . . publicly in Paris and everywhere, printed and reprinted with the name and reputation of the author, who was considered learned," was withdrawn from sale by royal order because it had created such a scandal.[61] It is obvious that on this point he was innovative: he, who habitually cited dozens of authorities to support his

---

[58]In the previous article Sanchez had just stated that one must refuse fornication even under pain of death.

[59]He also asserted—and this shows his cleverness in the discussion—that in the event of a grave peril, one could interrupt legitimate intercourse, even if this involved an ejaculation *extra vas*; for one has a greater duty to one's own life than toward the potential life of a child which might be born.

[60]See Sanchez, *De sancto matrimonii sacramento*, bk. 9, dispute 19, q. 7.

[61]See André Martin (ed.), *Journal de l'Estoile* (Paris, 1960), vol. 3, p. 230, under the date of March 16, 1611. L'Estoile and his contemporaries were not scandalized by what Sanchez says about coitus interruptus, but by the numerous and very explicit pages devoted to sodomy.

or contrary opinions, cited no one here to support his thesis. I do not, however, consider this sufficient evidence for us to ignore his opinion. I have no doubt that had the respectable ladies of Brantôme, and even their lovers, not found direct reassurance from the *De Matrimonio*, they would have found it through a carefully selected confessor.

Sanchez assuredly did not originate the ideas concerning contraceptive behavior described by Brantôme, since the *De Matrimonio* came after *Livre des Dames*. Although no cause-and-effect relationship has been established, the fact that the quasi legitimation came later is of no small interest to the historian. But, and we have stressed this several times, the principles which permitted Brantôme and the ladies of his day to precede Sanchez on this question had already long existed in the doctrine of marriage and sexuality.

*   *   *

Therefore, I do not wish to suggest that the late sixteenth century witnessed a major step in a moral evolution. The idea of illicit relations has always involved the idea of sterility, and the penitentials had already indicated that contraceptive intercourse mitigated the guilt of fornication. Moreover, in lay tradition, long before the gallant ladies of Brantôme, did not the rules of courtly love tend in the same direction, separating love from marriage and procreation?

The relationship between the bards singing of this "pure love" and the Cathar heresy have often been stressed. But the crime of the Cathars, like that of the Manichees in the fourth and fifth centuries, or the Gnostics of the second century, was to attack the sacrament of marriage.[62] It is because they likened marriage to fornication—or adultery—that they recommended sterile intercourse within a marriage. By contrast, Sanchez or Brantôme, like the troubadours, pushed to the extreme the contrast between marriage and fornication which the Church Fathers had developed since the second century.

Under pain of heresy, contraception could only be envisaged extramaritally. Under pain of scandal, illicit relations had to be sterile. And demographic statistics, within the limits of current research, indicate —only for the seventeenth and eighteenth centuries, and then only in France—practically no contraception in marriage, but a very low, indeed too low, illegitimate birth rate.

These statistics also indicate, during the same period, a late marriage age, on the average more than ten years after puberty. These late marriages are justifiably seen as a means of birth control, which was

[62]See the whole of Noonan's *Contraception*, and especially chaps. 3, 4, and 6.

not—without going into detail—a manifestation of the collective will of a society struggling against the threat of overpopulation, but rather of the individual necessity, valid for women as for men, of having sufficient capital to start a family. To an extent which we still cannot document, this capital was acquired by domestic, artisanal, or agricultural labor, and took time to acquire. Are we to believe that the majority of these prolonged celibacies were chaste?[63] We may doubt it, when we recall the virulent hostility manifested in the early sixteenth century[64] toward ecclesiastical celibacy, a hostility which the Protestant reformers took up in their turn, or when we think of the difficulty the Catholic Counter Reformation encountered in imposing chastity upon the secular clergy.[65] Instead, I believe that those who could not afford to have children found an outlet for their sexual impulses in illicit and sterile practices, including both solitary practices[66] and fornication.[67]

[63]Although few historian-demographers explicitly assert this, let us recall that many infer it and that Le Roy Ladurie for his part states this clearly.

[64]Many texts, such as Marguerite de Navarre's *Heptameron*, come from authors favorable to the Reformation. Is this a reason to take exception with them? Though the reformed position is based upon deeper theological foundations, it is also explained by the shortcomings of ecclesiastical celibacy, and the reformers had no trouble using this hostility to celibacy in their propaganda.

[65]Pierre Goubert in *Beauvais et le Beauvaisis*, pp. 204–5, indicates that between 1650 and 1679, in the diocese of Beauvais, which included 432 parishes, more than 400 priests were the object of an inquiry or a law suit before the ecclesiastical courts. But breaking ecclesiastical celibacy constituted only one part of these misdemeanors, a part which Goubert calls "considerable" without giving statistics. E. Brouette, on the other hand, gave us a study on the "Excessus et incontinentiae clericorum, dans l'archidiaconé liégeois de Hainaut (1499–1570)," *Revue belge de philologie et d'histoire*, 1956, pp. 1067–72. According to my calculations, between 1499 and 1504 for the entire diocese, each year, about 15 percent of the resident *curés* were fined for *excessus et incontenentiae*. The proportion decreases after the middle of the century, but this was a troubled time in which surveillance was perhaps lax.

[66]For example, we find the following dialogue in the *Caquets de l'accouchée*, written in the reign of Louis XIII: "Who began the quarrel? It was the newly delivered woman's mother, who was sitting next to the bed, at her daughter's right hand, and who replied to the question of how many children her daughter had, and whether this was the first one?—My word, Mademoiselle, it is the seventh, and I am very astonished about it. If I had thought that my daughter would get to work so quickly, *I would have let her scratch her privy parts until the age of twenty-four without getting married*" (ed. Marion and Flammarion [1890] p. 12). Concerning the marriage of domestic servants, we find in the same text: "'And I; said a servant . . . 'I am more to be pitied than you others: for in the past when we had served eight or nine years, and we had saved up a half a belt of silver and a hundred crowns in cash . . . we would find a good sergeant to marry, or a good mercer-shopkeeper. And at present, for our money we can get only a coachman or a palfrey, who makes us three or four children without stopping, then, being unable to feed them on their meager salary, we are forced to go serve as we did before'" (ibid., pp. 14–15).

[67]In the fourteenth century the Dominican John Bromyard observed in one of his sermons that when he reproached fornicators for not getting married, some replied that such as they were they could not have a wife; others said that they would marry "if they had a house to which they could take her"; others that they would not have enough to support

In short, I believe that illicit relations were not the deeds of restricted groups on the outskirts of society, and that they involved contraceptive measures.[68] Before the massive introduction of contraception into marriage, these techniques were learned in "sin."[69]

One problem remains which is apparently more difficult to solve now than at the beginning of this article: if, for centuries, contraception was a characteristic of illicit relationships and if marriage itself was only for procreation, how can we explain the free consciences of those Christian couples which, without doubt since the eighteenth century, sinned in good faith? First let us recall that this contrast between marriage and pleasure was found among both theologians and courtiers; we have not proved that it existed on all social levels and in every region of the Christian West. But, for those circles in which this dichotomy existed, the innovation was to behave in marriage as one did outside marriage. Through this innovation the husband behaved toward his wife as he would with a mistress, and the wife "behaved toward her husband as toward a lover." Good faith would therefore mean that marriage is an amorous relationship legitimized as such by the sacrament. And the sin lay in believing this a century too soon.

---

children. *Summa praedicantium* (Nuremberg, 1485), "Lechery," 28, cited by Noonan, *Contraception*, p. 229.

[68] I mean that unmarried persons of all ages had to seek sexual satisfaction in adultery and in such "unnatural" practices as homosexuality, bestiality, solitary masturbation, elaborate caresses, etc. Concerning all these practices we have a quantity of judicial, ecclesiastic, literary, medical, and folkloristic documents. I have indicated a few of them in an earlier article (*Annales: E.S.C.*, Nov.–Dec. 1972, pp. 1351–78). This illicit and infertile behavior also included coitus interruptus—undoubtedly used with increasing frequency from the sixteenth century up to the middle of the nineteenth century. It must be given special attention since it—rather than the contraceptive measures passed down from prostitute to prostitute ever since Antiquity—was used by Malthusian French households during the nineteenth century.

[69] Even though it appears simple and efficacious, coitus interruptus could not be reinvented by just anyone, in just any milieu, in just any period. In order for the "Malthusian revolution" to occur in France, an ensemble of favorable circumstances was required, including familiarity with this technique. I am suggesting here that before employing it in marriage, the couples of the second half of the eighteenth century learned the technique from a certain type of illicit relationship—a relationship in which the man is ready to make a sacrifice in order to please the woman. And since it appears that coitus interruptus was used in aristocratic circles before it was employed by the common people, I surmise that servants played an important role in the history of its spread. But this is still merely a hypothesis.

3
The Plague
in the Early
Middle Ages

J.-N. Biraben
and Jacques Le Goff

The plague, that "great protagonist of yesterday's history" (B. Benassar), has begun to reveal its secrets only for the great epidemic beginning in 1348. The two other pandemics—those of Antiquity and of the early Middle Ages—are still waiting at the threshold of historiography. General histories of the early Middle Ages either ignore this important and long-lasting event or simply mention it in passing. This silence or semi-silence is not just a matter of ignorance or intellectual laziness on the part of historians. To some extent it is due to the difficulty of obtaining reliable facts. Texts are scarce and vague;[1] the historiography of the plague is encumbered by studies of doubtful scientific value; and the chronology and geography of the phenomenon are not easy to establish.

Annales: E.S.C., Nov.–Dec. 1969, pp. 1484–1510. Translated by Elborg Forster. The translator wishes to thank Susan P. Baker and Timothy D. Baker of The Johns Hopkins School of Hygiene and Public Health for their kind help with the medical part of this article.

This article is the outcome of the encounter and the confrontation of two research projects undertaken independently of each other. Dr. J.-N. Biraben, under the auspices of the Institut National d'Etudes Démographiques, has just finished a general study of the plague in the history of population (and the *Annales* are grateful to him for publishing some of his findings here) and J. Le Goff, in his seminar at the VIe Section of the Ecole Pratique des Hautes Etudes, had studied the plague of the early Middle Ages in the West as one of the components in the formation of the medieval consciousness. This article has been incorporated into a forthcoming book: J.-N. Biraben, *Les hommes et la peste*, vol. 1 (Paris: Mouton, to be published in 1974).

[1] Is it too much to hope that advances in archaeology, physical anthropology, and prehistoric demography will some day shed light on the history of the plague in the early Middle Ages? Studies of cemeteries and skeletons from very early eras (two samples of which appear in *Annales: E.S.C.*, Nov.–Dec. 1969) give rise to a certain optimism.

The present essay seeks only to survey the documentation, to establish a definite, or at least likely, chronology, and to sketch out the geographical area of the pandemic. Problems visible at the horizon will be touched upon, though not explored in depth, and some hypotheses which could account for the breadth and the importance of this phenomenon will simply be set forth.

Two preliminary remarks: The plague of the early Middle Ages, like that of the fourteenth and fifteenth centuries, was "worldwide," i.e., it spread from its original African center to North Africa, Asia, and Europe, thus affecting parts of three continents. While not disregarding the history of the scourge in the Byzantine Empire and the Islamic world, our essay will concentrate on laying the foundations for a study of the epidemic in the barbarian West, which, in this respect as in others, appears to have been interdependent with the East as well as the terminus of the Mediterranean trade routes.[2]

A study of this kind confronts us with a highly significant fact for historical research and reflection, namely, the silence of the written sources. First of all, there is silence in the texts written between the end of this pandemic and the beginning of that of the fourteenth century. For five and a half centuries, there is silence on the plague—complete silence as far as the medical literature is concerned,[3] and almost complete silence in the historical texts. Once the phenomenon had disappeared, the people were incapable of grasping it in its past dimension. This finding calls for some adjustment in the notion that the medieval scribes blindly wrote down everything they had read or heard.[4] As for the contemporary sources—

[2]Certain contemporary authors—especially those of Byzantium—noted the worldwide character of the epidemic. One of them was Victor, bishop of Tunis, who wrote his chronicle in exile at Constantinople circa 564–65 and who, for the year 542, had this to say about the epidemic: "Horum exordia malorum generalis orbis terrarum mortalitas sequitur et inguinum percussione melior pars populorum voratur" (Monumenta Germaniae Historica, Autores antiquissimi, vol. 12, pt. 2, p. 201). We would like to thank E. Patlagean for furnishing us with valuable indications for the Byzantine area and we also thank André Miquel for showing us where to start our research on the plague of the early Middle Ages in the Islamic world. These two areas (Byzantium and the East) will be treated more fully and in greater detail in the forthcoming work by Dr. Biraben and, perhaps, in a later complementary article as well.

[3]We have examined the 121 early medieval Latin medical texts from French libraries as given in Wickersheimer's catalogue. Their dates are distributed as follows: seventh century, 3; eighth century, 3; ninth century, 50; tenth century, 27; eleventh century, 35; twelfth century, 3. In these published texts, we were unable to find a single mention of the plague or of any sign that might refer to it.

[4]It is true that some of the Western authors of the period after the Justinian Plague do mention this epidemic. However, we felt that most of these references were doubtful, and we therefore systematically excluded them, except in cases where one can be reasonably sure that the author's information was reliable. In the West, this is the case with Paul the Deacon, who incidentally, experienced the end of the pandemic.

those at the disposal of Gregory of Tours, well-informed and attentive writer that he was—they were often silent, even though their authors must certainly have seen the phenomenon at the height of its virulence. This must have been the case, for example, with Isidore of Seville or the author of the *Liber Pontificalis*.[5] Once again, these facts are a warning for the historian to handle *arguments ex silentio* with extreme caution, especially for the remote past. People see only what they are able to understand, and they write down only what they consider worthy of being passed on to posterity.

Outline of the Present-Day Medical and Epidemiological Conceptions of the Plague[6]

The Microbe. Discovered in Hong Kong by Yersin in 1894, the plague microbe "pasteurella pestis" is an ovoid bacillus 1 to 1.5μ long, bipolar staining, immotile, encapsulated, usually aerobic, occasionally anaerobic, which grows *in vitro* at an optimal temperature of 25° C.

Three natural varieties of this microbe are known. The variety most frequently found today in the Orient, in America, and in various ports is called "orientalis" and was responsible for the last pandemic starting in China at the end of the nineteenth century. Another variety, found in Asia, is called "medievalis" because it is believed to have caused the Great Plague of 1348 and the following centuries. Finally, a third variety, called "antiqua," exists around the great African lakes whence the epidemics of Antiquity and the early Middle Ages are believed to have come. These three varieties are equally pathogenic for man and have a genetic kinship with Malassez and Vignal's bacillus of which we will speak later. While all these plague bacilli are toxic to man, their toxicity nonetheless varies from one strain to the next: aging or the action of a bacteriophage may reduce their virulence, but rapid passage from host to host very quickly selects the most active strains.

The plague bacillus easily penetrates the mucous membranes, but it is unable to penetrate healthy skin, unless an excoriation—even infinitesimally small—makes it possible.

It was long believed that certain germs were antagonistic to the plague bacillus and that their development arrested that of *pasteurella pestis*. This

---

[5]In the case of the written sources of the history of Ravenna in the early Middle Ages—L. Muratori (ed.), *Spicilegium Ravennatis historiae*, 28 vols. (Milan, 1723–51), vol. 1, pt. 2, and Agnellus, *Liber Pontificalis seu Vitae pontificum Ravennatum*—one may wonder whether the silence is due to the sources written at the time of the plague or to later compilers.

[6]We are extremely obliged to Professor Henri Mollaret who, on several occasions, was kind enough to answer our questions, and to Mme. J. Brossolet who very willingly gave us

is probably a misconception, because the disappearance of the plague bacillus seems to precede, rather than accompany, this second infection. A second infection was nonetheless sought and provoked even in Antiquity, for it was considered a possible sign of recovery.

The life span of the plague bacillus is quite variable. In frozen cadavers it can survive for years, in putrefying cadavers for a few days only; in the ground it dies rapidly, but in the micro-climate of rodent warrens it can stay alive for several months and even years under certain conditions. The latter fact may account for certain cases of local persistence of which more will be said later.

The Disease. In man, the plague bacillus has an intense toxic effect. It causes cell necrosis, generalized vaso-dilatation, and sero-albuminous reactions. Furthermore, even when ingested by polymorph nuclear leucocytes, plague bacilli are not digested but continue to multiply and are thus disseminated throughout the body. Massive accumulations of bacilli obstruct the capillaries, which become distended and hemorrhage; sanguinous edemas infiltrate the nerve endings of the swollen lymphatic glands, causing the terrible bubonic pain. Finally, secondary infections, which were frequent until the nineteenth century, form large abscesses.

Clinically, a distinction must be made between two essentially different forms, depending on whether the germ enters through the skin or through the pulmonary mucous membrane.

In the bubonic form, resulting from cutaneous entry, the incubation period is one to six days. In very rare cases the disease may remain benign, but generally a very abrupt onset with temperatures of 39 or 40° C is observed. A pustule forming at the point of inoculation (usually a flea bite) necrotizes rapidly, developing into a black gangrenous patch called a plague carbuncle. Within two or three days a large, hard, very painful swelling appears in one of the lymphatic glands, in most cases in the groin, but sometimes also in the armpit or at the neck. This is the bubo.

The general signs are variable, but nervous and mental disturbances are frequent, particularly headaches and cloudy sensorium. After eight or ten days, the disease may take a turn for the better[7] and convalescence may begin.[8] Otherwise, generalized septicemia will bring visceral complications (heart, lung, kidneys), the temperature will reach 40 or 42° C, and death will ensue. If the patient lives longer, embolism may produce more pustules and more boils, spontaneous hemorrhages may occur, causing large

---

access to the archives on plague research at the Institut Pasteur. The "Outline of the medical conceptions" which follows is the work of Dr. J.-N. Biraben.

[7]See the passage by Procopius, cited later in this article (*Bellum persicum*, 2: 22 ff).

[8]Depending on the particular epidemic, the recovery rate varies between 20 and 40 percent.

subcutaneous bruises,[9] occasionally digestive troubles,[10] and especially mental disturbances—dizziness, hallucinations, and delirium, or sometimes somnolence. These symptoms will suddenly be cut short by coma and death.

Sometimes this same sequence of events leads to death within twenty-four to thirty-six hours even though there is no visible bubo. Some authors have called this development the septicemic form of the plague; in these cases, which are not infrequent, the swollen lympathic gland—a mesenteric lympathic gland, for example—lies too deep to be palpated or else has not yet fully developed, but there is no question that this is the bubonic plague also.

In certain cases, a pulmonary plague abscess develops *secondarily* and the coughing patient can transmit the disease: the bacilli are inhaled and pass through the mucous membranes of the recipient. The plague contracted in this manner has very different characteristics. It is called pneumonic plague.

In the *primary* pneumonic form, the incubation period is only one to three days. The onset is very abrupt with temperatures of only 38–39° C, but with pulse rates of 90–120. At first, the patient complains only of retrosternal discomfort and pain in the side, but he soon begins to cough, at first moderately with some sputum, then violently with blood-stained sputum. He chokes, must sit up to breathe, coughs more and more and finally suffocates, with neurological concomitants, such as motor incoordination. Death ensues within two or three days in 100 percent of the cases.

The plague bacillus is pathogenic to most mammals, and in man no natural immunity is known. However, survivors have an acquired relative immunity which may last a year or even longer.

Today, Girard's live vaccine gives protection for several years, and the treatment of the disease is based on streptomycin, which appears to be very effective.

EPIDEMIOLOGY

Contamination and Epidemiological Forms. The carrier responsible for the epidemic spread of the plague is the flea (Simond, 1898), which imparts the disease to man by its bite. The classic mechanism of this

[9]The hemorrhagic form showing large subcutaneous bruises seems to have been more frequent in the Middle Ages and up to the nineteenth century than it is at present.

[10]Digestive troubles such as diarrhea and vomiting are rare today but were very frequent in the past and even in the nineteenth century. This was probably related to the diet of the patients.

transmittal is the following: In the infected flea a plug of bacilli and blood blocks the proventriculus, a kind of sac located on the esophagus. When the flea bites, the blood it sucks comes in contact with this plug, mixes with it and is then regurgitated, infected, into the wound. But fleas without a proventriculus can also transmit the disease, and contamination can occur even without a bite if the infected excreta of a flea enter through excoriations of the skin. Even aside from the flea, the disease can be contracted by eating infected game or, sometimes, from bedbugs and lice.

The infective power of the flea varies greatly, even in a state of starvation. Under the most favorable conditions a flea can live up to one year. It can therefore be a reservoir of germs, whether it lives in the fur of a rodent or in the dust of the soil or flooring.[11]

The different species of fleas are strictly adapted to a single host: cat-fleas live only on cats, dog-fleas on dogs, and so forth.[12] There is only one important exception which, alas, has given plague epidemics a very wide range. *Xenophylla cheopsis*, the rat-flea, can, if necessary, and in the absence of its normal host, also live on man. This flea is responsible for passing the disease from the rat to man, and it was long believed that it alone caused all the epidemics because to this day its role is considerable. But *pulex irritans*, which lives only on man, can also transmit the disease, especially if it is present in great numbers.

The flea can only survive in strictly limited conditions of heat and humidity. It lives well in temperatures of 15 to 20° C with 90 to 95 percent humidity—in body clothing, for example. Cold limits its activity and heat arrests its reproductive function, but the degree of humidity regulates its life span. At 20° the flea dies if the humidity drops to 70 percent, and it survives only seven to eight days at 80 percent. In the natural state its life span thus varies between two days and one year; its activity is weak in winter but very high in summer.

For some strange reason, the flea is attracted by white and is therefore commonly found in white materials such as bed sheets and clothing. On the other hand, it is repelled by the smell of certain animals, such as horses, cows, sheep, goats, or camels, which, though susceptible to the plague germ, do not have fleas. Fleas also dislike the smell of certain cooking oils made from olives, nuts, peanuts, etc. These facts were discovered empirically by the people of the Middle Ages on several occasions, but they do not seem to have been used in Antiquity or in the early Middle Ages.

Whereas the flea spreads the bubonic plague, the pneumonic plague is transmitted from person to person by droplets of saliva projected by

[11]At Madagascar, their role in the persistence of the epidemic was proven by capturing infected fleas living in the dust of the mud floors of human dwellings.

[12]The fleas of mice sometimes bite rats, but they never bite humans.

speaking or coughing. If the atmosphere is cold and humid, the infection in these droplets will remain in suspension for a considerable length of time and can be inhaled, thus entering the body through nasal, buccal, or pulmonary mucous membranes. Infection can also ensue when hands soiled by cutting up infected animals come in contact with mucous membranes. The pneumonic plague can thus enter through the eyes, the nose, or the mouth, but this form occurs essentially in cold areas or during the winter in temperate zones. Under all other circumstances it is exceptional or very limited. It should be emphasized again that pneumonic plague is highly contagious and that it is 100 percent fatal.

RESERVOIRS OF INFECTION

The black rat was long considered the only source of the plague epidemics. In their publication of 1894, Roux and Yersin did not hesitate to write: "The plague is a disease of the rat which in an incidental fashion may also be transmitted to man." It wasn't until about 1925 that Ricardo Jorge introduced the notion of the sylvatic plague, that is, the plague of wild rodents. The latter can maintain permanent centers of infection. Examples are the large marmots, called *tarabagans*, of central Asia, near Lake Baikal; the jirds of the Near East, Iran, and Turkestan; the ground squirrels of North America; and, probably, certain rats around the great lakes of central Africa.

An analysis of the permanent centers in the Near East has given us a first insight into the problems of their persistence. We now know that the bacilli survive very well in the soil of the warrens, whose micro-climate is well suited to their requirements, and that they infect neighboring rodents which, once the weather has improved, come to occupy the warrens left vacant by the death of their former occupants. Meanwhile, smaller rodents may have passed through the warrens, providing sustenance for the fleas and thus ensuring the survival of the infected fleas. It is also known that the resistance of the jirds to the plague is largely determined by the way in which they have been infected. They can usually survive the plague if it is inoculated under the skin, by a flea bite for example, but they die if they contract pneumonic plague by burrowing in an infected warren.

In present-day India, the plague is spread from warren to warren by field rodents. Taking an unpredictable path, it infects the village rats along the way, causing rat epizootics which are followed by human infection; but it leaves certain villages unharmed in the midst of the general infection. This epizootic is very seasonal, in keeping with the ecology of the rodents and the biology of the fleas. At the end of May, the rodents enter into aestivation; they dig their tunnels and live on the reserves accumulated in their warrens. At that point the plague ceases to spread; it subsides in the villages where it had reigned for several months and does not last long in the villages recently affected. The rat epizootic can very rarely maintain the infection from one season to the next. In mid-October, after the end of the rainy season, the rodents emerge, invade empty but contaminated warrens, and the epizootic resumes, followed by the rat plague and eventually human plague.

Persistence of the disease can also be due to a somewhat rarer, but very real, process, in which wild rodents have contracted the disease and formed an encysted abcess which is dormant for several months, then suddenly becomes reactivated and kills the animal. This has been shown to happen in the tarabagan during hibernation; Dujardin-Beaumetz has noted the same phenomenon for the Alpine marmot.

Outside of these permanent sylvatic centers, there are, finally, temporary centers of infection, generally cities or ports where two species of rats that have contact with man are found today. One of them, the black rat (*rattus rattus*), has been settled in Europe at least since the Middle Ages, though it is not known whether it was present in Antiquity or in the early Middle Ages. It is extremely sedentary. It has never been found further than two hundred meters away from a building and lives mostly in granaries and on ships, where it is almost invariably found. It never moves from one village to another or from one port to another, except when passively transported. In Europe it was this rat, which is highly susceptible to the plague, which usually contaminated men. The other species, the gray rat (*rattus norvegicus*) originated in eastern and central Asia and appeared in Europe only at the end of the eighteenth and the beginning of the nineteenth century. It has much less contact with men. Habitually living in caves and sewers, it is very rare on ships, but it sometimes migrates across open fields. One account even reports a colony in the open country living in warrens by a stream, six hundred meters away from a village. The gray rat is slightly less susceptible to the plague than the black rat, but its fleas also attack man; it should be kept in mind that these fleas (*xenophylla*) themselves may constitute the reservoir of bacilli under certain circumstances.

MALASSEZ' AND VIGNAL'S BACILLUS OR
PASTEURELLA PSEUDOTUBERCULOSIS
(discovered in 1893 by Malassez and Vignal at
Paris in a guinea-pig)

Related to the plague bacillus, from which it can evolve or which it can produce by mutation, this bacillus has been closely studied only since 1954.

Its pathogenic effect in man is relatively benign and affects mostly children, in whom it may provoke mesenteric adenitis with abdominal pain, diarrhea, and sudden fevers. It is sometimes mistaken for acute appendicitis and usually subsides spontaneously within a few days. Clinically unrecognizable cases are much more frequent in adults, although a number of serious cases of septicemia in persons over thirty have been reported.[13]

In rats and mice the bacillus does not appear to provoke a disease, so that the animals become healthy carriers. Other rodents, however, are highly susceptible (rabbits and especially hares often develop fatal forms of the disease), and many other mammals, such as deer, monkeys, cats (which often contaminate humans), and birds (turkeys, chickens, pheasants, quails) are also very susceptible. By contrast, pigeons are very resistant and seem to be carriers, like rats.

Animals and humans eliminate the germ in the stools and contamination almost always occurs by way of tainted food, such as raw vegetables grown with the aid of human fertilizer, since the bacillus survives very well in the soil.

This infection is of great interest to our subject because of the fact that even without clinical manifestations the disease provides 100 percent immunity against the plague bacillus in rats and humans. (Studies by Schutz, 1922). For this reason it was hypothesized that this new disease was responsible for the disappearance of the great plague epidemics. Unfortunately there are still too many unknown factors concerning the time and place of its appearance to permit any definite conclusion; but it appears that it began to spread only very recently. While it existed in France and Germany as early as the end of the nineteenth century, for example, it appeared in Tunisia only in 1927, whence it reached Morocco—by way of Algeria—in 1943. To this day it is unknown in Turkey, Lebanon, and Israel, and in southeast Russia its progression is being observed year by year on the lower Volga and north of the Caspian Sea. On the other hand, it appeared very early in some distant ports. It was observed in Japan as early as 1910, in Dakar in 1933, in Vladivostok in 1959, in South Africa in 1960, and in Canada and New Zealand in 1963.

Under these circumstances, and in view of the devastation caused by the plague in Western Europe until the eighteenth century, it seems very unlikely—although not impossible—that pseudotuberculosis played any role in the disappearance of the plague in the early Middle Ages.

*   *   *

[13]It should be noted that aureomycin greatly stimulates the virulence of Malassez and Vignal's bacillus: a single dose administered to a guinea pig, hitherto only a healthy carrier, is sufficient to bring on a septicemia that will kill the animal in two or three days.

If the ancient authors—the Greeks, Indians, or Chinese—have left us descriptions so vague that it is difficult to recognize the plague in them, the authors of the early Middle Ages are not much more explicit. For the Justinian Plague, very few have provided us with sufficient details to answer all our questions. One of those who did was the most precise of them, the Greek Procopius. "Those in whom the bubo," he wrote, "grew to the largest size and suppurated while ripening usually survived, no doubt because the malignant property of the already weakened boil was annihilated. Experience had proven that this phenomenon was an almost sure sign of impending return to health. . . ."

In the most detailed, or perhaps we should say least vague, passage, Gregory of Tours expressed himself as follows: ". . . Since soon no coffins or biers were left, six and even more persons were buried together in the same grave. One Sunday, three hundred corpses were counted in Saint Peter's basilica [of Clermont] alone. Death was very sudden. A snake-like wound appeared in the groin or in the armpit and the poison affected the patients in such a way that they gave up the ghost on the second or third day. Furthermore, the power of the poison robbed people of their senses. . . ." Elsewhere, he only speaks of a disease in the groin, calling it "*lues inguinaria*." And as P. Richet has shown, the other authors are no more precise; the pseudo-Fredegarius refers to "*clades glandolaria*," Marius of Avenches to "*infirmitas, quae glandula, cujus nomen est pustula*" (this last term raises some doubt), and the Chronicle of Saragossa uses the term "*inguinalis plaga*." The most impressive description among Latin authors is that of Paul the Deacon.[14]

---

[14]"Huius temporibus in provincia praecipe Liguriae maxima pestilentia exorta est. Subito enim apparebant quaedam signacula per domos, hostia, vasa vel vestimenta, quae si quis voluisset abluere, magis magisque apparebant. Post annum vero explctum cocperunt nasci in inguinibus hominum vel in alilis delicatioribus locis glandulae in modum nucis seu dactuli, quae mox subsequebatur febrium intolerabilis aestus, ita ut in triduo homo extingueretur. Sin vero aliquis triduum transegisset, habebat spem vivendi. Erat autem ubique luctus, ubique lacrimae. Nam, ut vulgi rumor habebat, fugientes cladem vitare, relinquebantur domus desertae habitatoribus, solis catulis domum servantibus. Pecuda sola remanebant in pascuis, nullo adstante pastore. Cerneres pridem villas seu castra repleta agminibus hominum, postera vero die universis fugientibus cuncta esse in summo silentio. Fugiebant filii, cadavera insepulta parentum reliquentes, parentes obliti pietatis viscera natos relinquebant aestuantes. Si quem forte antiqua pietas perstringebat, ut vellit sepelire proximum, restabat ipse insepultus; et dum obsequebatur, perimebatur, dum funeri obsequium praebebat, ipsius funus since obsequio manebat. Videres seculum in antiquum redactum silentium: nulla vox in rure, nullus pastorum sibilus, nullae insidiae bestiarum in pecudibus, nulla damna in domesticis volucribus. Sata transgressa metendi tempus intacta expectabant messorem; vinea amissis foliis radiantibus uvis inlaesa manebat hieme propinquante. Nocturnis seu diurnis horis personabat tuba bellantium, andiebatur a pluribus quasi murmur exercitus. Nulla erant vestigia commeantium, nullus cernebatur percussor, et tamen visum oculorum superabant cadavera mortuorum. Pastoralia loca versa fuerant in sepulturam hominum, et habitacula humana facta fuerant confugia bestiarum. Et haec quidem mala intra Italiam tantum usque

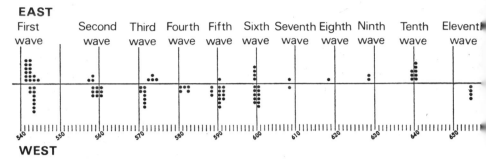

Figure 1. The Plague in the Mediterranean Area from the VI to the VIII Century.

We are counting only those texts which call the plague by one of its precise names, using the adjectives *inguinarius* or *glandolarius* or those which, in the absence of a real description, note one of the major symptoms. In this manner, we may have excluded some of the texts actually referring to the plague; but then it is also possible to feel that we are not being too critical and that the terminology used by the authors of the early Middle Ages was more precise than we might assume at first sight.

However, the chronology and the progression of this second cycle of the plague, that of the early Middle Ages, can be followed much more easily than that of Antiquity. Geographically, it extended throughout the regions surrounding the Mediterranean, although its development on the eastern side, beyond Persia in the direction of Turkestan and India is not known.

The great Justinian Plague began in 541 in Pelusium, an Egyptian port on the Mediterranean at the eastern mouth of the Nile whence it had come, according to Evagrius, from Ethiopia. From there, it spread to Egypt, reaching Alexandria, Palestine, and Syria. In the spring of 542, or perhaps even in the autumn of 541, it appeared in Constantinople, where it lasted for four months. Thanks to fragmentary data from local chronicles, we can summarize its progression as shown in Figure 1. It can be observed that at the end of the Middle Ages, and even in modern times, the plague still progressed in great successive waves.

The first wave of the early Middle Ages, from 541 to 544, was a catastrophe of such proportions for Byzantium that certain authors

---

ad fines gentium Alamannorum et Baioariorum solis Romanis acciderunt." (Monumenta Germaniae Historica, *Scriptores rerum langobardicarum et italicarum saeculi VI-IX* [1878], p. 74).

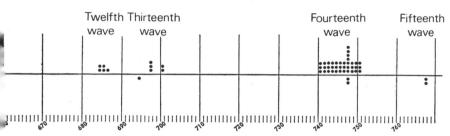

Number of localities and areas affected. Each dot represents a place cited by contemporary sources. Note the periodicity of the epidemic waves, whose peaks occur at nine- to twelve-year intervals.

consider it to be the major reason for the arrest and the failure of Justinian's policy of reconquest.[15]

Yet at that point, the West was, comparatively speaking, slightly affected in the regions bordering the Mediterranean. Arriving probably by way of Genoa, Marseilles, and an undetermined Spanish port, the plague proceeded inland only as far as Clermont and Reims and subsided rather quickly.

The second wave, between 558 and 561, started in Constantinople, entered the West by way of Ravenna and Genoa, and seems to have been confined to Italy. The third wave entered the West again by Marseilles and Genoa in 570, even though these ports are nowhere mentioned by name. This time the West was affected more severely than the East, especially Italy and the eastern half of Gaul. Constantinople was touched in 573–74.

The same pattern seems to obtain for the fourth and fifth waves, which held sway from 580–82 and 588–91 in the West only. The fact that they started in the port of Narbonne makes it very likely that they were of Eastern origin, although we cannot be certain; furthermore, it should also be noted that these two epidemics still remained confined to the Mediterranean areas of Europe, Spain, Gaul, and Italy. Their effects appear to have been quite severe, especially since they were combined with a violent epidemic of smallpox (variola), probably the first in Europe,

[15]Colnat, *Les épidémies et l'histoire* (Paris, 1937), pp. 33–34; J. C. Russell, Seminar on Historical Demography, Meeting of the Population Association, April 28–29, 1967, Cincinatti, Ohio (abstract in *Population Index*, July–Sept., 1967); J. C. Russell, "That Earlier Plague," *Demography*, vol. 5, no. 1 (1968), pp. 174–84. The latter article, which came to our attention only at the last moment, is interesting, but unfortunately marred by an uncritical acceptance of the sources and by an excessive number of rather hazardous hypotheses.

which apparently struck all of continental Europe about the year 570. (Gregory of Tours, *Historia Francorum*, 4: 14, 15; Marius of Avenches?)

The sixth wave of the plague, in 599 or 600, again entered the West by way of Ravenna, Rome, and Marseilles; but it does not seem to have proceeded very far inland, and the losses it caused were no doubt less considerable.

The subsequent waves, those of 608, 618, 628, 640, 654, 684–86, 694–700, 718, and 740–50, affected the West only sporadically and in a limited fashion. Rome, Pavia, Marseilles, and the province of Arles were touched about 654, Narbonne and the surrounding area in 694, Sicily and Calabria (after Carthage) in 746, Naples and southern Italy in 767.

This overview, while very brief, nonetheless provides us with certain characteristics of the plague which can also be observed, in identical form, during the third cycle of the plague extending from the fourteenth to the eighteenth century. In particular, it shows the spontaneous subsidence of the disease in Western Europe and its periodic rekindling in the ports that were in contact with the eastern Mediterranean. The resemblance is so close that the description of the plague of 588 in Marseilles by Gregory of Tours[16] can be repeated word for word to describe the plague of 1720 in the same port: arrival by a merchant ship, the illness contracted by those who bought these goods, the first house emptied of its inhabitants, and then, after a period of latency, the unleashing of the disease in all sections of the town at once, the flight of the inhabitants, the return to his flock of the bishop who had been traveling, prayers and preaching by the clergy, the subsidence of the disease, return of the population, and a relapse— everything is already present in this sequence of events which, unhappily, was destined to be repeated many times between these two dates.

The beliefs and attitudes developed in response to the plagues of the early Middle Ages were shaped by the medical traditions of Antiquity, by the Bible, and by the deepest recesses of an ancestral collective mentality. But they were modified, brought into sharper focus, and enriched during the sixth century. While the plague turned these decimated populations back to their still lively pagan superstitions (as Gregory of Tours reports, in

---

[16]"Interea navis ab Spania una cum negucio solito ad portum eius adpulsa est, qui huius morbi fumitem secum nequiter deferebat. De qua cum multi civium deversa mercarentur, unam confestim domus, in quo octo anime erant, hoc contagio interfectis habitatoribus, relicta est vacua. Nec statem hoc incendium lues per domus spargitur totas; sed, interrupta certi temporis spacio, hee velut in sagittem flamma accensa, urbem totam morbi incendio conflagravit. Episcopus tamen urbis accessit ad locum et se infra basilice sancti Victoris septe contenuit cum paucis, qui tunc cum ipso remanserant, ibique per totam urbis stragem orationibus ac vigiliis vacans, Domini misericordia (m) exorabat, ut tamdem cessante interitu, populo liceret in pace quiescere. Cessit vero plaga valde mensibus duobus; cumque iam securus populus redisset ad urbem, iterum succidentem morbo, qui redieraent sunt defuncti. Sed et multis vicibus deinceps ab oc interitu gravata est."

Liber de virtulilus sancti Juliani, 46a, they had recourse to a *hariolus*, a sorcerer), it mainly had the effect of making them more amenable to certain Christian beliefs and practices. Seen as one element in a whole set of calamities and signs, the plague settled in peoples' minds a concrete expectation of the Last Judgment (exegesis of Luke 21), explained calamities as retribution for collective sin, instilled notions of a wrathful God (and Gregory of Tours reports that the Arians objected to this notion), and gave rise to an apocalyptic and millenarian mentality. The faithful reacted to it with a hitherto unknown deployment of pilgrimages and processions. Examples were the prayers at the tomb of Saint Julian of Brioude, which were instituted by St. Gallus, and above all, the litanies at Rome, which were ordered by Gregory the Great. Gregory the Great, whose influence was to be felt throughout the entire Middle Ages, was obsessed by the plague and by the coming of the Last Day, as can be seen by everything he did and wrote. He was truly the Pope of the Plague. For him, the sores of Job were buboes.

This upheaval in popular consciousness became a factor in the social unrest of the time, just as it was to be in the fourteenth century. The pseudoprophets, to whom the plague gave large audiences and eager disciples, channeled the fear and resentment of the people against the rich and the powerful, even though the epidemic showed, or so it was believed, that the hand of God was upon the rich and the poor alike, contrary to His usual ways.

The antichrists of whom Gregory of Tours speaks (*Historia Francorum*, 9: 6–7, and above all, that woodcutter from Berry [590] in *Historia Francorum*, 10: 25) were popular leaders who exploited the confusion of people decimated by epidemics and food shortages and, especially, terrorized by the inescapable ravages of the plague.[17]

Yet we must keep in mind that the plague of the early Middle Ages, however important its psychological repercussions, was above all a demographic phenomenon of the first order. Its points of entry into the West, the routes it took to proceed inland, and the areas it affected reveal some of the fundamental aspects of the barbarian West of the sixth and seventh centuries A.D. The geography of the epidemics confirms the existence of urban centers since contagion cannot spread without them. It also confirms the fact that trade from Alexandria, Byzantium, and Africa continued to flow toward Ravenna, Rome, Genoa, Marseilles, and Narbonne, which were the gates of the plague precisely because they were

[17]Aside from flight and prayer, no steps appear to have been taken against the scourge, at least in the West. Only one isolated text, the letter from Gallus, bishop of Clermont, to Didier, bishop of Cahors, indicates that the bishops occasionally attempted to halt the advance of the disease by means of physical barriers.

the gates to the East (recall that Genoa and Marseilles were to pay that price until the seventeenth and eighteenth centuries). Furthermore, it indicates that communication by river, especially by the Rhône-Saône axis, was very important. The hagiographic texts—specifically the miracles of the patron saints—reveal the northern limits of the scourge: the Loire, the Marne, the Rhine, and the Alps mark the points where the impact of the disease was broken as well as the limits of the urbanized zones and the terminal points of the Eastern trade routes.

How many people did these epidemics kill? The lack of attention given to numerical estimates by the writers of the early Middle Ages and their fondness for symbolic or exaggerated figures whenever they did attempt a quantitative evaluation make it difficult to give even a very approximate answer. According to Evagrius, the plague of 542–44 in Constantinople took 300,000 victims, which would have been one-half or one-third of the inhabitants. Others speak of "*melior pars populorum*" of the world (Victor Tunensis), of "*innumerabilis populus devastatus*" (Marius of Avenches for Italy and Gaul in 570–71), of "*tota paene Hispania contrita*" (Chronicle of Saragossa for 542–43). As we have already indicated, the plague of the early Middle Ages in the West—especially by comparison with the Great Plague of the fourteenth to the eighteenth centuries—was relatively limited as to geographical expansion and concentration in time. But while it did not kill—as it did in the fourteenth century—a third or a fourth of the population of the West, there is no question that it did perform a severe demographic pruning. There is every reason to believe that in the Mediterranean area, despite, perhaps, a certain recovery of a limited and local nature, the great plagues of the sixth century, combined with smallpox,[18] caused a catastrophic demographic slump. Some authors feel that this collapse was the final transformation of a slow demographic decline begun in the late Empire and accelerated by the barbarian invasions, while others feel that it reversed a recent and still tentative upward trend brought about by the barbarian invasions. However that may be, it can be assumed that under the impact of this epidemic complex the demography of the West must have reached its lowest point since the early Roman Empire in the seventh and early eighth centuries.

It is perfectly legitimate to speculate on the demographic, financial, and political consequences of the Justinian Plague in the wide area it affected. Some authors have blamed it for the decline (and how easy that is in the

---

[18]In the more northern areas, which were not affected by the plague, the population seems to have been growing until that period. See the optimistic picture of Merovingian Paris until about 570–80 in Fleury, *Paris, croissance d'une capitale. Paris du Bas Empire au début du XIII siecle* (Paris, 1961), pp. 73–96.

sixth century!) of the Byzantine Empire. But it can also be seen as one of the circumstances attracting Slavic populations into the Balkans and Greece, where the epidemic may have created a vacuum and an opportunity for new settlers. One may also think that the decline in tax revenues due to the plague caused great disarray in the finances of the Byzantine Empire. Moreover (and Paul the Deacon already pointed this out), the epidemic could have favored, and even given rise to, the invasion of Italy by the Lombards, who had long been stationed along Italy's northern borders. And in North Africa (as Corippus asserts) the Berbers, who had escaped the plagues, seized the opportunity to revolt against the Byzantine Empire. Would it be unreasonable to suppose that the plague had something to do with the rather unexpected success of Arab revolts in the East and in North Africa?

As for the West, there is one tempting hypothesis. It is a fact that the British Isles, northern Gaul, and Germania were, for the most part, spared by the plague. Could not this have been one of the reasons for the shift of power in Europe from the south to the north, from the Mediterranean to the North Sea? If we dared pursue this idea further—too far, no doubt—we might advance the hypothesis that the Justinian Plague, having contributed to an explanation of Mohammed, can also explain Charlemagne.

*   *   *

The problem of the disappearance of the plague from the Mediterranean basin is all the more difficult as the texts are not very explicit. In the West, the last unquestionable mention of the disease refers to southern Italy in 767; in the East, the last instance is the plague at Smyrna, where buboes are expressly mentioned for 740–50. The state of the documentation unfortunately does not permit us to know the exact place and date of the last manifestation of the disease in the early Middle Ages with any certainty, and even less to determine the cause of its temporary disappearance until the fourteenth century.

Texts Referring to the Plagues of the Early Middle Ages

It should be kept in mind that in other texts the silence of the authors does not necessarily mean that nothing happened.

Here are some examples of texts we have not included because it is almost certain that they do not concern the plague.

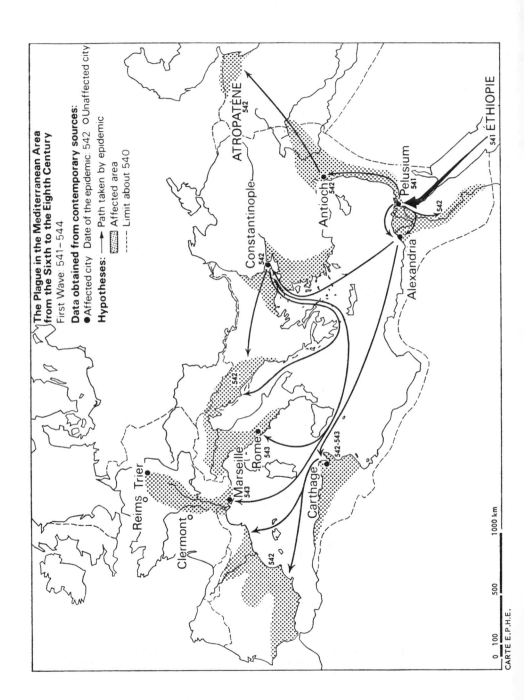

The Plague in the Mediterranean Area
from the Sixth to the Eighth Century

First Wave: 541–544

Data obtained from contemporary sources:
● Affected city   Date of the epidemic: 542   ○ Unaffected city

Hypotheses: → Path taken by epidemic
▨ Affected area
‑ ‑ ‑ Limit about 540

ATROPATÈNE
542

ÉTHIOPIE
541

Antioch
542

Constantinople
542

Pelusium
541

Alexandria
542

Reims
Trier

Clermont

Marseille
543

Rome
543

Carthage
542-543

542

542

0 100   500   1000 km

CARTE E.P.H.E.

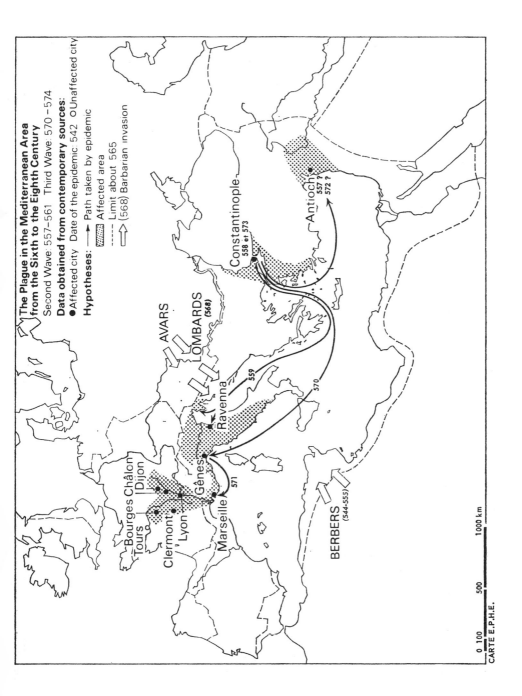

The Plague in the Mediterranean Area
from the Sixth to the Eighth Century

Second Wave: 557–561   Third Wave: 570–574

Data obtained from contemporary sources:

● Affected city   Date of the epidemic: 542   ○ Unaffected city

Hypotheses: ⟶ Path taken by epidemic

▨ Affected area

---- Limit about 565

⟹ (568) Barbarian invasion

AVARS

LOMBARDS
(568)

Ravenna

Gênes

Bourges Châlon
Tours Dijon
Clermont
Lyon

Marseille

Constantinople
558 et 573

Antioch
557 ?
572 ?

559

570

571

BERBERS
(544-555)

0 100   500   1000 km

CARTE E.P.H.E.

65

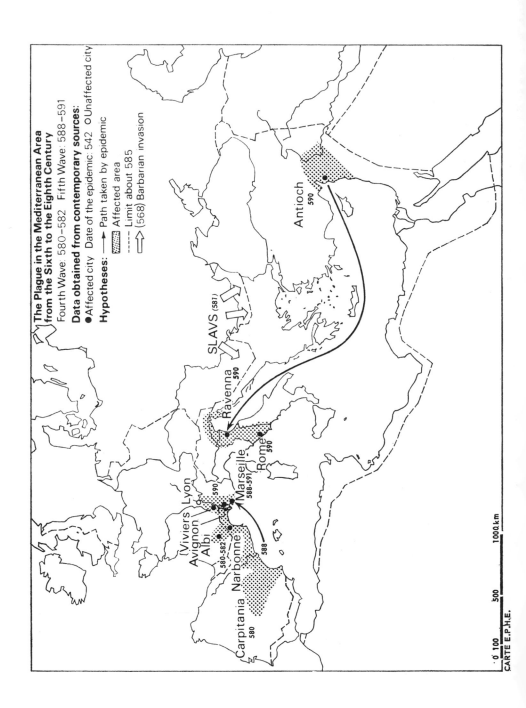

The Plague in the Mediterranean Area
from the Sixth to the Eighth Century

Fourth Wave: 580–582 Fifth Wave: 588–591

Data obtained from contemporary sources:
● Affected city Date of the epidemic: 542 O Unaffected city

Hypotheses: ⟶ Path taken by epidemic
▨ Affected area
––– Limit about 585
⇧ (568) Barbarian invasion

Antioch
590

SLAVS (581)

Ravenna
590

Rome
590

Lyon
590

Viviers
Avignon
Albi
580–582

Marseille
588–591

Narbonne
588

Carpitania
580

0 100   300   1000 km

CARTE E.P.H.E.

66

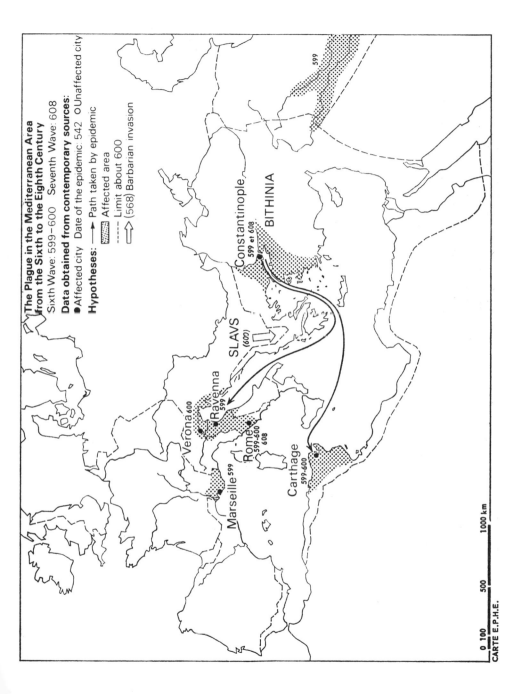

The Plague in the Mediterranean Area
from the Sixth to the Eighth Century

Sixth Wave: 599–600   Seventh Wave: 608

Data obtained from contemporary sources:

● Affected city Date of the epidemic: 542 ○ Unaffected city

Hypotheses: ⟶ Path taken by epidemic

▨ Affected area

--- Limit about 600

⟹ (568) Barbarian invasion

Constantinople
599 et 608
BITHINIA

599

SLAVS
(602)

Verona 600
Ravenna
599
Rome
599–600
608
Marseille 599
Carthage
599–600

0 100   500   1000 km

CARTE E.P.H.E.

67

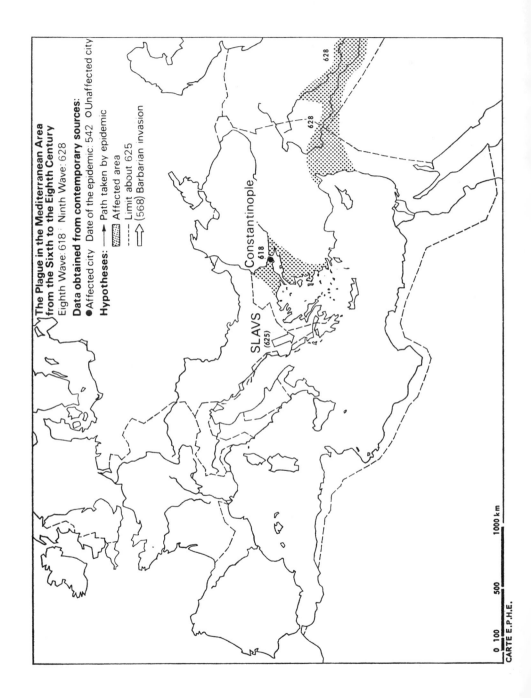

The Plague in the Mediterranean Area from the Sixth to the Eighth Century

Eighth Wave: 618 : Ninth Wave: 628

Data obtained from contemporary sources:
● Affected city   Date of the epidemic: 542   ○ Unaffected city

Hypotheses: ⟶ Path taken by epidemic
▨ Affected area
--- Limit about 625
⇨ (568) Barbarian invasion

Constantinople
618

SLAVS
(625)

628

628

0 100   500   1000 km

CARTE E.P.H.E.

68

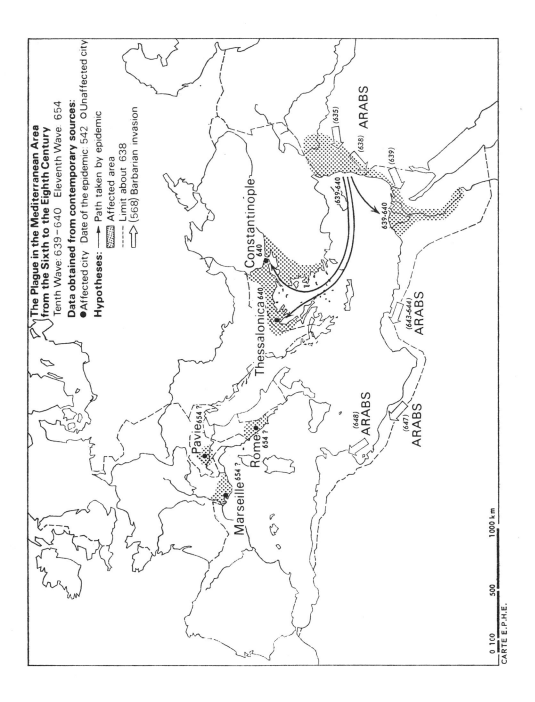

The Plague in the Mediterranean Area from the Sixth to the Eighth Century

Tenth Wave: 639-640   Eleventh Wave: 654

Data obtained from contemporary sources:

● Affected city   Date of the epidemic: 542   ○ Unaffected city

Hypotheses: ⟶ Path taken by epidemic

▨ Affected area

- - - Limit about 638

⟹ (568) Barbarian invasion

Constantinople 640

Thessalonica 640

Pavie 654 ?

Rome 654 ?

Marseille 654 ?

ARABS

(635)

(638)

(639)

639-640

639-640

(643-644)

(648)

(647)

0 100   500   1000 km

CARTE E.P.H.E.

69

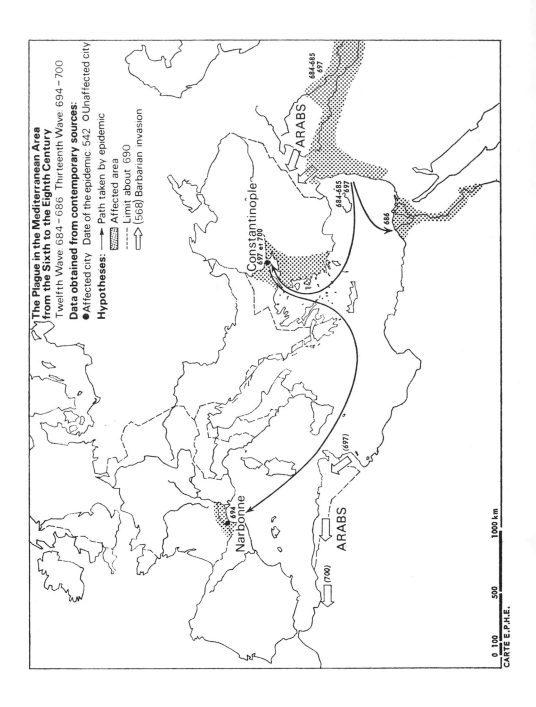

**The Plague in the Mediterranean Area
from the Sixth to the Eighth Century**

Twelfth Wave: 684–686   Thirteenth Wave: 694–700

Data obtained from contemporary sources:

● Affected city   Date of the epidemic: 542   ○ Unaffected city

Hypotheses: ——➤ Path taken by epidemic

⬚⬚⬚ Affected area

– – – Limit about 690

⇧ (568) Barbarian invasion

ARABS

684-685
697

684-685
697

686

Constantinople
697 et 700

Narbonne
694

(697)

ARABS

(700)

0 100   500   1000 km

CARTE E.P.H.E.

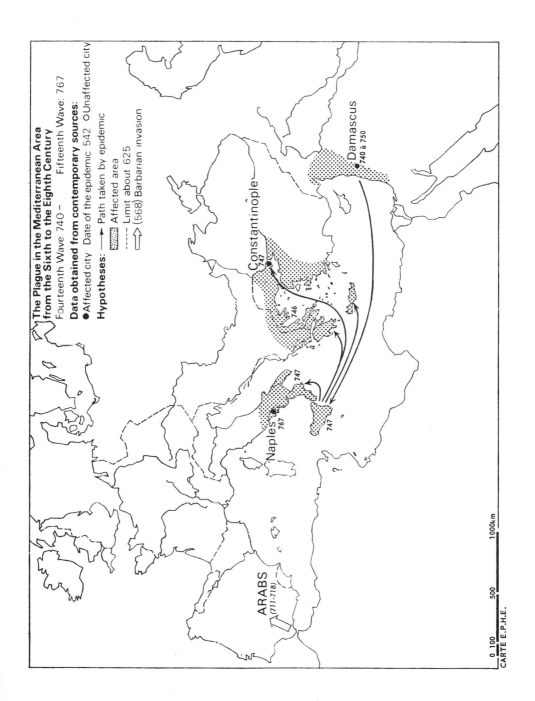

The Plague in the Mediterranean Area
from the Sixth to the Eighth Century

Fourteenth Wave: 740 –   Fifteenth Wave: 767

Data obtained from contemporary sources:
● Affected city Date of the epidemic: 542 ○ Unaffected city

Hypotheses: —→ Path taken by epidemic

▨ Affected area
--- Limit about 625
⇨ (568) Barbarian invasion

Damascus
740 à 750

Constantinople
747

746

747

747

Naples
767

ARABS
(711-718)

0 100   500   1000km

CARTE E.P.H.E.

71

Sticker, for one, describes an epidemic in the Soissonais in 550 and calls it "*Inguinarium*," following the *Vita Sancti Banderini* in the *Acta Sanctorum*, although that word does not appear there. This seems to have been a strictly local epidemic which broke out in 545, not 550, in the wake of a food shortage, and there is nothing in the texts to justify its inclusion among the plagues. This is also true for the epidemics ravaging Alamania in 552 and 618, the epidemic mentioned by Theophanes in his *Chronographia* (6048), as well as for an epidemic in Constantinople (555), described by Malalas in his *Chronographia* (448,4).

The epidemic referred to by Gregory of Tours (*Historia Francorum*, 10:30), which seriously affected Tours and the region of Nantes, also cannot be called a plague just because it mentions headaches.

And the epidemic in Rome in 618, described in the *Liber Pontificalis*, was not the plague either; the chronicler expressly says: "Post haec clades in populo, percussio scabearum, ut nullus poterat mortuum suum recognere"; so this was a very puriginous disease, but not the plague. Nor does this same source have any evidence that Rome experienced an outbreak of the plague in 686, even though a number of authors who copied each other often refer to it.

Finally, the epidemic described by the Venerable Bede, which ravaged the British Isles in 664, cannot have been the plague; in his time the terms "*pestilentia lues*" and "*clades pestis*" designated any serious epidemic but gave no clue as to its precise nature. According to W. P. MacArthur, what is meant here is smallpox. Also, we did not feel that we should consider the chronicle of Kleinlauel (which speaks about a "plague[?]" at Strasbourg in 591) or that of Sigebert of Gembloux (plague in 560 "in Italiam") because they seem to be too late.

Documentation of Plagues, by Date and Location

DATE	LOCATION	SOURCE
541	Ethiopia; Oct., Pelusium	(Evagrius, *Histoire écclesiastique*, 4: 29.) (Procopius, *Bellum Persicum*, 2: 22.)
541 or 542	Egypt, Alexandria, Palestine	(*Id.* Evagrius and Procopius.)
	Antioch	(Evagrius, *Histoire écclesiastique*, 4: 29.)
Spring 542	Constantinople	(Procopius, *Bellum Persicum*, 2: 22 ff.) (Theophanes, *Chronographia* for 6034.) Justinian edict 7 of Mar. 1, 542.

Notes: M.G.H., AA   =   Monumenta Germaniae Historica, Auctores Antiqui.
    SS.RR.MM.   =   *Scriptores rerum merovingicarum.*
    SS.RR.LL.   =   *Scriptores rerum langobardarum.*

Documentation of Plagues, by Date and Location (continued)

DATE	LOCATION	SOURCE
	Illyria	(Auctuarium Marcellini, M.G.H., AA, vol. 11, pt. 2, p. 107.)
542	Province of Africa (Tunisia and eastern Algeria)	
	Spain	(Corippus, M.G.H., AA, vol. 3, pt. 2; vols 16, 18.) (Chronicle of Saragossa, M.G.H., AA, vol. 11, pt. 2, p. 201: 542 or 543?)
543	Atropatene (Adjerbaidjan)	(Procopius, *Bellum Persicum*, 2: 22.)
	Constantinople	
	Province of Africa	(Auctuarium Marcellini, M.G.H., AA, vol. 11, pt. 2, p. 107.)
	Italy	
	Spain	(Chronicle of Saragossa.)
	Province of Arles	(Gregory of Tours, *Historia Francorum*, 4: 5.) Reaches the borders of the diocese of Clermont; St. Gallus institutes prayers to stop it. (Gregory of Tours, *Liber in gloria martyrum*, vol. 1, pt. 3; and *Liber vitae patrum*, vol. 6, pt. 6.) Ravages Germania and reaches the limits of the diocese of Reims, where the relics of St. Remy stop it (Gregory of Tours, *Liber in gloria confessorum*, 78, M.G.H., SS.RR.MM., vol. 1, pt. 2, pp. 795–96) and perhaps also the borders of the diocese of Trier (the text of Gregory of Tours, *Liber vitae patrum* 17: 4, which attributes the miracle to the bishop Nicetius, can be dated only from the episcopate of Nicetius, which lasted from 525 to 585).
544	Constantinople	Novella of Emperor Justinian of March 23, 544, declaring the plague ended and ordering prices to be put back to the level of before the epidemic.
About 557–58	Antioch	(Evagrius, *Histoire écclestiastique*, 4: 29.)
558	Constantinople	Feb. to July (Theophanes, *Chronographia* for 6050; Agathias, *Historia*, 5: 9; Evagrius, *Histoire écclesiastique*, 4: 29.) (Procopius, *Bellum Persicum*, 2: 23.) (Glycas, *Annales*, 4: 270.)

Documentation of Plagues, by Date and Location (continued)

DATE	LOCATION	SOURCE
About 559–60– 61	Ravenna	
	Istria	(Paul the Deacon, *Historia Langobardorum*, 4: 4.)
	Grado	
570[1]	Liguria	Spreads throughout Italy and stops at the borders of the Alamani and Bavari (Paul the Deacon, *Historia Langobardorum*, 2: 4.)
571	Lyon, Bourges,[2] Chalon-sur-Saône, Dijon, Clermont	Affects all of Auvergne and stops at the limits of the diocese of Tours (Gregory of Tours, *Historia Francorum*, 4: 31; *Liber de virtutis sancti Juliani Brivatensis*, 46a, M.G.H., SS.RR.MM., 1: 582.) (Marius of Avenches, M.G.H., AA, 11: 238. It is probable that one of these passages designates the plague and the other smallpox.) (Gregory of Tours, *Liber vitae Patrum*, vol. 9, de sancto Patroclo.)
572–74	Antioch	(Evagrius, *Histoire écclesiastique*, 4: 29.)
573	Constantinople	(John, abbot of Biclara, *Chronica*, M.G.H., AA, vol. 11, pt. 2, pp. 213–14.) (Michael the Syrian, 9: 28, and 10: 8.)
574	Constantinople	The plague ceases when Tiberius Caesar ascends the throne (John, abbot of Biclara, *Chronica*).
580	Spain; Carpetania, region of Toledo	(Gregory of Tours, *Historia Francorum*, 6: 33.)
	Narbonne	(Gregory of Tours, ibid., 6: 14, 33; and 7: 1.)
581	Narbonne	
582	Narbonne, Albi	
588	Spain, Marseilles	Arrives by a ship from Spain; travels along the Rhône valley as far as Octave (Saint-Symphorien d' Ozon near Vienne) and approaches Lyons: Gregory of Tours, *Historia Francorum*, 9: 21, 22.

[1]563 according to Sticker; 564–65 according to Corradi; 565, 566, or 570 according to Hecker. Given the testimony of Marius of Avenches, we are inclined to adopt 570.

[2]In his *Histoire de la peste à Bourg-en-Bresse* (Paris, 1933), p. 1, J. Guiart claims that what is meant is Bourg (rather than Bourges) and says that this plague took place in 563.

Documentation of Plagues, by Date and Location

DATE	LOCATION	SOURCE
590	Antioch	(Evagrius, *Histoire écclesiastique*, 4: 29.)
	Rome	Begins in mid-Jan. and ends in April (Gregory of Tours, *Historia Francorum*, 10: 1). Pope Pelagius II dies of it, Feb. 8. The epidemic ceases after processions are ordered by the new pope, Gregory the Great, in Apr. 590. (These major litanies were later celebrated on Apr. 25.)
	Viviers, Avignon	(Gregory of Tours, *Historia Francorum*, 10: 23.)
About 590 or 591	Ravenna, Grado, Istria	(Paul the Deacon, *Historia Langobardorum*, 4: 4; same situation as thirty years earlier, about 561.)
591	Marseilles	(Gregory of Tours, *Historia Francorum*, 10: 25.)
599	Constantinople, Bithynia, Asia	(Michael the Syrian, 10: 23.)
	Mesopotamia	(Elias bar Shinaya, Metropolitan of Nisibis, *Syriac Chronicle*.)
599 or 600	Marseilles, Province of Arles	(Pseudo-Fredegarius, vol. 18.)
	Ravenna and its littoral	(Doubtful, given by Paul the Deacon, M.G.H., SS.RR.LL., 121.)
599 and 600	Carthage, Africa, Rome	(Letters from Gregory the Great to Dominicus, bishop of Carthage, dated Aug. 599 and Aug. 600: 9: 232; 10: 20; M.G.H., *Epistolae*, 2: 288, 255.)
600	Verona and surrounding area	(Paul the Deacon; same doubtful text.)
608?		
Between 602 and 610	Constantinople (under Phocas)	(Theophanes, *Chronographia* for 6100.) (Zonaras, *Epitome*, 14: 14.) (Glycas, *Annales*, 510, 18.)[3]
608	Rome	(G. Sticker, *Drüsenpest*, p. 33.)

This is one example of the unfounded claims we find so often in the historiography of our subject.

[3]Was this really a plague? See E. Rebouis, *Etude historique et critique sur la peste* (Paris, 1880).

Documentation of Plagues, by Date and Location (continued)

DATE	LOCATION	SOURCE
618	Constantinople	(Nicephorus Patriarcha, *Breviarium*, ed. de Boor, p. 113.)
628	Syria, Mesopotamia	(A. von Kremer, *Seuchen des Orients*.)
639 and 640	Palestine (plague at Emmaus), Syria, Egypt	(Tholozan, *Histoire de la peste bubonique en Mésopotamie*.) (Sticker, *Drüsenpest*, p. 33.)
640	Constantinople	Plague (?) of Heraclius.
	Thessalonica (between 610 and 640)	(Sticker, *Drüsenpest*, p. 33; J. Mahé, in *Dictionnaire encyclopédique des sciences médicales*, p. 643.)
Between 630 and 655	Marseilles, Province of Arles	Letter from Gallus, bishop of Clermont, to Didier, bishop of Cahors (M.G.H., *Epistolae*, 1: 214.)
654	Rome, Pavia	July to Sept. (Paul the Deacon, *Historia Langobardorum*, 6: 5.)[4]
684 and 685	Syria, Bassorah	(Tholozan, *Peste en Mésopotamie*, with some reservations on the nature of the epidemic.)
686	Egypt	(*Beulenpest*, according to A. Von Kremer.)
694	Gaul	Region of Narbonne, very probably (17th Council of Toledo, ed. G. D. Mansi, *Sacrorum conciliorum nova et amplissima collectio* [Florence, 1759–98], 12: 95).
697	Constantinople	(Theophanes, *Chronographia* for 6190; Cedrenos, *Synopsis*), lasts four months.
	Syria, Mesopotamia	According to A. von Kremer (?)
700	Constantinople and "the East"	(Theophanes, *Chronographia* for 6192.) (Cedrenos, *Synopsis*, A 2.) (Leon Grammaticos, in *Corpus scriptorum historiae byzantinae* [Leipzig, 1828–97], 167: 1.) This epidemic may well not be the plague.
740–50	Syria, Damascus, Jordan valley	(Tholozan, *Peste en Mésopotamie*. This was a real plague, where the buboes were properly described. Was it the last for the Levant?)

[4]The date 679, which is given by the editor and reproduced by P. Richet, is completely unfounded. We are adopting the date 654, following the chronicle of Segebert of Gembloux (end of the ninth and beginning of the tenth centuries), who used the manuscripts of Paul the Deacon.

Documentation of Plagues, by Date and Location (continued)

DATE	LOCATION	SOURCE
746	Sicily, Calabria, Peloponnesus, continental Greece, Greek Archipelago, Constantinople	(Theophanes, *Chronographia* for 6238 = the year 6 of Constantine I.) (Anastasius, *Historia ecclestiastica*, Venice ed., 20: 75.) (C. Porphyrogenetes, *de Thematibus*, 2: 6.) (Nicephores the Patriarch, B.) (Glycas, *Annales*.) (Cedrenos, *Synopsis*, C 6.) (Zonaras, *Epitome*, 15: 6.) (Paul the Deacon, *Historia Miscella*, vol. 22, in Muratori, I: 156.)
767	Naples, southern Italy	A very violent outbreak; coming from North Africa or the East? John the Deacon (M.G.H., SS.RR.LL, 425): "quae medicis inguinaria vocatur."

Selected Bibliography

I. STUDIES WITH A PREDOMINANTLY MEDICAL POINT OF VIEW

Biraben, Jean-Noël. "Les conceptions médico-épidémiologiques actuelles de la peste." *Le Concours médical*, Jan. 26, 1957, pp. 619–25.

———. "La peste dans l'Europe occidentale et le bassin méditerranéen: principales épidémies, conceptions médicales, moyens de lutte." *Le Concours médical*, Feb. 2, 1963, pp. 781–90.

———. Remarks in *Actes du Colloque International de Démographie historique*. Liège, Apr. 18–20, 1963. In P. Harsin and E. Helin. *Problèmes de mortalité*. Paris: Génin, n.d.

Girard, Georges. "La Peste, situation actuelle et inconnues épidémiologiques." *Revue Médicale française*, Jan. 1957, pp. 5–15; good bibliography.

———. "Une lueur nouvelle dans l'épidémiologie de la peste. Peste tellurgique et peste de fouissement." *La Presse médicale*, May 30, 1964, pp. 1623–25.

Hirst, L. Fabian. *The Conquest of the Plague: A Study of the Evolution of Epidemiology*. Oxford, 1953.

Jorge, Ricardo. "Summa epidemiologica de la peste." *Bulletin international d'hygiène publique*, Mar. 1933.

MacArthur, W. P. "The Identification of Some Pestilences Recorded in Irish Annals." *Irish Historical Studies*, no. 6 (1949), pp. 169–88. (These are not plagues.)

Pollitzer, R. *Plague*. Geneva: World Health Organization, 1954.

Rath, G. "Modern Diagnoses of Historical Epidemics." *German Medical Monthly* and *Deutsche Medizinische Wochenschrift*, 1956.

Wickersheimer, Ernest. *Les manuscrits latins de médecine du Haut Moyen Age dans les bibliothèques de France. Documents, études et répertoires.* Paris: Institut de Recherche et d'Histoire des Textes of the C.N.R.S., 1966.

II. STUDIES ON THE CARRIERS
OF THE PLAGUE

Barnett, S. A. "Rats." *Scientific American*, Jan. 1967, pp. 79–85.

Guiard, Jules. *Les parasites inoculateurs de maladies.* Paris, 1911.

Hinton, M. A. C. *Rats and Mice as Enemies of Mankind.* 3rd ed. British Museum (Natural History), Economic Series no. 8. London, 1931.

Jorge, Ricardo. *Rongeurs et puces.* Paris, 1928.

MacArthur, W. P. "The Occurence of the Rat in Early Europe." *Transactions of the Royal Society of Tropical Medicine and Hygiene* 51, no. 1 (1957): 91–92.

III. STUDIES WITH A PREDOMINANTLY
HISTORICAL POINT OF VIEW[19]

Autran, A. *Les épidémies de peste à Marseille.* Marseille, 1894.

Colnat, A. *Les épidémies et l'histoire.* Paris, 1937.

Corradi, A. *Annali delle epidemie occorse in Italia dalle prime memorie fino al 1850.* Bologna, 1863.

Genton, M.-P. "Contribution à l'étude historique de la peste dans la région toulousaine, au XVIIIe siècle en particulier." Medical thesis, Paris, 1929.

Guiart, J. *Histoire de la peste à Bourg-en-Bresse.* Paris, 1933.

Haser, M. *Lehrbuch der Geschichte der Medizin und der epidemischen Krankheiten.* 3rd ed. Jena, 1882. Vol. 3.

Hecker, J. F. C. *Die grossen Volkskrankheiten des Mittelalters.* Berlin, 1865. Reprint. Hildesheim, 1964.

Le Coz, J. *Considérations sur quelques épidémies en Bretagne.* Lyon, 1936.

Mahé, J. "Peste." *Dictionnaire encyclopédique des Sciences Médicales*, edited by A. Dechambre. Paris, 1887. Vol. 23, pp. 641–752.

[19]We have verified all the sources given in these books on the plagues of the early Middle Ages for the West only.

Papon, J.-P. *De la peste ou époques mémorables de ce fléau et les moyens de s'en préserver.* Paris, 1800. Vol. 1.

Rebouis, E. *Etude historique et critique sur la peste.* Paris, 1880.

Riché, P. "Problèmes de démographie historique du Haut Moyen Age (V - VIIIe siècles)." *Annales de démographie historique,* 1966, pp. 37–55.

Russell, J. C. "Late Ancient and Medieval Population." *Transactions of the American Philosophical Society* 48, no. 3 (1958).

————. "That Earlier Plague." *Demography* 5, no. 1 (1968): 174–84.

Sarlat, P. L. *Contribution à l'histoire de la thérapeutique de la peste dans la haute vallée de la Durance,* 1936.

Seibel, V. *Die grosse Pest zur Zeit Justinians und die ihr voraus und zur Seite gehenden ungewöhnlichen Naturereignisse.* Dillingen, 1857.

Stein, E. *Histoire du Bas Empire.* Paris, 1949. Vol. 2.

Sticker, G. *Abhandlungen aus der Seuchengeschichte und Seuchenlehre.* Vol. 1, *Die Pest.* Pt. 1; *Die Geschichte der Pest.* Giessen, 1908.

Tarbé, T. *Histoire de Sens.* N.d.

IV. STUDIES ON THE PLAGUE IN ASIA

Sourdel-Thomine, J. "'Amwâs (Emmaus)." *Encyclopédie de l'Islam.* New ed. Vol. 1, p. 474.

Tholozan, J. D. *Histoire de la peste bubonique au Caucase, en Arménie et en Anatolie.* Paris, 1874.

————. *Histoire de la peste bubonique en Mésopotamie.* Paris, 1874.

————. *Histoire de la peste bubonique en Perse.* Paris, 1874.

Von Kremer, A. *Über die grossen Seuchen des Orients nach arabischen Quellen.* (*Sitzungsberichte der Kaiserlichen Akademie, philosophisch-historische Klasse,* vol. 36.) Vienna, 1880.

V. SELECTED STUDIES CONCERNING THE ROLE OF THE PLAGUE IN HISTORY

Benassar, B. *Recherches sur les grandes épidémies dans le Nord de l'Espagne à la fin du XVIe siècle. Problèmes de documentation et de méthode.* Paris: SEVPEN, 1969.

Braudel, F. *Civilisation matérielle et capitalisme.* Paris, 1967. Pp. 62–65.

Carpentier, E. "La peste noire: Famines et épidémies au XIVe siècle." *Annales: E.S.C.,* 1962, pp. 1062–92.

————. *Une ville devant la peste: Orvieto et la peste noire de 1348.* Paris: SEVPEN, 1962.

Guibert, S. "Au XVe siècle: un conseil municipal face aux épidémies." *Annales: E.S.C.*, 1968, pp. 1283–1300.

Manselli, R. "L'escatologia di S. Gregorio Magno." *Ricerche di Storia religiosa* 1 (1954): 72–83.

Mollaret, H.-H., and Brossollet, J. "La procession de saint Grégoire et la peste à Rome en l'an 590." *Médecine de France*, no. 199 (1969).

Mols, R. *Introduction à la démographie historique des villes d'Europe, du XIV au XVIIIe siècles*. Louvain, 1955. Vol. 2, pp. 426–59.

Renouard, Y. "Conséquence et intérêt démographique de la peste noire de 1348." *Population* 3 (1948): 459–66.

Siegfried, A. *Itinéraires de contagion. Epidémies et idéologies*. Paris, 1960. Trans.: *Routes of Contagion*. New York, 1965.

Winslow, C. E. A., *The Conquest of Epidemic Disease: A Chapter in the History of Ideas*. Princeton, N.J., 1944.

4
Disease and the Sick at the End of the Eighteenth Century

Jean-Pierre Peter

What a fantastic adventure it is to plunge into the ancient archives of the Société Royale de Médecine.[1] And I purposely say fantastic, for if you are looking for the picturesque, the pathetic, and the tragic, you should betake yourself to the judicial archives of the nineteenth century. But here you enter a world where the very color and shape of things is expressed with words that are no longer ours. And one already begins to wonder. One wonders so much, in fact, that one is no longer sure that it is only the hermetic language which blurs all objects and gives a bizarre hue to their contours and meaning. Could it be that their reality

Annales: E.S.C., July–Aug. 1967, pp. 711–51. Translated by Elborg Forster. The translator wishes to thank William R. Coleman of The Johns Hopkins University for helping her to understand certain aspects of this article.

This article offered the first outline of a research project which continued during the next five years. Not all of my initial hypotheses coincide with today's conclusions. But the publication of the latter has been deferred due to circumstances beyond my control. As it stands, the older text nonetheless gives a general picture of the sources and of the techniques used. Besides, a research project should also be judged by its history, that is, by its uncertainties, its false starts, its adjustments. The method of investigation and the evolution of the problems stated are in themselves of scientific value and significance. I should therefore like to ask the reader to consider the article below in that light, as one phase in a research project and as one of the keys to understanding it. It is, in short, a link in a chain and a testimony which will make it easier to forgive some inevitable inaccuracies. [J.P.P., 1974.]

[1]Académie Nationale de Médecine, Archives de la Société Royale de Médecine, cartons 85–201 (hereafter cited as SRM).

itself refuses to conform to any measuring device we might wish to apply? We find ourselves in a land where the unthinkable constantly crosses our paths. Humans soon cease to be human when we see them helplessly exposed to a proliferation of all the ills to which we are susceptible and when we see the surfacing of latent traits we carry within us, which would destroy us if we had not learned to contain them, now that we have become wise and well armed: lurking worms, of which no one was free at that time, consuming disease, and hunger so desperate that it made a mother capable of devouring her own child, as if to defy destiny.[2] We also see a close alliance between man and beast, one in which man patterned his own physical resistance on that of the animal to such an extent that he based the very choice of the medications he was willing to take[3] on the standards of animal equilibrium (which is to say, in the end, on his being one with the animal). This crucible of incoherent forces and upside-down logic, this unregulated universe (if by this we mean the absence of the most subtle of regulations, self-control), these hysterias of epidemic proportion, this collapse of reason, and this full-fledged delirium which

[2]From Lorentz, first physician of the Strasbourg hospital, "Mémoire sur une maladie qui a régné à Schlestatt en l'anneé 1785," manuscript, 36 pp., SRM 143, no. 6, we learn about the extreme distress of the poor and their great number. In certain quarters of the town, "one stove" (meaning "one household") commonly served to house two or three families, so that 120 square feet [about 13 square meters] of floor space were sometimes occupied by ten, twelve, and even fifteen individuals. These people were prime targets for misery and despair. "I shall never forget," the observer says, "two miserable persons I found half naked, eaten away by their own excrements, and crawling with maggots. I can say that disease was usually the least of the evils that came before my eyes. . . . These extremes must be seen to be believed." In this state of utter destitution, families became even more miserable when one of their members fell ill, and the poor eventually gave up: "I saw the complaints ceasing only at the point when the people felt ill, for then they hoped to die." Twenty years later, in an equally miserable hut near Sélestat, a woman "admitted without emotion that in her extreme want she had killed her child with a meat cleaver, cut off one thigh and boiled it. . . . Interrogated as to the reasons that made her commit such an act, she indicated that it was poverty, adding that God had forsaken her." Neither before nor after the crime did she show the slightest sign of mental disturbance. Yet, at the time of the murder she still had vegetables and some chickens in her house. But she was completely overwhelmed by her impending destitution and the cries of the starving child. Furthermore, she declared "that she had known that the act would not remain undiscovered, but that she did not care in which way she would perish, since she would soon die of poverty, anyway, especially now that the inundation caused by the flooding of the Rhine had destroyed her last hopes." Reisseisen, "Cas extraordinaire d'infanticide," *Annales de Médecine Politique de Kopp* 11 (1817). I have republished this last case in "Ogres d'archives," *Nouvelle Revue de Psychanalyse* 6 (1972): 249–58.

[3]"[Given the peasants' unwillingness to take any medicines], I know from experience that the shortest and surest way of all is to give them *theriac* from time to time, for since they regard it as a universal remedy against all the diseases of their animals, they imagine that you could give them nothing better against any disease that might befall them." Laservolle, physician at Montignac, to Vicq d'Azyr, Dec. 1777, SRM 143. (*Theriac* is a medicine containing dried and powdered rattlesnake meat mixed with some sixty other ingredients.)

we today feel compelled to constrain and tranquilize—to all of this we are given the key when we enter a small cubicle at the Académie de Médecine, where the correspondence received by Vicq d'Azyr between 1774 and 1795 has been sleeping a long sleep.[4]

Beyond this impression of strangeness, to be sure, there emerges a very real, very down-to-earth territory where we can conduct our research, once we have surveyed it and planted our signposts. The history of health, physical condition, and morbidity; the identification of diseases masked by an unfamiliar vocabulary; the geographic distribution of these diseases; and the ways of life and hygienic conditions in town and country —this is the knowledge we hope to gain through work now under way; and with every step we realize that we are only at the beginning. The future will tell whether it is possible to make these honeycombs yield all their honey.

Descriptive History of a Document

The Société Royale de Médecine was a child of the Enlightenment. Its birth was due to the cooperation of two groups, one of which was the Académie des Sciences. At that time, the academic medicine of France was one of the most backward in Europe, and some of the more progressive physicians found that they could gain a favorable hearing in the forward-looking Académie des Sciences, which soon inspired them with the desire, soon to become a project, to found their own academy, or society. Quite a few of these physicians were in charge of hospitals and, therefore, were less worldly minded than the rest. Hence, their thinking tended to go in two directions. The number and the anonymity of their patients, as well as the highly visible suffering they constantly encountered, convinced them of the importance of research. This aim, they felt, could be attained by more careful and more positive observation; perhaps, we can already call it experimentation. In this notion of hospital as laboratory lies the origin of the scientific approach. But the suffering masses of humanity they were treating also sharpened their collective, statistical, or as we would say today, social concern for public health. These physicians thus became the link between the two groups involved in founding the Société Royale: on the one hand, the Académie des

---

[4]While the Vicq d'Azyr collection (SRM) is the core of my research effort, I have also used other sources, such as samplings in Departmental Archives (Series C, Registers of Intendancies), municipal libraries (manuscripts), and medical literature of the eighteenth and nineteenth centuries.

Sciences, and on the other, the Royal Administration, which had a natural concern in this area.[5] Under these twin auspices, the new society was to become the meeting ground for a new theoretical way of thinking and for far-reaching efforts to conduct applied research on behalf of the "public good." Hence it had a twofold program: *"practical" or "observed" medicine* (theory) and *the investigation of epidemics* (practical application).

Yet, at the time of its founding in 1776, the members of this antifaculty, which was angrily denounced almost immediately by the Faculty [of Medicine of the Sorbonne], were not aware that their academy was carrying the seeds of a definite mutation of medicine. In this area as in others, the coming political and social revolution was to play the part of the midwife. They did not know—and would have been distressed to know—that their investigation, a vast clinical picture of France which, had it not been for August 10, was to give them a kind of code of the laws governing the appearance and the course of diseases, unfinished and then forgotten, was to become the delight—and the terror—of historians who were to study it after almost two centuries had passed. There is one paradox, however. Whenever one reads the periodic reports handed in by the so-called "epidemic" physicians throughout the nineteenth century to the prefects, the Commission on Hygiene, or the Académie de Médecine, one sees clearly that their model, their method, their spirit, and also certain of their ideas are taken from that old investigation. Its light shines through the bushel and shows us an enduring reality. And because of that reality, the historian's work can proceed through time in a homogeneous, continuing fashion. Disease and states of health, in short, are the supporting pillars of their own history.[6]

[5]Turgot was the originator of this movement. When he became controller general, he was thinking of organizing medical services for the people. To this end, it was necessary to bring into the countryside physicians who were not prisoners of the scholastic ways of the medical schools. The latter, incidentally, were hostile to any kind of reform. They were not pleased, therefore, when Turgot created a commission of medicine charged with studying epidemics and epizootics by an *arrêt du conseil* of Apr. 29, 1776. This commission became the Société Royale de Médecine under Necker, and its function was (1) to establish the facts concerning epidemics, (2) to discuss and interpret them, and (3) to prescribe the best remedial steps to deal with them. This, then, was a separate medical body, connected with the government and, theoretically, invested with authority over the entire medical profession.

[6]Given this continuity, I would like to apply my research to a longer time span. Samples taken in a number of Departmental Archives (including Deux-Sèvres, Vienne, Seine-et-Oise) have convinced me that the series 5 M1 (*Santé Publique et Salubrité*), 6 M2 (*Maladies épidémiques*), and 10 M (*Statistique médicale et sanitaire*), if they exist, are often very rich. In any case, this is a valuable source, containing a continuous, homogeneous series until 1914. Moreover, the Académie de Médecine has carried out its own investigation of epidemics since 1826 (see the reports of the Commission on Epidemics to the minister of the interior, published every five years in the *Mémoires* of the Academy). Unfortunately, the documents used to draw up these reports, namely, the statements sent from each of the

Only a year ago, Jean Meyer gave us, in the pages of *Annales: E.S.C.*, a very pertinent outline of the history of the archival collection with which we are concerned.[7] I am taking the liberty of referring the reader to that article, since the author not only presents a kind of general inventory of the wealth of material in the collection but also paints a lively picture of the work done by these provincial physicians, corresponding members of the Société Royale, in the face of severe handicaps and despite many false starts. Meyer shows that the unexpectedly large number of precise memoranda received and the detailed sequences of clinical observations and meteorological measurements—many of them kept up for fifteen years and more—attest to the fact that a real need was met when the appeal went out to the competence of these men. This was the first time they were given the opportunity to break out of their provincial isolation and to look at their own experience from the outside, as it were. It was the first time they were able to treat their patients, thanks to their collective efforts, with a working knowledge of the spatial interrelations—the cosmic and organic configurations which, to their thinking, guided the course, development, and sequence of diseases everywhere, as well as in the particular perimeter of their practice.

Jean Meyer attaches great importance to the scientific climate that brought about this investigation. In this connection, it is not the least of his contributions to point out that "contrary to widespread prejudice, great discoveries are not necessarily explained by a new perception of the problems." In this case, innovative physicians, some of whom can be called precursors of modern medicine, based their thinking on old ideas. Just as the Reformation went back to the Bible, medicine in its search for renewal and change went back to the writings of Hippocrates. Thus the most influential of the theoretical hypotheses leading to the investigation is the idea that the rhythm of the changing seasons is one of the decisive factors of health and, to an even greater extent, of disease.

Once this premise was established, it was a matter of discovering the precise nature of the correlation between climate and disease. This was the purpose of the immense *summa* planned and then executed by the Société Royale de Médecine. At that point, however, the purpose somehow went awry. The hypothesis governing the investigation came to

---

departments by the physicians in charge of epidemics, are now stored in a depot connected, not with the Archives, but with the secretariat of that Academy. There they are inaccessible and, besides, they are piled up in the greatest disorder. Every year, a fair number of them is discarded in order to make room. What can be done to save these treasures?

[7]Jean Meyer, "Une enquête de l'Académie de médecine sur les épidémies (1774–1794)," *Annales: E.S.C.*, 1966, no. 4, pp. 729–49. Jean Meyer is the first author to have brought this repository of medical archives to the attention of historians.

interfere with its results. To be sure, the investigation found what it was looking for, but it could find *only* that, having postulated the relationship it purported to investigate as a fact from the outset. In this manner, it became self-enclosed. And since this was the case, a whole rigid layer of intellectual categories came to constrict the reality, immobilizing it in a structure. Whatever was seen was placed under a grid of classifications, operations, and totally fictitious combinations. Does this compromise the lessons to be drawn from the investigation? And do these presuppositions rob the document of all its value? I have asked myself this question, and the present article is really nothing but an attempt to answer it. At a certain level of the analysis at least, essential information was gathered, for these physicians scrupulously noted temperatures and air pressures and described the sequence of changes wrought upon the body by disease so carefully that they wrote down everything—including things they did not understand either as to their nature or to their cause. It is only at the next level of analysis that the contemporary theoretical point of view seriously distorted matters. It must also be said, however, that there are the additional stumbling blocks of imperfect meteorological instruments and a medical language to which we have lost the key. All of this will have to be dealt with at considerable length.

Jean Meyer, for his part, was more concerned with the technical problems posed by the ancient *measures* and, therefore, discussed the possibilities of using the statistical, meteorological, and economic data [of the collection] under that aspect.[8] Since I have assumed the task of bringing to light, by means of this source, an archaeology of disease, I quickly came to realize that, led astray by the ambiguity of the texts, I was running the risk of ending up, unawares, with a geology of medical perception. But it so happens that this study has already been made, and made once and for all;[9] there is no need to come back to it. It falls to me—a traveler who, trapped in a labyrinth he tries to understand, must not permit himself to be taken in by the play of its mirrors—to reach the open space beyond words, an open space which our sources, beneath all their veils and distortions, do indeed reflect. It is the space where, in a very rigorous and material sense—without metaphors but through the scientifically translatable interplay of their own organs, their cells, and

---

[8]The meteorological data are being processed in view of a quantitative study (E.P.H.E., VIe Section, Centre d'Etudes Historiques, under the direction of Emmanuel Le Roy Ladurie).

[9]Michel Foucault, *Naissance de la clinique. Une archéologie du regard médical* (Paris: P.U.F., 1963), vol. 15; trans. A. M. Sheridan Smith, *The Birth of the Clinic: An Archeology of Medical Perception* (New York: Pantheon Books, 1974).

their defense mechanisms—the lives, the deaths, and the suffering of several million people were played out.

* * *

Some one hundred and fifty physicians corresponded with Vicq d'Azyr in this vast census-taking operation. About fifty of them followed the investigation over a period of more than ten years. Month after month they filled out two-part, printed forms. On one side they would enter three daily readings of the thermometer, the barometric readings, the monthly average of these measurements, the amount of sunshine, humidity, and rain, the direction of the wind, its velocity, and all other relevant meteorological information. The other side, entitled "nosology," had room for medical observations, but the physician was entirely free to decide what he wanted to report. Here one of them might briefly note the five or six diseases he had most often treated in the course of the month; another might describe in a detailed note how these diseases had broken out, what symptoms they exhibited, how they followed each other, how serious their effects were, how many of them had ended in death, and what treatment he had followed. Frequently, correspondents would illustrate their observations by giving precise examples concerning a certain man of such and such age, whose illness took such and such a form, which might be either classic or unusual; or a certain girl, or woman, or person who had been saved or had died. Occasionally, a physician would consult the members of the Société Royale on the subject of some rare or even unknown disease, some exceptional occurrence, or any other noteworthy observation. All of this amounted to a restraining discipline; and, in contrast to the printed forms for the meteorological tables whose very arrangements called for systematic measurement, this monthly medical statement was subject to very few rules and therefore obliged the corresponding physician to condense and to choose. It also obliged him to break up continuous cycles of epidemics, so that their underlying unity was apt to be masked by the fact that they were reported piecemeal every month. This part of their task, which looked so simple, therefore presented quite a problem to the correspondents.

For this reason, we find a great many appendices. Many of these are letters sent along with the forms or instead of them. ("Monsieur, I am sending you my observations for the last three months of 1782." "I have put off for some time sending the Société Royale the forms which . . . ," and so forth.) Quite frequently these letters contain a penetrating commentary which, by way of excuses or explanations, leads us right into the teeming reality of the conditions in which the physician worked—into the social and human milieu where he practiced, beset with various difficulties ranging from complete frustration to overwork and lack of assistance. Too busy to fill out the printed forms on time, he would attempt to synthesize a whole year of treatments, cases, and epidemics in a long letter or a report. Sometimes he would mention sudden disasters, villages overwhelmed by death, mysterious illnesses to which there was no clue and which he tried to stem as best he could. This kind of situation furnished the perfect subject matter for a special memorandum of five or twenty or fifty pages, which was particularly opportune if it could fill a gap left by tardiness[10] or if there was hope that it might be read publicly during a session of the Société Royale, published in its Annals,[11] or be rewarded with some token, a medal, or perhaps even a prize. Anything to break out of the anonymity of confinement in the provinces!

It is therefore no coincidence that the number and the quality of these writings is far superior to the ordinary meteoro-nosological tables. In the end, the matters surrounding the investigation became more important than the investigation itself; they now constitute its most valuable core. In them and through them medicine has taken its place as the expression of a "world."

Meanwhile, the Société Royale de Médecine clung to its original definition of the investigation. Receiving medical observations differing greatly among themselves, it decided to publish them every year in the form of a month-by-month résumé which was to include only the contents of the "tables." In the opinion of the editors, the résumé would be sufficient to give the reader, at a glance, all the information on the meteorological measurements, which were printed exactly as they had appeared in the forms. They felt this information would clearly establish the correlation between climate and disease.

These statistical elements, which are useful for the history of climate and are easy to use, since they are printed, first attracted the attention of Emmanuel Le Roy Ladurie. They were the starting point for the project undertaken under his direction by the Sixth Section of the École Pratique des Hautes Études. In the course of this project of recording the climatic data, the printed medical data—the résumé made by Vicq d'Azyr—were

[10]". . . since time did not permit me to write down my nosological observations of the last trimester, I have the honor of sending you, under the present cover, a small *mémoire* concerning an observation which warrants the attention of the profession. I would therefore like to ask you, Monsieur, to read it to a session of the Société Royale and to ask that assembly of enlightened practitioners to state their opinion of it. . . ." Jean-Gabriel Gallot to Vicq d'Azyr, Nov. 21, 1784, SRM 189.

[11]*Histoire et Mémoires de la Société Royale de Médecine* for the years 1776–98, 10 vols., in -4° (Paris, 1779-An VI).

also collected and coded.[12] These latter data were then given to me; they are full of enigmatic things and conceal a great many traps.

There was no hope of using these data profitably before I had come to grips with a number of prejudicial questions relating to the following:

1. The manipulation of the basic documents before they were published as a resumé; in other words the value of that resumé.
2. The archaic medical terminology, which is incomprehensible at first sight.
3. The need for utilizing part or all of the manuscript documents (tables, observations, letters, and reports) which potentially support the data but are not included in them.
4. Biases in observation resulting from subjecting the reality the physician thought he was reporting to a doctrinaire "aerist" (or "climatist") point of view.

As a first precaution, therefore, a sampling of every hundredth printed table was made in order to determine whether or not the printed version or resumé faithfully reflects the monthly observations of the correspondents (in the manuscripts). It turned out that these two bodies of documents have very few points in common. The filter interposed between them permitted only a minimum of information to reach publication. What, then, was to be done? First, it became clear that I was dealing, not with two versions of the same source, but with two different sources, and that they must be considered as such. One of them, which is vast and concerned with a hundred different topics, could be explored and sampled at leisure, gradually and piece by piece; while the other, because it is perfectly straightforward, could be used to assess a situation quickly, with the understanding that its particularities and patterns could be worked out later with the help of the general *fonds*. Second, and conversely, it also became clear that the obscurities of the data could only be resolved (by evaluating the resumé, translating the nosology into modern diagnosis, etc.) by constantly referring back to its own source, that imposing mass of letters and documents. Hence, the work entails a constant back and forth between the two.

The published resumé takes the form of a long list of diseases, presented in chronological order. To give one example, we have the following as some of the entries for December 1783:

Aix: Fluxes, colds, rheumatism, vertigo, pleuropneumonia, smallpox.
Argentat: Cold, pleuropneumonia.
Bordeaux: Intermittent fevers, puerperal fevers, smallpox.

[12]With a view to an eventual use of the computer.

Brest: Measles, intermittent fevers, smallpox.
Chinon: Bilious fevers, chest congestions, fluxions.[13]
. . . and so forth

There is no need to burden the reader with the thirty-five-hundred
cards from which these five examples are taken. Let us turn instead to
what can be learned from the data as a whole.

1. The published résumé restricts the detailed manuscript observations, reducing them to a dry list of names of diseases.[14]
2. By doing so, it curtails the amount of significant content. It treats as
slag things one can rightfully consider to be essential.
3. Since it "processes" the documents, however, it at least erases the
diversity in observation and point of view. It restores homogeneity to the
documents and presents them as a "set" in which every item can be
compared to every other item.
4. And yet the résumé, in turn, imposes its own point of view. For it
could not be made without *translating*. It shows the dominant influence
of a school. Certain terms are modified, and prolix symptoms are
grouped together under one word designating a single morbid entity.[15]
We might say that the information given, once it is pressed into the mold
of a specific code of nosological terminology, is more convenient to use

[13]*Histoire et Mémoires de la SRM*, vol. 5, for the first part of 1783 (Paris, 1787), pp.
300 ff, table 25. Published tables exist only for the years 1776–86, inclusive.
[14]Bret, a physician, said in his "Observations" about Arles in Sept. 1783: "Measles have
continued, and especially this month a number of children have died, not while they had the
measles, but from their aftereffects, such as diarrhea, dysentery, or tenesmus, attended by a
continued low fever, which flared up without producing shivers. This untreated diarrhea . . .
brought them to a state of marasmus, and they eventually perished in the third and fourth
week, sometimes even later. In all of the cases of death I observed, the measles were
accompanied by whooping cough. . . . During this month, no other disease has prevailed,
and the number of various other diseases has not been considerable." The *printed* version
reads: "Intermittent fevers, diarrhea, measles."
[15]Poitiers (De la Mazière, physician), June 1782, SRM 184. The correspondent says, in
essence, that intermittent fevers were the principal complaint, and that the patients
discharged a great deal of bilious matter. He mentions double tertian fevers and tenacious,
obstinate quotidian fevers, as well as obstinate catarrhal fevers. He also notes "a great many
eruptions," which he attributes to the heat having "rarefied the blood." Malignant putrid
fevers of long standing are still present, but have not had any serious consequences. A few
sudden deaths have occurred. The Société publishes the following entry: catarrhal affections, intermittent fevers, eruptive putrid fevers. Evidently, this last expression combines the
two notations "a great many eruptions" and "malignant putrid fevers," although it is not
clear how this principle of association was developed. In March of the same year, one
expression was used to synthesize four different terms, but here the procedure seems clearer.
Since the correspondent had described colds, catarrhal affections, whooping cough in
adults, and catarrhal fevers, all of which presented analogous symptoms of pulmonary
congestion or bronchitis, Vicq d'Azyr simply translated them as "chest fluxions."

exactly because of the extent to which it has been distorted by being translated.

5. The published lists are incomplete. Vicq d'Azyr and his team shied away from a superhuman task[16] and published only the following: (a) Observations forming a fairly regular sequence over a fairly long time. (b) Observations presented in a sufficiently clear and well-written manuscript. (c) Observations conforming to the uniform pattern of the prepared "tables" printed and distributed by the Société Royale.

6. Consequently, the following materials were eliminated: (a) Scattered observations. (b) Observations written on blank paper (letters, reports, etc., except in cases where the physician reproduced the printed form by tracing columns with his quill). (c) Observations not conforming to the norm. Certain physicians did indeed prefer to hand in only one report per year. They approached the subject matter either by season or by major blocks of diseases or epidemics. It should be noted that these reports were generally more intelligently written and are therefore more consistently interesting. (d) Special memoranda concerning a particular epidemic. These came from very busy physicians who did not have time to write every month and who were often interested only in the impact of epidemics affecting large segments of the population. (e) Monthly tables punctually filled out for the meteorological part, but lacking any mention of disease so long as the health situation was normal (i.e., when only the usual diseases were present). These physicians only sent in their observations when they felt that things had taken a turn for the worse (in the presence of a serious epidemic or a high incidence of various diseases). Hence there is a seeming irregularity in their work, but this irregularity only indicates that they had a different conception of the purpose of the investigation. To them, a "blank" did not mean "observations: none," but "nothing special to report," while others felt that they should mention all their routine cases of eczema, gout, or colds.

The choices and transpositions made by Vicq d'Azyr are not the only ones that must be taken into consideration. If this were all, it would be a minor matter, since in addition to the truncated publication we do, after all, possess cartons and cartons bulging with manuscripts. For our purpose, it is much more critical that the physicians themselves, depend-

---

[16]When it wanted to resume this task after 1826, the Académie de Médecine instructed a committee to publish a comprehensive report on this investigation of forty or more years earlier. After four years of work on the *Mémoires* preserved in the Archives, the committee had been able to analyze only those concerning a single one of the new departments, the Ain. The project had to be abandoned. (See *Mémoires de l'Académie de Médecine* [1833], 3: 377 ff.)

ing on their understanding of the project and especially on their training or, rather, the school of medical thinking to which they belonged, contributed to the ambiguity and the hidden disparity of the material at our disposal. In the manuscripts, any given term does not always carry the same weight in terms of value, despite its identical appearance. Everything has a double meaning. Some names ("continued fever" or even "colds") will not designate the same disorder depending on the physician using them. What can we trust? The concern becomes even more acute when we discover that in the tables some physicians listed only the diseases they themselves had treated in their area, which was obviously only a part, but the part they felt called upon to report.

Here, for example, is the observation of Morel, physician at Villefranche-sur-Saône, for January 1785: "Whooping cough has finally ceased. . . . Measles have appeared in a few subjects, but have not been more serious than the smallpox whose epidemic continues at the same level as in the preceding months. The other prevailing diseases have been *indispositions arising from individual idiosyncrasies* rather than caused by atmospheric conditions, which have been fairly healthful."[17] As we can see, the matter was perfectly clear to this observer: he was concerned with epidemic diseases only. He based his assumption on three reasons which we can deduce as follows: (1)The Société Royale de Médecine is primarily interested in epidemics (evaluation of the project). (2) Epidemics affect a large number of people and therefore fall into the domain of collective medicine; for this reason they alone have a quasi-statistical value which makes them the material of choice for an investigative report (objective investigation). (3) They, and they alone, are dependent on climate (theoretical interpretation). The choice is coherent, but oriented in a specific direction; and the sands are shifting.

A colleague applying another grid will come to different conclusions. He will have a different interpretation of the criteria of the Société Royale. Contrary to the first correspondent he will be convinced that every disease is in one way or another governed by climatic factors. He will therefore give us observations like the following, where the small change of isolated or insignificant accidents is carefully placed into the kitty: ". . . old people and languishing patients have perished in a few days without warning, having had only a little fever" (Poitiers, Feb. 1784);[18] ". . . several eruptions upon the body are making the patients very hot" (ibid., July 1782); ". . . darkening of the mental faculties" (Laigle, May 1787);[19] and "abscess on the knee" (ibid., July).

[17]SRM 194, italics mine.
[18]SRM 184.
[19]SRM 152.

Now let us return to the printed version, which gives a résumé of these diseases. There are three cards, one of them (Villefranche-sur-Saône) mentioning "smallpox . . . measles"; the second (Laigle), "tertian fever . . . continued remittent fever . . . madness"; and the third (Poitiers), "colds . . . intermittent fevers . . . rheumatism . . . eruptions." Without very careful research on the respective systems of the physicians, however, we are not aware that these data are of differing importance. Once they have been processed by a computer, we will most certainly make mistakes. The benign eruption of one and the single case of madness of the other will weigh as heavily as the murderous epidemic of measles of the first. On one and the same card the abscess on the knee is given equal importance as the continued comatose fever, which must have consumed the population of Laigle with a very different flame; for from our vantage point we can assume that it was actually typhus. Finally, any question asked for the purpose of determining whether madness or eruptions occurred in, say, Villefranche can only be answered "no," even though it is quite possible that cases of that kind did arise there. The accounting is lopsided.

*   *   *

The physicians, then, "sorted" their evidence. Some based their reports on the idea that they were supposed to record *any incidence* of a disease, regardless of the number of cases it produced. Others felt that only those diseases that struck many people should be reported. This means that the former placed the emphasis on the various kinds of diseases—on *disease* as such, in the final analysis—while the latter placed it on the population or, better, on the "big" phenomena affecting it. In this manner, the collective and the distributive approach get in each other's way, and the investigation takes its clues from points in the total picture which do not correspond to each other.

Yet these clues are all we have. What is sadly lacking in all of this material is any kind of effort at measuring. The fact is that we never know *how many* people had red fever, or *how many* children contracted smallpox. The printed version, by its very nature, is silent on this point. The manuscripts sometimes do furnish a few figures of mortality for the most serious epidemics, but fail to relate them in any meaningful way to the number of people affected, or to mention the size of the population as a whole.[20] In the rare cases when we are given figures for one village, one

[20]"Catarrhal fevers . . . have stricken some of our cantons with an absolutely frightening power. They have now prevailed for fifteen or sixteen months, and have wrought havoc wherever they have appeared. The first village to be attacked was that of Caisses and its

town, or one section of a city, we would still like to know the size of the
area covered by the reporting physician and how far he went for his calls.
Except in a few instances, we will never know. This being the case, we will
follow the example of the physicians whose efforts provided us with these
documents and confine our curiosity to the total picture. Our work will be
concerned with disease rather than with the sick person. It will not worry
about the individual, at least not as a demographic unit. We will find out
which diseases were endemic and which were recessive; we will know
which of them raged locally and which, on the contrary, blazed a fiery
trail; we will be able to find clusters, cycles, isolated outbreaks, and tidal
waves. But we will still not have any statistics concerning the number of
sick people.

Altogether, then, we are dealing with a document riddled with gaps:
gaps in time, gaps in space,[21] gaps in content. Yet I am glad to have it, and
I accept it as it is. It is true that all the physicians did not report the same
kinds of observations (two lines, two pages, twenty pages); it is true that
the subsequent reduction of the manuscripts caused them to reach us in
an abbreviated, corrected, and therefore distorted form; and it is also true
that many rich sources did not find their way into the printed version and
our data. But despite all of this, I am willing to say, "I don't care!"

For why should we permit ourselves to be blinded by discontinuities
that can be retrieved and therefore corrected? Why should we neglect an
important source simply because we know it to be distorted by theoretical
presuppositions? As I already pointed out, there are too many advantages
to this double recording (the printed and the manuscript version) not to
make the effort of coping with its confusing aspects as well. To that end,
our data can serve us like a digging tool. From the printed version, which
is helpful despite and, indeed, because of its compressed nature, an
elementary cartography of the diseases will emerge (though it will usually
show the symptoms rather than the diseases). It will also give us a first
picture of the rhythm and the routes by which epidemics proceeded.
Having learned this much, we will be in a position to delve into the

---

surrounding hamlets. Twelve persons were carried off in this rather large parish. . . . This
disease killed very quickly. Most of these persons died at the end of the fourth day; some of
them even perished on the third day. . . . In the village of Laqui in the parish of Carlepont
[these diseases] struck more than a third of the inhabitants. A great number of them had
already died by the time [I was called]." Dufour, physician at the hospitals of Noyon, in
charge of epidemics, "Mémoire sur la ville de Noyon," 1782 manuscript, 20 pp., SRM 159.

[21]The localities for which we have consecutive monthly reports over more than five or six
years are rather evenly distributed over the French territory, with the exception of three
major gaps: the western part of Brittany and Lower Normandy, the northwestern part of the
central highland, and the alpine region of the southeast are represented by only one constant
correspondent each.

overwhelming mine of information formed by the *fonds* Vicq d'Azyr at the appropriate points.

The only real obstacle I thought I could not overcome was the ancient medical terminology. This was the problem that turned everything into a riddle. To skirt the issue, to leave it in suspense, heavy and opaque behind me, would have meant to grope in the dark forever. So I had to face it head on and to cope with it.

On the Names of Diseases

The concern that prompted this study is not one that originated with our generation. Already in the last century, there was some awareness that any set of diseases affecting a given group of humans has its own history.[22] However, no one took the trouble of tracing the chronology of that evolution back very far; and if the documents studied here are among those which can help us in this endeavor, they also present immediate obstacles. For example, in view of our interest in the high incidence of cardio-vascular troubles in our own day, we might want to know what that situation was two centuries ago. What would our archives tell us? Nothing. What about mental illness? Just as little. And more or less the same would be true for viral hepatitis, tuberculosis, micosis, leukemia, and many other diseases. Why is this so? There are two reasons.

First, what we know about the various diseases has changed. New knowledge, new terms. It sometimes looks as if the diseases had split apart or contracted, depending on the physicians' ideas of them and the conceptual basis by which they were diagnosed. Diseases which fell under a single diagnosis in the past have since been differentiated into several new entities. Thus, the term "asthma" used to include disturbances which had nothing to do with allergic asthma as we know it, among them respiratory difficulties due to cardiac decompression.[23] On the other

[22]The elder Bertillon, pleading for a statistics on the causes of death, already wrote: ". . . one of the reasons which will make these documents so valuable in the future is the fact that they will enable future generations to study in what ways time, civilization, and science have modified the interrelationship and the intensity of diseases. Is it not one of the most regrettable gaps in our knowledge that we are unable to evaluate the real or imagined progress brought about by our efforts in the fields of hygiene, therapeutics, and social economy? . . . Therefore these archives of the causes of death will be closely examined by our sons, for they will wish to study the history of human pathology and will try to find out whether the various species of disease acted with greater or lesser intensity in their time than in ours." Bertillon, "Considération sur la statistique des décès," *Union Médicale*, 1856, p. 534.
[23]There was no symptomatology of the heart before 1806. The distinction between cardiac and pulmonary disorders was made by Corvisart.

hand, a variety of infectious diseases, among them typhus, have all been brought into the same category, once it was discovered that they are caused by a common microbic agent, namely, the *rickettsiae*. Everyone knows that what was called "pernicious anemia" meant—among other things—what we now know to be a cancer of the cells regulating the production of blood corpuscles.

But it so happens, and this is the second reason for the shift in terminology, that the diseases themselves have changed. Not only their incidence, their very nature—or at least their character—has become different. Like societies, diseases are subject to laws of perpetual change. How risky it must be, then, to try to identify a disease as we know it under an archaic term! Will it really be the same disease? Clearly our effort is threatened by ambiguity on all sides. The *specific* morbidity of any given historical population is not present in the old diagnoses.

At first sight, therefore, the outlook was rather gloomy. By going through the data based on Vicq d'Azyr's printed version and by gathering together the monthly statements of the names of diseases current in the various localities, I soon found myself in possession of a list of 420 medical terms. They should be transcribed in order to let the reader judge for himself. As an indication, here is a tiny sample:

Abcès gangreneux	gangrenous abscess
Affection catarrhale	catarrhal affection
Affection chronique	chronic affection
Affection vaporeuse	vapors
Anasarque	dropsy
Angine couenneuse	membranous angina
Angine putride	putrid angina
Asphyxie	asphyxia
Bouffissure	swelling
Colique bilieuse	bilious colic
Colique du Poitou	Poitou colic
Convulsions	convulsions
Coup de sang	apoplectic fit
Coup de soleil	sunstroke
Cours de ventre	running bowels
Crachement de sang	bloodspitting
Démangaisons	itch
Dépôts	complication of humors
Dévoiement	looseness
Diarrhée	diarrhea
Douleurs de poitrine	chest pains

Dysenterie	dysentery
Dysenterie bilieuse	bilious dysentery
Dysenterie inflammatoire (etc.)	inflammatory (etc.) dysentery
Ebullition du sang	boiling of the blood
Eruption aux viscéres	eruption in the bowels
Fluxion catarrhale	catarrhal flux
Frissons	shivering fit
Passion iliaque	iliac passion

The list goes on, with the column "fever" giving 128 titles, such as fit of fever, acute f., autumnal f., bilious f., bilious inflammatory f., continued f., continued acute (or continued bilious, continued exacerbating, or continued inflammatory bilious) f., ephemeral f., exanthematic f., intermittent f., malignant f., putrid f., every one of which can be used in conjunction with any or all of the adjectives.

It is a word puzzle. The hiatus revealed here is related to a historical fact. Beginning with the years 1840–50, medical thinking underwent a radical mutation; and this evolution had an impact on the very definition of disease. Henceforth, medical diagnosis—good or bad, and even if only provisional, waiting to be confirmed by new means of investigation or new discoveries—rests upon an *anatomical* and *etiological* conception of disease, while the nosography I have taken it upon myself to decipher is defined by the fact that it isolates and examines the distinctive characteristics of a given disease on the basis and with the help of *symptoms* and *syndromes*. Consequently, it is neither possible nor right to match every old word exactly with a modern medical term, i.e., to translate it. The two systems of reference simply do not have a common logical basis. This is so true that for a time I considered giving up. Physicians whose advice I solicited advised me against "pouring old wine into new bottles." Yet some of them suggested ways of getting around the difficulty. What had to be done was to treat matters at a different level, one that is more modest, but also more fruitful.[24]

This is why I decided to take each term to the point where it ceases to be a constituent part of a system. Once the distorting glow of the system is dispelled, each term can furnish us some information, however elementary, on the real morbidity. While many of these terms only skim the surface, others lead us right into the soil, to the very roots. And if the latter will give us a somewhat better idea of what diseases people had, the former will also help us to know, better than ever before, and humble as

[24]I should like to thank the following persons for their valuable help: Professor Huard, Drs. J.-N. Biraben, M. D. Grmek, P. Chavanne, L. Dulieu, and A. Carré. All of them carefully answered my questions, and some of them patiently suffered through repeated and sometimes lengthy "consultations" with me.

this approach may seem, how people's health was or, rather, in what ways it was bad.

Among the seemingly simplest, most encouraging, but also most devious terms are, first, those that are still nosological entities, "diseases" of today. They are aphthae, angina, lead poisoning (or, as we would say today, saturnism), smallpox (variola), measles, influenza, lumbago, boils (furunculosis), mumps, sciatica, hives, and a few others. There are not many of these.

Now, as we have seen in the case of asthma, the names have often been kept, but the contents have changed. The old term "angina" (or its synonym, "synanche") designated the whole gammut of pharingitis, tonsillitis, red angina, Vincent's angina, and even the first and only evidence of an incipient but surmounted poliomyelitis. The old physicians used the term "scorbutic affection" to designate a whole series of analogous and partially analogous clinical signs which, today, would point to many other disorders than just scurvy. Whenever they saw receding or bleeding gums, painful joints, and ecchymosis (bruises), all of this combined with generalized weakness, they would write down "scurvy," although we now know that these conditions might also be arthritis, alveolar pyorrhea, anemia, cardiac insufficiency, and possibly septicemia. The old "jaundice" could be, not only what this term still implies, but also infectious icterus, bleeding icterus, as well as the sign of spirochetosis or cancer of the liver or of the head of the pancreas. "Phthisis" [consumption] is not necessarily pulmonary tuberculosis. And so forth.

On the other end of the spectrum there is an abundance of more general terms designating simple symptoms or limited accidents which do not permit us to make a diagnosis. These are things like nosebleed, rashes, asphyxiation, cephalalgy (headache), sunstroke (what we call insolation), hoarseness, eruptions, fluxions (discharge) from the head or the eyes, indigestion, stomach-ache, cough, vomiting. I am mentioning so many of them because my supply is ample. Here, it is impossible to be precise. Who can tell whether "torminal diarrhea" refers to a gastric upset, dysentery, parasitosis, food poisoning, typhoid, or any number of other things? "Blood spitting" is apt to lead us a little further, though it is still ambiguous. Cancer of the lungs or of the larynx or an infection of the trachea may have caused it. But statistically it is more likely that it was a matter of hemophthysis connected with pulmonary tuberculosis. And the case of "paralysis" is similar. While there is every justification for hesitating and for considering either syphilitic tabes, multiple sclerosis, an attack of poliomyelitis, or various lesions of the spinal marrow, everything (and especially the manuscript memoranda which I sampled in this connection) indicates that we must understand this term to mean motor troubles accompanying and pointing to vascular injuries at the brain level.

In short, these series of symptoms require that we proceed with a great deal of caution. But, at whatever level they may be useful, the indications they can provide are not to be rejected. They speak to us. Sometimes low, sometimes loud and clear, their voices add to a rich discourse offering us the makings of a day-to-day history of states of health.

Finally, there are those expressions that make no sense at all. This medical terminology seems to be pure gibberish. What are "*porcelaine*" and "Saint Anthony's fire"? What can be meant by "malignant bilious petechial putrid fever"? What might "putrid red fever" be? Such stumbling blocks confirm once again that there is an element of detective passion in all research; the missing explanation becomes like a lock which gives us no peace until we have discovered how it works.

But in this case there was a strong temptation not to try. It looked as if there were no door and no secret, as if it were an illusion that there is a riddle to be solved. I was given to understand that the truth lies elsewhere, because these strange words of the ancient medicine are the very core of a system of thought, both its support and its product. Outside of that system they lose their meaning and their value. If the relationships these words have among themselves are coherent, and therefore intelligible, one must conversely also see that these relationships, and they alone, give them that coherence. This, I was told, is proof that any relationship between these words and organic reality can only be allusive, illusory, and in the final analysis, indecipherable. For in terms of structure—or, better, of structural analysis—those who adopt this position (for my part I am only wondering whether the system that hampers my movements was really all that rigid) cannot admit any possibility of transfer or mobility. Every moment constitutes its own prison. It has no future. It is settled once and for all in its coherence. "Hominal" is not synonymous with "human." Cuvier will never be superseded by Geoffroy Saint-Hilaire and Darwin. "Membranous synanche" is trapped in a network of significations which assigns it to its place. It can never be the equivalent of any of the diseases we know, because it is only its own name, which imprisons it. The mind that named it did not have the same syntax as ours.

I refuse to accept these strictures. But then it behooves me to justify my refusal; and this is why I must ask the reader who might be intrigued by "mucous synochus" to bear with me just a little longer. Before I can legitimately identify it and discuss it as typhoid, I must pay off one last mortgage.

* * *

The body of documents formed by the responses to the investigation of the Société Royale captures a unique moment in the history of medicine. For here we see medical perception in the act of giving birth, unaware though it was of its own adventure. What we sense is the emergence of a new insight into the relationship between life and disease. Standing at the crossroads where these two meet, the physician began to realize that his role would have to change, both as to its direction and to the area of its concern. For the first time, he could dimly perceive, beyond the vain imaginings of theory which still hid it from his view, the true object of his efforts, namely, disease as it was embedded and inscribed in the human body. Hitherto, disease had only existed for its own sake, unrelated to anything else. Now, gradually, the diseased organism emerged into consciousness and into view.

And yet, as we see it at the end of the eighteenth century, this school, which carried within it the seeds of the future, gave above all the impression of confusion. Wavering and compromising, it perched atop a system with two sloping sides; *class* and *constitution*. This very uncertainty is a sign that we are dealing with a system about to give way. Let us examine these two principles.

The system owed its basic vocabulary to the medicine of the morbid species. The lexicon of inflammation, hemorrhage, fevers, etc., organized the forms of diseases, distributing them into orders or *classes*. These entities are veritable beings. They exist as essences, independent of any circumstance, independent also of the sick person. The latter, while necessary to their incarnation, is never more than an unreliable vessel, for he adulterates the natural, pure form the physician is called upon to recognize under the duplicity of the flesh.

Yet the body, according to Bordeu, for example,[25] is an assemblage of organs, each of which lives its own life, moving, acting and resting in its own fixed ways. "The life of the body as a whole is the sum of the lives of these particular organs, each of which is endowed with its own particular movements. These movements are governed by the nerves, and the nerves in their entirety can be considered to be a polyp with roots or branches

---

[25]Théophile Bordeu, *Recherche sur les maladies chroniques* (Paris, 1775), theorems 1, 11 and 12. Bordeu was what is called a "vitalist." His ideas had a great influence on the Société Royale.

extending to the organs of the senses and to all parts of the body. The nerves will impart to each of these the kind of sensibility, activity, and vital movement with which the organs are endowed and which, in turn, are governed by sentiment. For life is only sentiment and movement." The brain, the heart, and the stomach are a triumvirate, the "tripod of life." By working together, they provide for the life of each part and for each function; and they are the three centers from which sentiment and movement originate and to which they return after they have circulated, for health is maintained through this continuous circulation.

Diseases result from disturbances in this vital principle. They are this disturbance. Sauvages in particular saw them as a reaction of the immaterial principle against interference.[26] "Just as cold tends to force humors toward the center," he wrote, "so the vital power will immediately be aroused and make every effort to reestablish the balance." The results are spasms, convulsions, or fever. In apoplexy, the obstacle is in the brain, and in that case the heart will be stimulated to clear it.

For this reason, diseases can be understood through groups of symptoms with which, in the final analysis, they are identified. It is therefore necessary to observe what is happening in the body, to know the essence of all the organs, their interrelations, etc., in order to distinguish clearly which of the symptoms are caused by organic support and resulting upsets within the body, and which ones indicate the presence of the pure nosological essence. Furthermore, each of these symptoms is somehow governed by dominant and more regular symptoms, which are like the leaders of a troup.[27] And these leading signs belong to three categories: functions, excretions, or qualities.

In this manner, for example, a *function* manifesting itself with so much force that it disturbs other functions constitutes in itself a morbid state. This is often the case with digestion. When the stomach is irritated by the presence of food, it upsets the entire body; it then calls all of its forces toward the interior, whence they are propelled toward the exterior. Thus, a laborious digestion is in essence the same thing as a fit of fever or the process of suppuration.[28] These symptoms are so closely related, in fact, that their outward appearances are interchangeable. A disease which first takes the form of digestive troubles may turn into suppuration and still remain the same disease. But for us, this view will make the terms used to designate it at one or the other of its phases most ambiguous.

[26]François Boissier de Sauvages, *Nosologia methodica* (1763); trans. Lyon, *Nosologie méthodique* (1772).
[27]"Symptomata magis obvia et simul constantiora agmen ducunt" (Sauvages).
[28]Bordeu, *Maladies chroniques*, theorems 17 and 19.

Another example is given by Barthez,[29] who defines regular gout as a depurative effort (*excretion*) aimed at "bringing to the surface earthy matter resulting from imperfect transpiration which is itself caused by a faulty constitution of the blood."[30]

Finally, in the category of *qualities*, we often hear of that "acrimony of humors," which brings about melancholia.

The catalogue of terms I enumerated above now assumes its full coherence. It is an ontology. In this arrangement of inductive categories the incarnation of the morbid entity matters less than its essence. Measles, rheumatism, and gonorrhea are but the avatars (or temporary incarnations) of a specific inflammatory entity, phlegmasia; and the analogy in appearance (redness, heat, pain, secretion) is a special bond uniting these classes. On the other hand, the divergence of form which places them into subgroups and differentiates them secondarily is a function of the characteristics they assume. Hence the various combinations of qualifications by which a tumor is designated as either serous or varicose or malignant, or by which pleuropneumonia is sometimes called putrid, sometimes humoral, also catarrhal, or even bilious. Nonetheless, these secondary forms all fall within the common model. Hemorrhage is a single phenomenon: it is the flow of blood. In the encompassing scheme, apoplexy is not fundamentally different from nosebleed. The only difference is that the former reveals a *plethora* [fullness] while the latter—an external (epistaxis) rather than an internal flow—is the result of "a particular direction, a manifestation of the vital powers in that part of the vascular system," the nose.[31] It is thus a *flux*. Blood spitting (hemophthysis), on the other hand, is related to a "general state of the bodily habitus"[32] characterized in terms of quality as lymphatic, thin, and burning. It is an *irritation* causing a *spasm*.

This, then, is the manner in which the medicine of classes and species operates. It is of such a nature that any direct question we might like to ask of it today—suppose we want a diagnosis of "inflammatory (or acute, catarrhal, bilious, gangrenous, etc.) disorder"—is bound to lose itself in this glass case where hundreds of well-labeled essences are lined up. Influenza, rheumatism, syphilis, and pleurisy are included in this term as particular aspects of a general class which subsumes, but also obliterates, them. This polymorphism (to our way of seeing) of a single term thus defies the very idea of translating it.

[29]Paul-Joseph Barthez, *Traité des maladies goutteuses*, 2 vols., in-8° (Paris, 1802).
[30]Quoted by F. Broussais, "Doctrine de Barthez," *Examen des doctrines médicales et des systémes de nosologie*, 3rd ed., 4 vols. (Paris, 1829; 1st ed., 1821), 3: 393.
[31]P. Pinel, *Nosographie philosophique* (Paris, An VI), 1: 207.
[32]Ibid., p. 209.

And yet, what distinguishes the group of men connected with the Société Royale is the fact that they too, for the first time, felt ill at ease in this universe. These physicians were too dismayed at the sight of their patients and their suffering to be able to disregard them in favor of some pure nosological essence that would provide all the answers. What did it mean to assert that diseases are caused by the *affection of the vital principle*, except that they are the disturbance of the unknown cause which regulates the existence of life in general? But then, they thought, if this cause is not known, its disturbances cannot be known either. And what is the use of looking for the cause of diseases in the disturbance of a thing of which we can have no knowledge, especially when the reality of the sick, the injured, and suffering organism is there for all to see?[33] As a result, these physicians, while still using the old vocabulary, eventually ceased to believe in it. They began to use these words in such a way that they no longer really interlocked with each other. The words no longer referred to the system from which they had issued. It is as if the theoretical framework had been lifted from these memoranda that were pouring into Paris in a steady stream. All that was left of it were allusions and a few residues.

This situation made for disintegration, on the one hand, but a new rigor, on the other. The new practice, while corroding the old framework, increasingly took its bearings from an ordered conception of the time and space in which diseases develop. Its space was that of the body and its organs, as well as the geographic locality, with its soil and its particular kinds of air and water. Its time was that which brought a sequence of natural or social phenomena—seasons, meteors, dearths—as well as the time of the organs themselves, which are attuned to these events. All of these relationships and encounters, it was felt, form a variable complex named a "*constitution*." The constitution carries within it and reflects "a consciousness of the disease in time and place."[34]

This term is purely technical and "practical"; it is light years removed from all classifying speculations. It designates the entire set of physical circumstances governing the particular characteristics of a particular disease at a particular time and in a particular place. As a result, and by the logic of this definition, any disease will assume a particular aspect, depending on whether it appears here or there, in one year or the next. Conversely, in a year with well-defined characteristics whose constitution

---

[33]On these critical ideas, see SRM 110 (miscellaneous correspondence concerning the investigation); 114 (opposition to the Faculty); and 115 (memoranda on the state of medicine in France and various views on the reform of the teaching and practice of medicine).

[34]Foucault, *Birth of the Clinic*, p. 21.

in a circumscribed area has been marked by exceptional putridity, all the diseases observed there—from the most ordinary to the most serious —will bear the stamp of a putrid component, i.e., a propensity for putridity. The very term "influenza" still reflects the role played by cosmic factors in past ideas of the conditions necessary for a universal propagation of disease.[35] "Malaria" (bad air) also reveals the notion that disease-giving powers are inherent in the *genius loci*, the "local constitution" of certain places.

What about circumstances?

After the winter of the Year II the diseases in the area as well as in this town consistently assumed a decidedly bilious character. The real or imagined shortage of food, its poor quality, the terror, the anxiety and all the things . . . which the storms of the Revolution had brought about, either by increasing the intake of bile-producing substances or by curtailing their secretion and elimination, made the humors susceptible to bilious degeneration. In addition, these conditions seriously affected the sensibilities so that nervous disorders greatly complicated the problem.[36]

And what of the abnormally high number of sudden deaths in Lower Poitou in 1776? Surely, they had to be attributed to the shocks of an earthquake.[37]

Atmospheric factors:

The remote causes which have brought about a disposition indispensable to disease . . . must unquestionably be related to the winds which during the month of January have always blown from the south or southwest. These naturally warm and humid winds have loosened the tone of the solids whose sustained action is neccessary to effect the equal distribution of the liquids. Because of their lack of movement, the liquids have thickened, and, due to their lack of serosity, they have contributed further to the loosening of the vessels and, hence, to conditions of stasis. As soon as a sustained north wind began to blow . . . the already very slack fibers, unable to offer the least resistence to such sudden and rigorous cold, were abruptly contracted. . . . In a number of patients, the result was chest congestion, which occurred on the very first day. . . .[38]

---

[35]See Mirko D. Grmek, "Géographie médicale et histoire des civilisations," *Annales, E.S.C.*, 1963, no. 6, p. 1076.

[36]J.–B. Laugier, *Constitution épidémique de Grenoble* (Grenoble, An IX), p. 1.

[37]Jean-Gabriel Gallot, physician at Saint-Maurice-le-Girard, "Observations sur les maladies regnantes . . . ," 1776, manuscript, 22 pp., SRM 189; earthquakes of April 14 and 30, 1776.

[38]Ayrault, physician at Mirebeau (Poitou), to Vicq d'Azyr, July 4, 1785: "Topographie du village de Marconnais et description de l'épidémie . . . ," SRM 163, no. 1. This was a case of epidemic pneumonia (Feb.–May 1785).

The body was believed to be attuned to the seasons.[39] If, in summer, dysentery "affects most particularly subjects of bilious, hot, and irascible temperament, that is, those who already have the disposition which the season would impart to them, [it is because] according to Hippocrates *summer boils man*; it heats him up by concentrating the most acrid principles which irritate the sensibility of the organs and thus provoke a reaction."[40]

For us, the most important aspect of the idea of constitution is its historical dimension. This, to be sure, is a rather modest dimension, for it only lines up clusters of circumstances in order to weave them together. We call the result *histoire à conjoncture*, history dealing with combinations of circumstances. Such history is interested in the fleeting color of the time and place and in the bilious overtones which will be fully orchestrated in the catarrhal register by the next season.[41]

But all of this is held together by the notion of time. This notion gave medical thinking a mobility which eventually was to sweep away its archaic moorings. Once this notion had come into play, the physicians interested in the so-called "practical" medicine of the Société Royale became increasingly aware of new medical concerns, especially of the social factors which vitally affect both the impact of disease and the role of the physician. The reality of these factors showed itself so powerfully that certain physicians were led to question the very notion of constitution. "Such a meteorological constitution," one of them wrote, "cannot be qualified as unhealthy.[42] Far from contributing to the slackening of the fibers, it has augmented their tone and their activity. . . . It would therefore be vain to look for the principle of the disease in this constitution of the air . . . and it would be all the more gratuitous [to do so] as the disease has always remained confined to the poor of the town."[43]

The fact is that the medicine of closed species and the medicine of the open social space could not be reconciled. Trapped between these two stages of medical consciousness, the physician became aware of the fragility, the vanity of all systems. He was of two minds; he felt torn.

[39]"The dry season has contributed greatly to sustaining disorders of the nerves . . . which are brought to the highest pitch of tenseness and rigidity. The heat and dryness which are so evident on the outside must certainly find the same disposition on the inside, and we cannot hope for any improvement until the nerves relax when the weather turns wet." Mirebeau, summer 1777, SRM 163, no. 1.

[40]Sydenham, cited in *Dictionnaire des Sciences Médicales, par une société de médecins*, 60 vols. (Paris: Panckouke, 1812–22) s.v. "colique" (colique bilieuse) by Pariset; italics mine.

[41]Louvemont (Lorraine), autumn 1786, in "Description de l'épidémie qui a règné . . . ," by Dr. Wacquart of Verdun, SRM 160.

[42]Dry, very cold winter, dry and chilly spring, cool summer, mild and sunny autumn, prevailing north wind.

[43]Lorentz, "Mémoire." "Putrid malignant petecchial fever": this is typhus.

Perhaps he was not always aware of his state and limped just a little. But he did limp. Consequently, he henceforth tended to trust only his own experience and such observations as eschewed grids of any kind interposed between the disease and the observer. Hence, we hear professions of faith like the following: "Experience, that torch which enlightens an attentive physician on the tortuous and difficult path of his practice much more safely than all the learned reasonings and ingenious systems brought forth in the study—*for these systems are more attractive to the mind than solid, and their falsehood can only be perceived at the bedside of a patient*—experience, I say, has caused me to rule out the practice of bleeding once and for all."[44]

The physician finally came to grips with the reality of the patient; he saw, freed himself, and entered the exciting open space of the body in the throes of its discomfort and its suffering. Here the physician read the message of a knowledge yet to come, which he tried to hang as best he could by the old nails, the old words. No wonder that the message became blurred in the process!

In this fashion, medicine made its way, from one state of imbalance to the next—toward the open space of physiology, the pathology of anatomy, and its final state as an experimental science. We must now reconsider the Société Royale, its team of correspondents, and its work in terms of this long perspective.

This medicine, I said, was caught up in history. The course of epidemics, atmospheric depressions, social and political upheaval—it closely followed all of these events. It is no coincidence that from the very beginning of the Revolution it aspired to a major role in the reform proposals for the medical care of the nation considered by the Comité de Salubrité.[45] And what of the very idea of "constitution"? Does it not smack of Montesquieu, and was it not destined to have a very unmedical future? The investigation with which we are concerned here was, after all, helped along by the subdelegates, supported by the central administration, and later continued on a similar basis under the Empire and even the

[44] Archives départementales, Deux-Sèvres, C 14 (hereafter cited as A.D. Deux-Sèvres). Subdélégation de Bressuire. Berthelot, doctor of medicine, "Topographie de la ville de Bressuire . . ."; italics mine. To be compared to the "Observations" for 1775 from Saint-Maurice-le-Girard: ". . . and furthermore, I am not too fond of theories, since most of them are usually doubtful, and often altogether erroneous" (SRM 189).

[45] The statistical approach of the Société needed and hoped to develop the institution of hospitals. However, its way was blocked by a whole faction within the medical profession opposed to hospitals as "gathering places of beggars." These opponents controlled the Committee on Mendicancy and prevailed over the other Committee (Public Health) thanks to political support from various quarters. On this point, see H. Ingrand, *Le Comité de Salubrité de l'Assemblée Nationale Constituante*, in-8° (Paris, 1934).

July Monarchy. Who can fail to see that it was a scientific undertaking with a parallel political purpose? It was the prerevolutionary medicine of a prerevolutionary decade.

Having been led this far, have I lost sight of my subject? On the contrary, I have come back to it at the end by way of a detour. This school, in the act of giving birth to a new medicine, this evolving system of thought, used words in such a way that they were shaken out of the rigid thinking where they had gradually congealed as the pearl congeals in the oyster. Presently they were swept along to the point where we can seize them, where we can finally make them amenable to translation.

Inasmuch as this medicine was able to make the transition from "before" to "after" by forcing the locks of its theoretical prison, and inasmuch as all of the work of Bichat and Laennec was already potentially there, it has handed down to us texts concerning epidemics and diseases where everything that could be seen was described. These texts will permit us to make our own diagnosis. To the extent, finally, that these obscure words broke out of their old classes in order to serve a new way of seeing, to the extent that they were changed, lost, renewed, and even used to advance the progress of knowledge, to that extent they will be intelligible. All we have to do is follow them. A good number of them, after all, are still found in today's medicine. They are like old furniture which is still in use, and not only for decoration. Inherited, worn out, rejected, rediscovered, and modified, they have their history. This vocabulary has passed through the mouths of many generations. Follow its traces closely, and you will gradually, through many mutations and transitions, come to understand what the various terms have meant in the various ages. You will know at what date a word began to waver, when it turned the corner, and when it disappeared; you will also know what words took its place if it did not eventually reappear. You will know this up to our own time. But this work entails perusing the entire sequence of dictionaries and treatises, for each age will furnish its own. Term by term we must follow the secular dialogue which took place between the physician and disease.

These names of diseases can be translated. But we must work as historians.

*　　*　　*

Miracles, of course, should not be expected. A nosebleed will never be anything but a nosebleed—either a pure symptom or a minor complaint. On the other hand, my chronological expedition through the dictionaries and treatises has permitted me to make certain discoveries.[46] "Cholera morbus" looked as if it were self-evident. Not so. Before the arrival in France of the "Asian" bacillus, that is, before 1832, the word "cholera" always designated dysentery. Similarly, in the course of the years 1820 to 1840, a whole series of terms (putrid angina, gangrenous sore throat, membranous angina) was fused into a common syndrome. The terrain was being prepared. But it was only after 1880 that the bacillus became known. It was diphtheria. An even more considerable tightening was achieved when the French school of the first third of the nineteenth century reduced the whole set of mucous, bilious, continued putrid, slow putrid, malignant, ataxo-dynamic fevers and their composite forms to what was first called entero-mesenteric fever, then dothienentery, and finally typhoid.[47]

What a wonderful feeling it was when the net was finally pulled in over influenza (the common flu), which had eluded it under the changing guise of catarrhal fever, inflammatory fever, or epidemic pulmonary catarrh. The latter, incidentally, should not be confused with simple pulmonary catarrh, which is bronchitis. It was a long time before "flying smallpox" for a time mistakenly considered to be a highly contagious form of smallpox (variola), found its rightful place as chickenpox.

The "malignant pustula" turned out to be anthrax. "Saint Anthony's fire" was a matter of ergotism, that is, food poisoning from ergot of rye causing damage to the nervous system. The unending sequence of so-called intermittent fevers (vernal, autumnal, quotidian, tertian, quartan, etc., fevers) eventually yielded paludism.[48]

---

[46]The works I used were the following: *Dictionnaire Universel de Médecine, de Chirurgie, de Chymie . . .* , *Précedé d'un discours Historique sur l'origine et le progrès de la Médecine*, 6 vols. (Paris, 1746–48) (Supplement to Diderot's *Encyclopédie*), in-fol.; Boissier de Sauvages, *Nosologia methodica*; W. Cullen (trans.), *Eléments de médecine pratique*, 2 vols., in-8° (Paris, 1785); C. de Selle, *Pyrétologie*, in-8° (Paris, An X); Pinel, *Nosographie Philosophique*; J. Capuron and P. Nysten, *Nouveau dictionnaire de médecine, de chirurgie . . .* , 2nd ed., in-8° (Paris, 1810); *Dictionnaire des Sciences Médicales*; Broussais, *Examen des doctrines médicales*; E. Bouchut and A. Desprès, *Dictionnaire de médecine et de thérapeutique médicale* (Paris, 1867); A. Deschambre et al., *Dictionnaire encyclopédique des sciences médicales*, 100 vols, in-4° (Paris, 1864–89); E. Brissaud et al., *Pratique medico-chirurgicale*, 6 vols., in-8° (Paris, 1907); *Collection Medico-chirurgicale à révision annuelle*, under the direction of Pasteur Valley-Radot and J. Hamburger, 35 vols. (Paris: Flammarion, 1948–66); *Encyclopédie médicale constamment mise à jour*, 47 vols. (Paris, 1929–66).

[47]P. Bretonneau, *Traité de la dothiénenterie* (Paris, 1822); and P. C. A. Louis, *Recherches anatomiques et pathologiques sur la maladie connue sous le nom de gastro-entérite, Fièvre putride . . .* (Paris, 1829). Contemporaries made the mistake of ignoring the first of these works almost completely, while the second enjoyed considerable notoriety.

[48]It is quite possible to see quartan fever as caused by *plasmodium malariae*, benign tertian fever by *plasmodium vivax* and quotidian fever by *plasmodium praecox*.

Such conversions were bound to entail some mishaps. One of these was the sound thrashing I received as I was going through the 1880s in my encyclopedias. The texts of that period point out and criticize the tendency of the physicians of earlier years (1830–50) to see typhoid everywhere, because it was the best and newest thing. It immediately struck me that I had made the same mistake as these physicians. After the discovery of Ebert's bacillus (1880) the diagnosis of typhoid became more strictly defined. This new rigor had to be applied to the old terrain as well. This meant that certain matters were not as easy as they had appeared to be. It also showed, beneath the vocabulary, a constant overlapping of typhus, typhoid, septicemia, and hemorrhagic variola. I had to start over. But it was profitable to do so. For suddenly all the comatose, putrid, petechial, slow, and nervous fevers fell in with the henceforth isolated typhus. The rest could be dealt with later. And yet, once I had set out to refine these diagnoses, it was time to break out of the narrow lexicological framework (the list of terms). Under the circumstances, the greatest satisfaction was to be had by dipping into the detailed memoranda. Once their vocabulary and the systems to which it refers is understood, these are a pleasure to peruse. These old physicians had very keen eyes indeed. Some of them have left us splendid observations. That diphtheria of Noyon, that typhus of Sélestat, that scarlet fever of Rouen are textbook epidemics.[49] Trait by trait they describe the classic stages of the diseases as we know them so well. Above all, they confirm most of the principal equivalents derived exclusively from the lists of words and the dictionaries and help to refine and adjust others. They also make it possible to erase certain mistakes. For example, I had long thought that red fever was simply a synonym for scarlet fever—which indeed it was in certain texts. But in fact it designated the "scarlet," the exanthema of typhus.[50] Thus one sometimes narrowly escapes these minor disasters which could have serious consequences.

And how grateful I was to a certain Dufour, physician at Noyon, who almost casually presented me with a valuable equivalent: ". . . by all of these symptoms . . . one was bound to recognize a malignant catarrhal fever of the most dangerous kind, or a false pleuropneumonia, as certain colleagues call it."[51] Goodness knows that this false pleuropneumonia had long been a puzzle. Pleuropneumonia, depending on its train of adjectives, and depending also on its symptoms, sometimes means bronchial

[49]SRM 159 (end of 1781); 146, no. 6 (winter 1785–86); 166 (Apr.–May, 1781), tables.
[50]Typhus or spotted fever; at this point it is impossible to decide.
[51]Noyon, "Constitution médicale pour 1782," manuscript, 20 pp., SRM 159.

pneumonia, and sometimes pulmonary congestion. But *false* pleuropneumonia? Only here, on the occasion of an epidemic that our archives show was very widespread in France between 1782 and 1785, do we find out, thanks to very exact descriptions, that it was an epidemic of pneumococcus-pneumonia. So much for the problem of false pleuropneumonia.

Enough of these anecdotes. Many other delicate distinctions should be mentioned. "Iliac passion," for example, points to a tripartite diagnosis: either intestinal occlusion, appendicitis, or peritonitis. There is no way to decide between these, except in specific cases. But the texts indicate that in most cases it was a matter of occlusion.

What, then, have we found out?

At the bottom of the barrel, we have a quantity of symptoms which can pertain to ten, to a hundred diseases. Yet they are useful. After that, there is a good armful of recognized infectious diseases. These are really the most convenient; they are also those which appear as epidemics; they are highly visible events which put great stress upon the fabric of society. Finally, there are the more elusive disorders of a properly organic nature, such as disturbances of the heart or circulation, troubles of the glandular or endocrine systems, gastrointestinal diseases of an infectious or noninfectious nature, cirrhosis, and so forth.

For there is a point beyond which we cannot go, given the nature of our documentation. Certain recently individualized entities, such as toxoplasmosis or nephrosis will never be found there, since they are broken up among a number of disparate symptoms which no one in the past would have thought of combining. We might perhaps find cases of nephritis; we will certainly find cases of edema (though of different origins) and possibly even of albuminuria. With a great deal of effort on our part, these diseases will appear in our densely packed manuscripts. But how can we tell whether these diseases had their origin in a nephritis which then caused the secondary symptoms? No one will ever know. Similarly, certain types of parasitosis with ambiguous symptoms can only be firmly diagnosed through a blood test. Here we are completely blocked. Finally, there is the universal presence of worms, wherever we look through the intermediary of our texts. These worms of varying kinds, which all autopsies found in great profusion in the stomach and in the lungs, and which fled the living body as soon as high fever set in through the stools and even through the nose and the mouth, must have considerably distorted every clinical picture. The symptoms of a condition described in good faith by a correspondent as "catarrhal bilious putrid verminous fever" might easily induce us to take it for a simple or atypical pneumonia accompanied by an infestation of worms. But every modern physician would also consider the possibility that it might be an infection related to the invasion of the lungs, the bronchi, and the entire system by thread worms.

Today we know the ataxo-dynamic states brought about by pneumococcal septicemia or acute staphylococcus infection. The former looks like typhus, while the latter takes on the appearances of typhoid. In the purely symptomatic descriptions of Vicq d'Azyr's correspondents, these signs can be misleading, but we have no way of avoiding these errors. Many related questions of this kind could be asked. How can we uncover the hidden cases of botulism, rickets, diabetes, and the various colibacillus infections?

There is nothing we can do. There are no leads, any more than there are leads for a number of major areas of morbidity (which I have already cross-checked), namely, the venereal diseases[52] and gynecological (fibromes, etc.) and osteological problems. There are only very tenuous indications for rheumatism and no mention whatsoever of acute rheumatoid arthritis. Nor do tetanus and rabies appear.[53]

These are the "blanks." Clearly they add up, but they do not in any way impair the abundant and well-defined material at our disposal. How shall we use this material?

First of all, recall the framework of the present project. We have a file in which every unit mentions a disease present in one month and one locality. Altogether, the entries cover ten years and 120 localities. The file is based on the tables published by the Société Royale.

This file will be put through the computer. That is, it will be stored in its memory. But this memory must also be given instructions which will permit it to select, interpret, and understand these raw data. To this end, a number of preliminary operations had to be accomplished.

1. The localities were classified and coded according to their identity and their characteristics, that is, by the province and the subdelegation in which they were located; rural or urban environment; plain, mountain, or seashore; northern, northeastern, central, western section of the country, etc.

2. The list of diseases was shortened, since certain terms are purely synonymous. Thus, one single term can be used to designate diarrhea, running bowels, intestinal fluxions, and looseness. Other equivalents are

---

[52]No doubt the investigation did not consider these diseases as falling within its scope, for they cannot be integrated into its "constitutions." By contrast, they are treated in many of the separate memoranda, but always in the context of individual cases.

[53]We do have numerous specific data on rabies, its frequency, etc., but they do not come from the investigation. See SRM 117, 119, and *Histoire et Mémoires de la SRM*, vol. 6, for late 1783 (Paris, 1784), passim.

gout, gouty affection, and gouty rheumatism, or pulmonary phthisis and consumption. In this manner 75 terms were merged with others, reducing the list from 420 to 345 items.

3. The list of terms was weeded out. Seven ambiguous or misleading terms were eliminated, for example, *température funeste aux valétudinaires* (temperature dangerous to the very sick), *morts de pulmoniques* (deaths of consumptives; or, died from consumption), and *suppression de transpiration* (supression of perspiration).

4. The list of words was divided into three major groups. Group A: General symptoms or symptoms pertaining to diseases not related to each other (exhaustion, chills, vertigo, inflammatory congestion, swelling, etc.). Group B: Symptoms linked to a specific organ, a specific part of the body, or a specific disease. Group C: Actual diseases.

5. These groups in turn were organized
   a. by types of attacks (in Group A and B)
      –pain and painful manifestations
      –breathlessness, oppression, dyspnea
      –indispositions according to seriousness, going as far as cachexia (general debility)
   b. by parts of the body and especially organs and organic systems (in group B and C)
      –head, including buccal cavity, brain, eyes, nose, throat and ears, parotid glands
      –digestive system, kidneys, obstetrics and its accidents
      –skin problems
   c. by types of diseases (or symptoms)
      –rheumatism, edemas, disorders of the nervous system, psychopathology, infectious epidemic diseases, diseases due to deficiencies or food poisoning.

Obviously, this is a rather curious curriculum for medical studies! But I must point out once again that this spotty and sometimes illogical arrangement is a function of the material at hand. Furthermore, certain terms will be found in several places. A pneumonia with secondary gastric symptoms (malignant bilious catarrhal fever) will appear under *lungs*, *gastric troubles*, and *infectious diseases*. A decision will have to be made.

6. Diagnoses will be reconstructed. Even today, a number of diseases are recognized by their symptoms (and then confirmed or adjusted by laboratory tests). These series of symptoms will be stored in the computer. If a locality shows indications of the presence of typhus, typhoid, or some other easily identified disease, the computer will go through the data for adjoining regions over the preceding and the immediately following months in order to retrieve the symptoms pertaining to some or all of the

characteristics of the disease. Epidemic sequences will thereby be brought to light.

Moreover, all these operations will have to be organized in such a way that the disparate nature of the original arrangement is corrected. It is hoped that diseases and symptoms can eventually be classified in a more modern way, for example, by disorders concerning (1) an organ (heart, kidneys, lungs), (2) a group of tissues (rheumatism), (3) the organism as a whole (infectious diseases), (4) the equilibrium of the systems relaying the organs among each other (nervous or hormonal system), and (5) the organization of the cells (cancer).

There is no doubt that in this respect the exploitation of our data will be somewhat disappointing, since these lists of names are totally schematic. Still, these findings will provide a general orientation. They will give us sequences of epidemics, bad years, the dominant trends of a few kinds of diseases, malarial zones, and a cartography of "poor" health.

More precise identification of the diseases, exact patterns of their incidence, and a better understanding of the most serious epidemics can only be achieved by means of sustained work with the manuscript memoranda of this collection. Consider, for example, one of my most recent investigations. The demographic historians are emphasizing the high death rate of the years 1782–84. This phenomenon appears to be unrelated to any food shortage.[54] Such a claim calls for verification. I am therefore in the process of conducting a thorough examination of the correspondence and the memoranda concerning epidemics for a short time span (1782–85). Sweating sickness of Languedoc, the so-called "Muscovite" influenza, viral pneumonia, murderous outbreaks of smallpox—what has come to light already is appalling. Here our curiosity plunges us into a thicket which is being cleared before our very eyes by the scythe of death.

Illness and Society

There are countless connections between illness and society. It is useful to recall that the notion of "malignancy," the focal point of every disease, is etymologically related to *malum*, or evil, which is at the core of every system of morality. Our concerns lie outside such complexities. Our archives, the first to deal with popular and collective medicine, speak to

[54]See E. Esmonin, "Statistique du mouvement de la population en France de 1770 à 1789," *Etudes et chroniques de démographie historique*, 1964, pp. 27–130.

us of much more direct connections, which are dramatic precisely because they are so simple. Their song is monodic. It sings of unending frustration. Once disease strikes, man is in its power. Even the physician must often acknowledge his impotence. His victories—for there are victories —are never final. What physician did not, at one time or another, tell us of his weariness? "To know all the bitterness of practicing amidst so much misery, one must have been in that position. If there is one point where a doctor is sorry to bear this title . . . and where he is so discouraged that he is tempted to flee [his profession], it would be in these deplorable circumstances . . . where he seems to be inexorably rebuffed by everything he encounters."[55] Not only did these men fight with weak weapons, they also could never escape from an unchanging terrain. Disease had only one face, and it never seemed to change. It was a monotonous sequence of coughs, infections, and fevers. It was monotonous, and it was deadly. The sick were huddled together, burning and eaten away, from the inside as well as from the outside, with putrefaction of the organs, rashes, ulcers, and scabs. This is the terrible impression conveyed by our texts. And this is why the thousand fine points of modern medicine really have no place here. With their bodies assaulted on all sides, these people were carried off before the more subtle disorders had a chance to strike. The more solid ones survived and could do without a physician. Delicate children were doomed from the start. The process of selection was devoid of all nicety. Medical science, therefore, necessarily went after only the big game. Hence the preponderance, in our texts, of "big" events, namely, epidemics and, for that matter, only a restricted variety of them. Indeed, "catarrhal fevers, putrid and malignant pleuropneumonia, intermittent and remittant, putrid and malignant fevers with exanthema, red fevers, smallpox and measles, diarrhea and putrid and malignant dysenteries are about all the epidemic diseases prevailing in the countryside."[56] In other words, we are dealing with influenza, serious pulmonary disturbances, malaria, typhoid, typhus, smallpox, and dysentery. For our purposes, this concentration has its advantages, for it enables us to study each one of them thoroughly.

This opportunity led me to undertake the study of a major epidemic of pneumonia which I first isolated between October 1784 and June 1785 in Poitou, where it flared up again in November of the same year.[57] But this

[55]Strasbourg, 1785, SRM 143, no. 6.

[56]*Description des épidémies qui ont régné* [*à Paris*] (1783), p. 22.

[57]Saint-Maurice-le-Girard, SRM 189; Poitiers, 184; Marans, 183; Saint-Maixent, 174; Mirebeau, 163; and J. G. Gallot, *Recueil d'observations ou Mémoire sur l'Epidémie . . . de la Chataigneraye,* in-4° (Poitiers, 1787); de la Mazière, "Observations nosologiques," 1775–1791, manuscript, 199 pp., Bibliothèque municipale, Poitiers.

epidemic originally revealed itself elsewhere. It first appeared at Noyon and at Bruyères in Lorraine in the spring of 1782, reaching Obernheim (Alsace) and Dijon during the following winter. By November 1783 it was found in the Pyrenees. It then came to Saint-Dié, continued through Burgundy (Seurre), and reached Montluçon at the beginning of 1784, whence it traveled to Rouen and Dunkirk. By this time Poitou experienced the first wave. In the course of the year 1785 there was a second outbreak in Noyon, Burgundy, and Saint-Dié, as well as in Lower Poitou.

The descriptions of some of these cases are so precise and conform so exactly to the *classic* picture of pneumonia, that one would like to transcribe them *in extenso*. They will be published in due course. What we have to note here is the high rate of mortality: 35 to 40 percent of those who contracted the disease died. Only the villages taken in hand by a physician saw this rate reduced to 20 or 15 percent. Today we know that, even without antibiotics, the prognosis of pneumonia is not too unfavorable. This consideration even made me wonder whether I had diagnosed this epidemic correctly. But I had! The descriptions leave no room for doubt, and there is only one conclusion. We must keep in mind, however, that the hygienic conditions in the countryside were atrocious, that clothing provided inadequate protection against cold evenings, that a very poorly balanced diet gave rise to a multitude of deficiencies, and that a hundred latent secondary infections were always ready to develop. For these and other concurrent reasons, the invasion of the pneumococcus wrought complete havoc in the weakened organism. The repercussions were felt throughout the body, a chain reaction of complications set in, and the whole edifice collapsed. It can therefore be said that pneumonia is *no longer* considered to be a disease whose prognosis is apt to be fatal, except in special cases. But this must be taken as a recent development in the history of disease. In the eighteenth century pneumonia was a killer.

The frailty evidenced here makes us understand why the country people who went into the towns in search of work in the following century and lived there under very precarious conditions constituted such a prime target for the ravages of tuberculosis. To be sure, the peasants of 1840 were no longer those of 1780. Their standard of living had changed. But the reports of the physicians in charge of epidemics do not leave us any illusions as to the conditions of hygiene and nutritional imbalance. The organism was still fragile.

Yet the problem can also be stated in a different way. A number of autopsies performed during the epidemic in Poitou revealed that the lungs, which, indeed, showed evidence of damage caused by the pneumococcus-bacillus, also exhibited lesions that can easily be read as being of tubercular origin. These cavities must have contributed to the fatal outcome. Thus, there is reason to wonder whether the inhabitants of the countryside did not suffer from tuberculosis more often than we realize. Recall that the physician only came to them when there was a serious epidemic. The rest of the time they were not under his care. They dealt with "charlatans," "quacks," and "surgeons." They died, and no one knew of what. This was still true in the first third of the last century. But when they went into the towns, the medical profession took note of them; physicians kept records of the cases. Going to town also meant crowding, exhaustion, and spreading contagion. In such a melting pot the virulence of the bacilli went out of control. This situation was to bring together all the preconditions of the great tuberculosis endemic of the first industrial revolution which is particularly well known to us because the medical profession was concerned about it. *Mal du siècle* (spleen, melancholia) only partially explains the spread of the scourge in urban areas, namely, the contamination of the upper classes. But these germs did not suddenly spring up from nowhere. They no doubt came from that great pool of misery of the Old Regime so starkly depicted in the medical archives.[58]

These archives also suggest another hypothesis. It is striking to note how often these observations mention convulsions as a complication of diseases which normally do not admit of them. In a number of places this happened in the pneumonia epidemic I have just mentioned. Convulsions also accompanied a case of scarlet fever at Rouen and a case of diphtheria at Mirebeau. Here again, these anomalies would make us question the diagnosis if the evidence were not so conclusive. What is the answer?

It so happened that certain physicians were interested in nervous disorders. At least their correspondence with Vic d'Azyr often refers to that subject. One of them described some veritable epidemics of hysteria: ". . . there also was a melancholic condition, especially in women. Its principal symptom was a fiery pain which, the patients claimed, they felt going through their frontal bone. They all wanted to throw themselves into a well. . . ." He prescribed cold baths. But some of the women did not improve. "This decided me to place one of the sick women next to a well from which four men continually drew water, pouring it on the bare head and the body of the patient, who only fainted after eighty buckets." The next day it took only fifty, whereupon she was "seized by an extremely violent fit of fever which ceased only with the onset of a most abundant sweat. Eventually, the machine calmed down. . . . Her de-

---

[58]There are numerous revealing texts. For example, Flaugerges, physician at Rodez, notes in June 1784, during a spell of very hot weather, "a rather high incidence" of blood spitting. Many of those so afflicted later discharged pus. "They are in the last stages of consumption" (SRM 148).

ranged reason regained its rightful place. . . . This woman, who had never had any children, has since given birth. . . ."[59]

Moreover, one can see that a number of these attacks of hysteria were provoked by the subconscious refusal to have any more children. One woman experienced a delivery lasting four days and four nights because her cervix was completely tightened up by the convulsive attack. This condition continued for two months after the difficult delivery, with the patient feeling in her stomach "a beating vessel; it was so tight," she said, "that it moved like an extremely taut violin-string."[60] Another woman in childbirth was seized by fits of convulsion and raving delirium broken by periods of coma. All of this continued for two days after the delivery. As soon as she regained consciousness, everything was fine. "She did not have the faintest idea of what had happened to her and was surprised to see her child."[61]

On the occasion of a thunderstorm in the spring of 1784 in Poitou, a bolt of lightning entered a spacious house, went through it, whirled about in a room where three servant-girls were working, and finally made its exit by breaking a window. The reactions of the three frightened women were of the hysterical type. Two of them had convulsions. The third was found in a faint under a bed. Later she swore that she did not betake herself there. Yet no one could explain how else she could have found herself in that place. Her legs at least remained paralyzed for two days. Subsequently she recovered completely. In terms of modern psychology, it is clear that this paralysis was used to obliterate the memory of that frightening experience. It could be translated as: "It is not true that I went to hide under a bed, because my legs are gone." Perhaps all of these incidents can furnish the key to one of the terms in the "lexicon" I was unable to translate: false paralysis. It was a frequent phenomenon, and it had no lasting consequences. After a few days, movement always returned and there were no relapses. Could this be hysterical paralysis?

I have spoken of these examples in some detail only because it seems to me that they point to a profound hysteroid tendency characteristic of the Old Regime, at least in the lower classes. A frightening encounter with disease, personal troubles, fear—all of these often evoked responses of the same type, namely, convulsions and even paralysis. These reactions had strong hysterical overtones. In our own time these reactions are different. They are more apt to be depressive or schizoid; although the sociological phenomena connected with rock 'n roll seem to indicate a return to the

[59]Mirebeau, Aug. 1777, SRM 163.
[60]Ibid., Nov. 1777.
[61]Meyer, physician at Mulhouse, Dec. 1784, SRM 166.

responses of the former type, collective hysteria. This is the first sign of a mutation brought about by our mass society.

However that may be, if we adopt the theses of modern psychiatry, we can say that the hysterical personality is characterized by an anomaly in the processes leading to the establishment of personal identity.[62] The personality becomes dissociated, as it were, if it lacks models of personal behavior. Hence the extreme plasticity in the emotive expression of the subject as he endeavors to put together his social role (to "play it" as upon the stage) in keeping with outside models which are transposed by the subconscious. This explains why collective events are so important. Here the individual submits to the image projected by the mass, to a collective superego. This fact is corroborated by the important role of suggestion in the etiology as well as the treatment of hysterical attacks.

Normally, as we know, personal identity develops as the subject assumes the role of the personality he or she tends to become. In a society where the functions, the sacred rights, and the prestige of the father were taken over once and for all by the seigneur, the priest, and, supremely, by the king, the ordinary man was, psychologically speaking, confined to a kind of perpetual childhood. He was the subject and the victim of a tutelage that could never be lifted, because this tutelage was the supreme institution. The simple man did not entirely own himself; he did not altogether exist. And this was even more true of the woman. The choice of their social being was not theirs to make.

Thus, in the last analysis, the permanence of hysterical components in the behavior of the lower classes says something about the nature of a society which, in fact, gave rise to these tendencies. Here again, the medical archives touch upon the very core of the social reality. The solemn execution of the father on January 21, 1793, was to create the conditions for a slow but sure shift in the tide of psychopathology.

* * *

And yet, even beyond that date, the physician was in constant contact with extreme distress. It was said of Saint-Romain-sur-Meuse in 1833: "The misery here has been so great that many parents refused to have their children treated unless they were also given the means of feeding them. In all candor, it must be said that some of them even hoped that the illness would carry the children off, thus delivering them from the woes to

[62]Dr. Henry Ey, "Introduction à l'étude actuelle de l'hystérie," *La Revue du praticien* 14, no. 11 (1964): 1417–31.

which they themselves had fallen prey."[63] Nor were conditions in the Lozère any better: "Covered with rags and owning hardly more than one change of covering, they live in miserable huts among the dungheaps which exhale an unbearable stench. . . . The air inside these dank and gloomy hovels is only renewed by the flue of the big fireplace, a broken-down door, or sometimes a small window; although some of the people have taken the precaution of having their windows walled in, in order to avoid paying a tax on them. A little straw, covered with an old piece of burlap and one wool blanket, usually serves as their pallet, which is often shared by a decrepit old man and a new-born babe, a girl and a boy, the sick and the well, the dying and the dead."[64] We have several series of similar testimonies for the eighteenth century.[65]

These more recent texts are doubly interesting. What the physicians of the Société Royale were saying might have been the fruit of the maudlin sentimentality of Jean-Jacques's contemporaries. We might have run the risk of making facile extrapolations and of generalizing La Bruyère's remarks about the peasants on that basis. As it is, these descriptions from the 1830s confirm our original impression. This abject poverty is no myth. The reports of men who already had a scientific approach to things testify to a situation that quite simply had not changed.

For our purposes, the essential feature to be noted is, again, the pervading lack of hygiene, which created so favorable a terrain for contagion, as well as the poor state of general health of the people, which made any onslaught of microbes so very dangerous. The water was not protected. The dungheaps adjacent to the houses were constantly kept wet by throwing all the waste water on them; in the cemeteries the dead were not buried deeply enough, so that violent rainstorms often uncovered the corpses; and vegetables were washed in stagnant pools. All the water, whether it came from rivers or wells, was polluted. The drinking water was alive with germs, and a great deal of it was consumed, because wine was rare on the tables of the poor. For this reason, typhoid was endemic in France up until the 1860s. It would strike the countryside every year, most particularly in the north and northeast of France. This localization

[63]*Mémoires de l'Académie de Médecine* 6 (1837): 406.
[64]Ibid., vol. 3 (1833). Commune of Vébron.
[65]See J. G. Gallot, "Observations" for La Rochelle, manuscript, 11 pp., SRM 189: "The dreadful state to which disease reduces these unfortunate people must be seen to be believed, especially in times of epidemics, such as dysentery. They have no food, no care, no change of linen. Most of the unfortunates whose deaths I witnessed were lying in straw still soaked with the first discharges of the dysentery. Sometimes three, four, five and even six individuals are huddled together amidst such filth."

can probably be explained by the presence of the manure-producing livestock and the abundant rain which leached the manure into the soil.[66]

Moreover, the houses were "low, damp, and so poorly aired that in three-fourths of our farmhouses it would be impossible to read without candlelight even at high noon."[67] Animals came and went freely; the pigs lived right in the room, their slops fermenting in buckets; and the bedding of straw or coarse feathers, covered with cloths that were never changed, harbored the whole gamut of vermin.

In Poitou, the peasants always worked barefoot in the wet soil. In Périgord, almost everyone had varicose, ulcerated legs with open sores. Everywhere wounds went untreated and became infected. Rough clothing irritated the skin. No wonder that heat waves gave rise to "epidemics" of rashes of various kinds, for the combination of filth, sweat, and skin irritation produced exanthema. This was true even in the towns.[68] In fact, no one's skin was ever healthy or smooth, except perhaps that of the "well-to-do," who kept themselves clean and wore "fine linen," which did not irritate the skin.

Besides, the food was of poor quality. The bread of Périgord was two-thirds freshly ground maize, which fermented in the flour and soured the bread. It was soaked in a vegetable soup, "usually seasoned with the oldest and most rancid lard, grease, or oil."[69] In the region of Embrun, an eruptive epidemic killed a great many people; it occurred "after the use of salted meat from oxen and cows dead of the boils"[70] (anthrax). The bread of the towns contained sawdust, starch, and toxic salts; cooking salt was mixed with plaster, dirt, toxic salts, saltpeter; even arsenic oxide was found in it. Absinthe was given its green color by copper oxide. The use of poorly cared for copper utensils, like the cooking pots that were in constant contact with acidic products such as sorrel and vinegar, kept the body in a permanent toxic state, predisposing the corroded digestive system to the most serious consequences in case of disease.[71]

All of this makes it plausible that there were many villages "where often not a single man of a military stature could be found."[72] "Want and poverty are great obstacles to the development of a strong and healthy

[66]"Rapport de l'Académie de Médecine . . . sur les épidémies," Paris, 1868.

[67]Bressuire, "Topographie . . . ," 1786, A.D. Deux-Sèvres C 14.

[68]See Poitiers, July–Aug. 1784, SRM 184.

[69]Montignac, "Observations" for 1777, SRM 143. In the preceding year, a typhus epidemic in the region had carried off one-fourth of the inhabitants in certain places.

[70]Montdauphin, Feb.–June 1784, SRM 146.

[71]See *Annales d'Hygiène*, vol. 7, no. 2 (1831), p. 198; vol. 8, no 2 (1832), pp. 250 ff. and 438.

[72]Commission on Epidemics, "Rapport général," *Mémoires de l'Académie de Médecine* 3 (1833).

constitution. Half naked all year long, and obliged to run through mud and ice in order to beg for their livelihood, how could these unfortunate children not suffer damage to their growth?"[73] All of them were constantly on the verge of physiological destitution, as we can see by unmistakable signs: "The girls in our countryside are very susceptible to pallor, and they rarely menstruate before they are eighteen, nineteen, and twenty years old. They frequently suffer from white flux and from edema in the legs and feet."[74]

All of this was so obvious that the physicians were perfectly conscious of the futility of their efforts. How could they treat people who did not have the physical resources to help overcome disease? They knew they would have to invent a different kind of medical practice. Did it really mean anything to speak of diet under these circumstances? "There was no point in forbidding fat bouillon when there was no meat and when bouillon—provided there was any—was hardly different from clear water."[75] Give them food first, then we will treat them; that is what these physicians kept writing. Furthermore, they also encountered resistance from the peasants themselves, who refused treatment. In this respect, the popular mentality reveals a prudence which is perhaps the fruit of long familiarity with the kind of cunning that makes survival possible. The peasants were opposed to all bleeding and purging which would in any way diminish their substance, even that part of it which was diseased. "Such patients should first be given one kind of purgative [an emetic] and then another [a vermifuge], but they do not want to take them. The reason they give is that their bellies are empty."[76] Were they really so wrong? It is true that all they had were worms. "Often our poor peasants kill themselves because they do not follow the doctor's advice."[77] And the reason is that "extreme poverty makes people stupid as well as tough."[78] Present-day studies on the pathology of poverty have confirmed that extreme deprivation leads to a lowering of the I.Q.[79] An illustration of this fact can be seen in the endless struggle of the physicians of Poitou to make their peasants adopt the potato. They constantly came up against a stubborn, imbecilic resistance, which was totally impervious to proof and evidence. The potato can feed man and beast; it grows well and is resistant to thunderstorms and rain; it can be made into tasty dishes, and those

[73]Saint-Maurice-le-Girard, "Observations," 1776, manuscript, 14 pp., SRM 189.
[74]Bressuire, "Topographic," 1776.
[75]Sélestat, "Memoires . . . ," 1785, SRM 143, no. 6.
[76]Montignac, letter of Dec. 15, 1777, SRM 143 (Laservolle).
[77]Saint-Maurice-le-Girard, "Observations nosologiques," second trimester, 1787.
[78]Sélestat, "Mémoires."
[79]See C. Richet and A. Mas, La famine (Paris: E.P.H.E., VIe Section, 1965); and C. Richet, Pathologie de la misère (Paris: S.D.M., 1957).

who grow it are prosperous. Very well and good, they would answer, but we don't want it. And they continued to go hungry.[80] On the other hand, these peasants were so credulous that the quacks, and the pharmacists as well, gave them phony drugs, patent medicines, arsenic pills and "kinkina" that was tampered with, even when it was prescribed by the physician.[81]

Above all, these people were resilient, despite the evidence to the contrary provided by the ravages of malaria, typhus, and smallpox. They were resilient in the face of the greatest odds, as numerous cases can attest. Some of them survived the most trying physical tests.

One young man, who must have been mentally unbalanced, was so afraid of being drafted into the militia that he decided to get out of it by cutting off his genitals. His family, having worked in the fields, found him only late in the evening. He was very weak. The physician, who lived far away, came late in the night. The loss of blood must have been considerable. Yet, the physician bled the boy three times, and again the next day. It is true that the shock of bleeding will produce a peripheral constriction of the vessels as well as a lowering of the arterial tension, both of which may stop the main hemorrhage. But at what tremendous risk! However, the mutilated patient recovered and was soon restored to "flourishing" health.[82]

One physician describes for us a case of "gangrenous infection," whose symptoms are those of arteritis. The patient's foot, no longer receiving any blood, had become gangrened. The physician was called only after the situation had badly deteriorated. He looked after the patient, but given the condition of the foot, it was better to leave it as it was. He simply waited for "the mortification of the limb." It eventually dropped off by itself, and the man recovered.[83]

At Neufchâteau in Lorraine, a servant-girl was attacked while her master was out.[84] Asked to indicate where the money was, she began to scream. A "choke pear" was placed in her throat to silence her; and while the thieves were beating and choking her with a rope, she swallowed the object. When the neighbors came, they found her unconscious, and she remained so for six hours. Upon awakening, she was seized by excruciating stomach pains, spasms, convulsions, and fits of fainting. This state

---

[80]Bressuire, "Topographie."

[81]See Auxerre, Sept. 1784, SRM 154; Tonneins, Sept. 1783, SRM 152; *Annales d'Hygiène*, vol. 7, no. 1, p. 195; A.D. Deux-Sèvres 6 M 21, 2.

[82]Noyon, 1782, SRM 159.

[83]Mirebeau, SRM 163, no. 1.

[84]Javelot, physician at the faculty of medicine at Nancy, "Histoire d'une maladie singulière," 1778, manuscript, SRM 188, no. 26.

lasted for four months, during which she brought forth, one by one, 264 pins and needles through the mouth, the urinary passage, the bowels, the skin, and the corners of her eyes. Each one of these needles was produced at the price of convulsions taking her again and again within inches of death. Yet, in the beginning, her masters believed that this was trickery, that she was in league with the thieves and simulating. So she was taken to Nancy, where she was strapped, naked and under constant supervision, to a bed without sheets in order to make sure that she was not cheating. The pins kept coming. Thus exonerated, she was sent home. But the jolting of the cart made her feel even worse. Now the remedy was found: it was decided that every day she should be taken for a ride over the rough country roads. The resulting crises would help her get rid of everything. After six months of this, she seemed to be recovered. Needless to say, she had been gagged with a pin box, whose metal covering she eventually brought forth as well.

Such people were tough. They were also closer to a certain natural balance which, however, was disrupted by their extreme poverty. But in the last analysis, all these physicians wanted to do was to reestablish that balance. Seen in this light, it seems to me that their climate-related medicine begins to make a certain sense. These people really did seem to be profoundly affected by hazards of the weather, the rhythm of the seasons, the varying degrees of hardness or sulphur-content of their water, the impact of moist or dry air. Remember that they were not protected by any town walls.

What is even more interesting and more surprising is the fact that the practicing physicians managed somehow to treat and to cure them. To that extent, they are certainly entitled to their halo. For it is a fact that in the areas devastated by typhus, typhoid, and pneumonia, where men, women, children, and old people died without knowing what was happening to them, the picture changed when the doctors arrived. Was it only because they took care of the people, that is, made them clean up the bedding and the houses, made them open the windows or at least let in some air,[85] because they told them to drink hot beverages, to keep warm or cool? They dug the patients out of the heaps of covers that had been piled on them in order to "make them sweat." They stopped them from drinking great quantities of alcohol which was supposed to cure all ills. Or was it also because their therapy was more appropriate than we might think? They gave homeopathic doses of drugs made from "herbs" and wisely managed fevers which in certain diseases must be maintained. Less

---

[85]As soon as somebody fell ill, the house was closed, candles were lit, and everyone crowded around the patient. This practice is described again and again.

than ten years ago, André Lwoff has quantitatively demonstrated—and thereby corroborated Pasteur's hypothesis—that fever plays a protective role in certain viral attacks (such as poliomyelitis and viral adenitis). Another very appropriate practice was the use of the very simple and very natural *limonade*, lemon juice, which makes up for vitamin C deficiency. Not to mention the medicine of temperaments, since modern genetic biology tells us that its intuitions were not necessarily absurd or poetic. Neither were these physicians' ideas on the dynamics of healing totally unwarranted. We now know that any infection presupposes a certain receptivity on the part of the organism and that any recovery demands the active participation of the body and the mental attitude governing it. A keen awareness of these factors was at the core of the work of these physicians undertaken under the difficult conditions we have come to know.

"It is very difficult, Monsieur, to practice medicine in the countryside as it should be practiced," one of them wrote. "In a hospital, a physician gives orders, and these orders are followed. He sees his patients two or three times a day. . . . But in the countryside, how can he observe the patient if he is moving from one hamlet to the next? And whom can he leave with the patient in order to be informed of the changes the disease has undergone? Some quack who hardly knows how to read."[86] What is needed in the countryside are hospitals, so that all these people can be protected from the charlatans to whom they are given over. "After all, the common people are the mainstay of agriculture, the right arm of the state." Or, as one of his colleagues says, "What is at stake is the life and the interest of the citizens most useful to the state, yet they are the victims of cupidity."[87]

In this world where human life was cheap, these physicians were the first to realize that each individual existence carries its own weight and its own value. All of these men who moved in the orbit of the Société Royale and made it flourish had a keen sense of economics and history, sometimes even a prophetic understanding of social welfare. What is more, they had hope. Their medicine cleared the way for the future.[88]

[86]Montignac to Vicq d'Azyr, Dec. 1777, SRM 143.
[87]Auxerre, Sept. 1784, SRM 154.
[88]Since the publication of this article, I have elaborated certain aspects of it in the following texts: "Les mots et les aspects de la maladie," *Revue Historique* 499 (July–Sept. 1971): 13–38; "Le corps du délit," *Nouvelle Revue de Psychanalyse* 3 (1971): 71–108.

5
An Essay on the Diet of the Various Classes in the Medieval Levant

Eliyahu Ashtor

The purpose of this essay is not to deal with the history of gastronomy, but rather to sketch out a few characteristics of the nutrition of certain classes in medieval Levantine society, based on information about food supplies in the Near East and the budgets of the salaried classes. We should begin by asking two questions: (1) Can we show that the nutrition of the lower classes underwent marked changes during this period? (2) How did the diet of the Levantines influence public health and demographic development?

A great variety of sources must be employed for such research. Beyond a few official documents and the travel accounts of pilgrims and other European travelers journeying through the regions beyond the sea during the later period of this study, we must seek our information chiefly in works belonging to the various branches of Arabic literature. It is true that studying cookbooks intended for the rich does not give us much information about the nutritional habits of the common people,[1] but the works of travelers, Arab geographers, and Levantine physicians included precious observations about the nutrition of their day. We will also

---

Annales: E.S.C., Sept.–Oct. 1968, pp. 1017–53. Translated by Patricia M. Ranum. *Translator's note*: For full names of Arab authors, complete titles of works in Arabic, and other editions of these works, see the "Bibliographie" to Ashtor's *Histoire des prix et salaires dans l'Orient médiéval* (Paris, 1969), pp. 2–34.
[1]V. M. Rodinson, "Recherches sur les documents arabes relatifs à la cuisine," *Revue des études islamiques*, 1949, p. 98.

use information contained in purely literary works. Although we do not
have "journals" of middle-class families, like those available to Western
medievalists, the other sources, mentioned above, permit us to discern a
few essential characteristics of nutrition in the medieval Near East.

*   *   *

In every Near Eastern country, wheat was the principal cereal during
the Middle Ages. Wheat production was so abundant in several regions
that it was exported to other countries. Egypt, which had been the
granary of the Roman Empire, supplied the Hidjaz with wheat in the time
of the caliphs. Moreover, at the end of the tenth century, al-Mukaddasī
also mentioned the exportation of wheat from Upper Mesopotamia.[2]
Relatively little barley was grown, in comparison with the countries
bordering the European coast of the Mediterranean, though we find in
the journal of a Persian traveler that in Palestine, in the region of Hebron,
barley was the cereal most cultivated.[3] This was probably an exception,
explained by the quality of the soil in that mountainous and very elevated
region (Hebron is 926 meters above sea level). Barley was rarely cultivated
in Egypt after the Hellenistic period, and then it was used as fodder for
cattle.[4]

A change occurred in cereal production during the period of the
caliphs: rice was introduced, or at least there was a considerable increase
in the amount of land on which it was grown. Rice had probably long
been grown in the marshes of Lower Babylonia, but according to Ibn
Haukal, the Hamdanids, lords of Upper Mesopotamia, introduced it to
the region in the middle of the tenth century.[5] In the last half of that
century rice plantations also existed in Palestine, notably in the Baisān
district.[6] In Egypt, during the same period, rice was abundant, especially
in the province of Fayyūm, where it was the chief cereal grown.[7] It seems
that rice was already cultivated in Egypt before the Arab conquest, but it
is more than likely that its cultivation was greatly expanded after the
conquest.[8] Nevertheless, we must not exaggerate the importance of this
change. While rice and rice-based dishes had apparently always been a

---

[2]al-Mukaddasī, *Kitāb Ahsan at-takāsīm*, ed. M. J. de Goeje (Leyden, 1906), pp. 136, 145, 195 (hereafter cited as al-Mukaddasī).

[3]Nāsir-ī Khosrau, *Sefer nameh*, trans. C. Schefer (Paris, 1881), p. 103.

[4]D. Müller-Wodarg, "Die Landwirtschaft Aegyptens in der frühen 'Abbāsidenzeit," *Der Islam* 32 (1955–57):21.

[5]Ibn Haukal, *Opus geographicum* . . . , ed. Kramers (Leyden, 1938), p. 213.

[6]al-Mukaddasī, pp. 162, 180.

[7]Ibid., pp. 201, 203, 208; Ibn Haukal, *Opus geographicum*, p. 160.

[8]Müller-Wodarg, "Die Landwirtschaft Aegyptens," p. 24.

part of the diet of the common people in Lower Babylonia, such dishes
remained luxury items in other regions until the end of the Middle Ages.
Ibn Kutaiba cited the famous philologist al-Aṣmaʿī (d. 828), who said:
"White rice with melted butter and white sugar is a dish not of this
world," that is, it is a dish which is eaten in paradise.[9] Cookbooks contain
numerous rice-based dishes which were considered delicacies.[10] Rice,
therefore, was by no means a food within the reach of the working
masses. It was too costly.[11]

Until the end of the Middle Ages, therefore, the majority of Levantines,
especially city-dwellers, ate a wheat *bread*, although we have reason to
believe that a little barley was added to it.[12] The physician Ibn Djazla,
who lived in Iraq in the eleventh century, listed various sorts of bread:
wheat bread, bread with middlings (*khushkār*), "washed" bread, bread of
the finest flour (*samīdh*), bread of the best sort of flour (*ḥuwwārī*),
unleavened bread, little-oven bread (*ṭābūn*) baked on pebbles,[13] bread
cooked on an iron plate (*ṭābiḳ*),[14] barley bread,[15] etc. But Arab authors
pointed out that wheat bread was eaten almost exclusively. During the
period of the Moslem conquest, bread in Iraq was baked of fine flour
called "from Isfahān."[16] We learn that in the first half of the tenth century

[9]Ibn Ḳutaiba, *Kitāb ʿUyūn al-akhbār* (Cairo, 1925–30), 3:200; on "samn maslī" see R.
Dozy, *Supplément aux dictionnaires arabes* (Leyden, 1881), 1:679.

[10]See H. Zayyat, "Le livre de cuisine" (of Djamāl ad-dīn Yūsuf b. Ḥasan Ibn ʿAbdal-
hādī), *al-Machrique* 35 (1937):371 ff.

[11]See our study "L'évolution des prix dans le Proche-Orient à la basse époque," *Journal
of the Economic and Social History of the Orient* 4:22–23; Mudjīr ad-Dīn al-ʿUlaimī, *al-Uns
al-djalīl* (Cairo, 1283), 1:59; 2:443; and Nāṣir-ī Khosrau, *Sefer nameh*, pp. 103–4, where we
find that in the sanctuary at Hebron on Friday peppered rice and pomegranates were
distributed, and on other days bread and lentils with oil; see also M. Canard, "Le riz dans le
Proche-Orient aux premiers siècles de l'Islam," *Arabica* 6:125 ff, and also Rodinson's article
"Ghidhā," *Encyclopédie d'Islam*, 2nd ed. (in French), 2:1087. On the other hand, it appears
that rice became so widespread in southern Europe that by the end of the Middle Ages it had
become a lower-class food, eaten by the poor. See F. Braudel, *Civilisation matérielle et
capitalisme* (Paris, 1967), 1:83.

[12]See our article, "Prix et salaires à l'époque mamelouke," *Revue des études islamiques*,
1949, p. 73.

[13]Dozy, *Supplément*, 2:27.

[14]Ibid., 2:25.

[15]See Zayyat, "Le livre de cuisine," p. 377.

[16]at-Ṭurtūshī, *Sirādj al-mulūk* (Cairo, 1935), p. 243. This study sheds light on the
changes which occurred in agriculture and diet in the Near East before the Arab conquest.
For in ancient Babylonia barley bread was eaten almost exclusively and wheat bread was
only baked on holidays. See B. Meissner, *Babylonien und Assyrien* (Heidelberg, 1920)
1:413. Spelt occupied the second place among cereals and was sold at approximately the
same price as barley, while wheat cost twice as much (Meissner, p. 198). According to
Herodotus, the Egyptians also baked bread from this cereal; see A. Ruffer, *Food in Egypt*,
Mémoires présentés à l'Institut de l'Égypte (Cairo, 1919) 1:46, 54 ff, which also cites and
examines other references found in Greek writings. In Palestine barley bread predominated.
One of Gideon's soldiers was shown dreaming of the victory of the peasants over the nomads

the vizier Ḥāmid b. ʿAbbās gave white bread to all his guests and servants, and even to his slaves.[17] In Palestine, the city of Ramla was known in the tenth century for its excellent white bread (huwwārī);[18] and three centuries later a Christian author observed that he had never eaten better bread than that offered him in Jerusalem.[19] As far as Egypt is concerned, al-Mukaddasī also told how only fine bread (huwwārī) was eaten there and that no other sort was baked.[20] European voyagers visiting Egypt in the late period also praised the excellent bread. In the 1420s the Irish monk Symon Simeonis described at length the white bread of Alexandria.[21] The Florentine Lionardo Frescobaldi, who went to Egypt in 1384, told how the bread was badly baked but white as milk.[22] His traveling companion, Simone Sigoli, while discussing their stay at Alexandria, also said that the bread there was excellent and cheap.[23]

Arab physicians recommended eating only white bread, and there is no doubt that in this context we cannot minimize the influence of such prescriptions. The famous ar-Rāzī (d. 925) included among the foods which provoke melancholy bread baked with flour from which the waste matter (nukhāla) had not been cleaned; that is why he warned against eating bread made with middlings.[24] Ibn Djazla contrasted unleavened bread, with its low nutritional value, and bread made from the highest quality flour.[25] Likewise, Hibatallāh Ibn Djumaiʿ (d. 1198), Saladin's personal physician, recommended white bread exclusively.[26] Maimon-

---

in the form of a cake of barley bread which rolled into the camp of the Midianites (the ideal nomads) and toppled the chief's tent; see Judg. 7: 18. But the cultivation of wheat spread throughout the entire Levant and the Mediterranean. The evolution of the diet in Greece and Italy is significant. While barley bread was eaten during the period from which our oldest literary sources date, later this bread was only given to slaves and to the poor: see Orth, "Kochkunst," in *Neue Bearbeitung*, ed. Pauly-Wissowa (Stuttgart, 1894–1919), vol. 2, cols. 948, 957.

[17]at-Tanūkhī, *The Table-Talk of a Mesopotamian Judge*, trans. D. S. Margoliouth (London, 1922), pt. 1, p. 14.

[18]al-Mukaddasī, pp. 151, 181; see translation by A. Miquel (Damascus, 1963), pp. 153, 219.

[19]Burcardus de Monte Sion, in *Reyssbuch des Heyligen Lands* (Frankfurt, 1584), fol. 464 b.

[20]al-Mukaddasī, p. 199.

[21]Symon Semeonis, *Itineraria Symonis Simeonis et Willelmi de Worcestre*, ed. J. Nasmith (Cambridge, 1878), p. 34.

[22]Lionardo Frescobaldi, *Viaggio di Lionardo di Niccolo Frescobaldi Fiorentino in Egitto e in Terra Santa* (Rome, 1818), p. 104.

[23]Simone Sigoli, *Viaggio al Monte Sinai* (Milan, 1841), p. 80.

[24]ar-Rāzī, *Kitāb al-Ḥāwī fī ʾt-tibb* (Haidarabad, 1955–62), 1:62, 84.

[25]Ibn Djazla, *Taḳwīm al-abdān fī tadbīr al-insān*, Bibliothèque nationale, ms. 2948, fol. 9b.

[26]Hibatallāh Ibn Djumaiʿ, *Kitāb al-Irshād li-maṣāliḥ al-anfus wa ʾl-adjsād*, Bibliothèque nationale, ms. 2963, fol. 49b.

ides, who lived during the same period, gave precise instructions on this subject: wheat bread must be baked when the wheat is completely ripe, but before it begins to spoil. Refined flour should not be used, but the flour should be passed through a sieve to eliminate the particles which might make it bitter. Bread should be baked of unrefined, but ground, wheat, and a great deal of salt should be added.[27]

Indeed, ascetics ate the other sorts of bread. We learn, for example, that the great poet and philosopher Abu 'l-ʿAlā al-Maʿarrī (d. 1057) ate barley bread once he had become an ascetic.[28] The well-to-do and middle classes of Iraq, Syria, and Egypt ate barley bread or bread of durra or millet only during periods of scarcity, that is, when extraordinary increases in wheat prices occurred or during sieges or other calamities.[29]

The predominance of wheat bread was therefore a characteristic of the Levantine diet, distinguishing it from the food of the West during the same period. For, until the period following the Black Death, almost every social class in the majority of European countries ate barley, rye, or mixed bread. It appears that in the East the cultivation of barley spread during and after the Crusades; the price of wheat became higher than that of barley, although there is no indication that barley bread began to be eaten in the cities.

In the case of *meat*, another food item of prime importance, we can also infer from numerous sources that the preference for mutton did not change over many centuries; it was eaten everywhere. But kids were also eaten. In Iraq, the province of Kaskar on the Tigris was known for its kid.[30] We are told that at the beginning of the Moslem era the governor of Kūfa ate kid.[31] During the reign of the caliphs there were such great flocks of sheep in several provinces of Syria that mutton could be exported. This is what al-Makuddasī tells us when describing Transjordania.[32] Various fourteenth-century narratives indicate that during this period native-grown mutton was also eaten within Syria. The Italian pilgrim Jacopo da Verona (1335) told how the Moslems ate sheep on the

[27]Maimonides, *Tractatus Rabbi Moysi de regimine sanitatis ad Soldanum Regem* (Augusta Vindeliciorum, 1518), fol. 2b ff; trans. H. L. Gordon, *The Preservation of Youth* (New York, 1958), p. 29.

[28]Nāṣir-ī Khosrau, *Sefer nameh*, p. 35; see also Sibṭ Ibn al-Djauzī, *Mir'āt az-zamān*, ed. Jewett, (Chicago, 1907), p. 357 (biography of Muḥammad b. Aḥmad Ibn Ḳudāma).

[29]Ibn al-Athīr, *Kitāb al-Kamil fī t-ta rikh*, ed. Tornberg (Leyden, 1851–76), 8: 285, 293, 311; Carl H. Becker, *Beiträge zur Geschichte Aegyptens* (Strassburg, 1902–1903), 1:51, 52; Abū Shāma, *Dhail 'ala 'r-raudatain* (Damascus, 1947), p. 178; al-Maḳrīzī, *Sulūk*, Bibliothèque nationale, ms. de Slane, 1727, fol. 84a; Ibn Iyās, *Die Chronik des Ibn Ijās*, ed. Kahle (Istanbul, 1931–), 3:44, 232.

[30]Ibn Ḳutaiba, *Kitāb 'Uyūn al-akhbār*, 3:252.

[31]Ibid., p. 260.

[32]al-Muḳaddasī, p. 180.

nights of Ramadān;[33] in addition, an Arab historian told how Damascus had a good supply of sheep, which apparently provided its principal food. This text dates from the second half of the fourteenth century.[34] Several European pilgrims and voyagers who visited Egypt during the later period described the excellent quality of Egyptian mutton. They told of the delicious taste of this long-tailed animal,[35] and one of them even said that the tail was so fatty that it weighed more than thirty pounds.[36] Indeed, many of these sheep were imported from Syria, where the Turkomans raised them.[37] Mutton was also salted to be used by travelers who undertook to cross the deserts.[38]

The preference shown for mutton over other sorts of meat agreed with the precepts of Arab physicians; it had also been characteristic of Arab nutrition during the pre-Islamic period. All great Arab physicians whose works have been preserved warned against eating beef and recommended mutton. According to ar-Rāzī, almost all meats, with the exception of mutton, cause illnesses.[39] In classifying the various foods, Ibn Djazla listed mutton and veal among the "heavy" foods, a small amount of which provides great nourishment. He advised against the meat of ewes, rams, and billy goats.[40] We could also cite Ibn Djumai', who recommended the meat of the milk-fed calf, the kid, and the lamb,[41] as did Maimonides.[42] All these physicians advised against eating chicken. Isḥāk al-Isrā'īlī, the famous ninth-century physician known in the West as "Isaacus" or "Judaeus," advised against eating beef, which is very dry, even more so than the meat of the ram, and which causes thick and murky blood.[43]

Among the fats, various sorts of *oil* were universally used. Olives flourished in Syria and Palestine, as indicated by numerous accounts by Arab geographers and European travelers, over a variety of periods and in almost every province.[44] Oil was so abundant in Syria that it was used

[33]Jacopo da Verona, *Liber peregrinationis di Jacopo da Verona*, ed. Ugo Monneret de Villard (Rome, 1950), p. 97; see p. 90 concerning the Bedouins.

[34]Ibn Kathīr, *al-Bidāya wa 'n-nihāya* (Cairo, 1351–58), 14:299.

[35]Symon Semeonis, *Itineraria*, p. 39; Poggibonsi, *Libro d'oltramare di Fra Niccolò da Poggibonsi*, ed. Bacchi della Lega (Bologna, 1881), 2:196.

[36]"Voyage du magnifique et très illustre chevalier . . . Domenico Trevisan," in *Le Voyage d'outremer de Jean Thenaud*, ed. C. Schefer (Paris, 1884), p. 210.

[37]al-Makrīzī, *Kitāb al-Sulūk li-ma'rifat duwal al-mulūk*, ed. M. Zaida (Cairo, 1934–42), 2:463.

[38]Poggibonsi, *Libro d'oltramare*, 2:105.

[39]ar-Rāzī, *Kitāb al-Hāwī fi't-tibb*, 1:62, 84.

[40]Ibn Djazla, *Takwīm al-abdān fī tadbīr al-insān*, fol. 9b.

[41]Ibn Djumai', *Kitāb al-Irshād li-masāliḥ al-anfus*, fol. 49b.

[42]Maimonides, *Tractatus Rabbi Moysi*, fol. 2b ff.

[43]Isḥāk al-Isrā'īlī, *Kitāb al-Adwiya al-mufrada wa 'l-aghdiya* (Hebrew translation), Bibliothèque nationale, ms. 1128, fol. 22a.

[44]al-Mukaddasī, pp. 162, 174; and A. Mez, *Die Renaissance des Islâms*, (Heidelberg, 1922), p. 409; Nāṣir-ī Khosrau, *Safer nameh*, pp. 62, 67; Burcardus de Monte Sion, in

to light lamps[45] and was exported.[46] As a result, olive oil represented a major component in the diet of the inhabitants of Syria. al-Mukaddasī told how sprouted beans would be fried in oil; once cooked they would be sold with olives.[47] Dishes prepared for fast days by Christians in Syria required such great quantities of olive oil that they were called "oil dishes."[48] Iraq and Egypt lacked large quantities of olive oil and people had to use other oils. In Iraq sesame-seed oil was used, and in Egypt, radish and turnip oil.[49] The physician 'Abdallaṭīf al-Baghdādī, who wrote at the beginning of the thirteenth century, told how in Egypt oil was pressed from turnip, colza (*brassica campestris*), and lettuce seeds.[50] Western travelers to Egypt during the late period commented upon the poor quality of the oil in the region.[51] They were, of course, referring to the locally produced oil. But the rich could pay for olive oil, which at that time was imported in great quantities from southern Europe.[52] Importation of oil from the Maghreb and Syria, the traditional sources of supply, continued after the Crusades.[53] Since foreign olive oil was a luxury item, it is not surprising that a French ambassador coming to Egypt in 1512 would offer some as a gift to the governor of Alexandria.[54]

The information available to us concerning the spread of the cultivation of *sugar cane* indicates that during the rule of the caliphs and in the period preceding the First Crusade, this important food became a native product in every Near Eastern country. In Iraq, at the time of the caliphs, a great deal of sugar imported from Khuzistan was consumed, but it was

---

Reyssbuch, fol. 456a; Jacopo da Verona, *Liber peregrinationis*, p. 134; al-Dimashḳī, *Nukhbat ad-dahr*, ed. Mehren (St. Petersburg, 1866), pp. 205, 211; Frescobaldi, *Viaggio*, p. 142; Stephan von Gumpenberg, in *Reyssbuch*, fol. 239b; Bernard von Breitenbach, "Beschreibung der Reyse und Wallfahrt Herrn Johann Graffen zu Solms," in *Reyssbuch*, fol. 65 b.

[45]al-Dimashḳī, *Nukhbat ad-dahr*, p. 193.
[46]al-Mukaddasī, p. 180.
[47]Ibid., pp. 183–84; see Miquel translation, p. 226.
[48]H. Zayyat, "*Le livre de cuisine*," p. 370.
[49]See Mez, *Die Renaissance des Islâms*, p. 409; and Müller-Wodarg, "Die Landwirtschaft Aegyptens," pp. 29–30, 64.
[50]'Abdallaṭīf al-Baghdādī, *Relation de l'Égypte*, trans. de Sacy (Paris, 1810), p. 311.
[51]Frescobaldi, *Viaggio*, p. 85.
[52]J. Day, "Prix agricoles en Méditerranée à la fin du XVIe siècle (1382)," *Annales: E.S.C.*, 1958, no. 16, p. 643; B. Krekić, *Dubrovnik (Raguse) et le Levant au Moyen Age* (Paris, 1961), nos. 476, 698, 706; E. Piloti, *L'Égypte au commencement du XVe siècle, d'après le traité d'Emmanuel Piloti de Crète, incipit 1420*, ed. Ph. H. Dopp (Cairo, 1950), p. 65; J. Heers, *Gênes au XVe siècle* (Paris, 1961), pp. 241, 246, 343; Marino Sanuto, *Diari*, vol. 1, col. 380, vol. 3, cols. 98, 1122–3, 1198, vol. 7, cols. 712, 765, vol. 12, col. 214; Reinaud, "Traité de commerce entre la république de Venise et les derniers sultans mameloucs d'Égypte," *Journal asiatique* 2 (1829):32; and see p. 28.
[53]Piloti, *L'Égypte*, p. 57.
[54]Schefer (ed.), *Voyage de Jean Thenaud*, p. 22.

also cultivated in the Sawwād, especially near Baṣra.[55] Indeed, a tenth-century physician, Abū 'Abdallāh Muḥammad b. Aḥmad at-Tamīmī,[56] wrote that in Iraq the whitest variety was called *"al-ḳand,"* and in Syria, *"al-Ahwāzī."*[57] In the tenth century there were great plantations of sugar cane along the Palestinian coasts of Syria.[58] They were even more widespread there during the Crusades and in the fourteenth century.[59] As for Egypt, A. Mez has concluded that sugar cane became widespread there in the eleventh century. But al-Mas'ūdī and Ibn Ḥauḳal had already spoken of sugar-cane plantations and the manufacture of sugar in Egypt, especially candy.[60] Nevertheless, it seems that Mez was correct in suppos-ing that the growth of this form of agriculture in Egypt occurred after the accession of the Fatimids. Numerous travel accounts and Arab histories indicate its great importance from the time of the Crusades until the end of the fourteenth century, a period when Egypt was still able to export great quantities of it.[61] Although the manufacture of sugar decreased considerably after the great economic crisis which shook Egypt at the beginning of the fifteenth century, there were still sugar-cane plantations at the end of that century.[62]

Nonetheless, there is every reason to believe that sugar was always a very costly item, whose consumption was beyond the reach of the poor.[63] Therefore they resorted to other foods, as a sort of ersatz sugar. In addition to honey, extremely sweet jams were eaten. One of these was *naida*, a jam prepared without sugar or honey, but very sweet; it was a sort of paste made with wheat grains which had been sprouted and soaked in water for a few days, then dried and ground, and finally cooked to a certain consistency.[64]

[55]Mez, *Die Renaissance des Islâms*, p. 410.

[56]See Brockelmann, *Geschichte der arabischen literatur* (Leipzig, 1909), vol. 1, pt. 2, p. 273.

[57]Abū 'Abdallāh Muḥammad b. Aḥmad at-Tamīmī, *Kitāb al-Murshid īlā djawāhir al-aghdiya*, Bibliothèque nationale, ms. 2870[1], fol. 10b (al-Ahwāz is the capital of Khuzistan).

[58]al-Muḳaddasī, pp. 162, 180.

[59]Nāṣir-i Khosrau, pp. 40, 46; Burcardus de Monte Sion, in *Reyssbuch*, fol. 464 a-b; "Ein niederrheinischer Bericht über den Orient," *Zeitschrift für deutsche Philologie* 19 (1886): 84 (three different sorts are mentioned: the black employed in pharmacies, the red for the kitchen, and the white which is the best); al-Dimashḳī, *Nukhbat ad-dahr*, p. 207.

[60]al-Mas'ūdī, *At-Tanbīh*, p. 21; Ibn Ḥauḳal, *Opus geographicum*, p. 142; and see Müller-Wodarg, "Die Landwirtschaft Aegyptens," p. 47.

[61]Nāṣir-i Khosrau, *Sefer nameh*, p. 150; Guglielmus of Boldensele, "Hodoeporicon ad Terram Sanctam," in H. Canisius, *Antiquae lectiones*, 6 vols. (Ingolstadt, 1604), vol. 5, pt. 2, p. 112; al-Makrīzī, *Sulūk*, ed. Zaida, 1:383–84; Ibn Duḳmāḳ, *Description de l'Egypte . . .* (Cairo, 1893), 4:41 ff; 5:32–33.

[62]Arnold von Harff, *The Pilgrimage of Arnold von Harff, Knight from Cologne*, trans. M. Letts (London, 1946), p. 99.

[63]Abulḳāsim, *Ein bagdader Sittenbild*, ed. Mez (Heidelberg, 1902) p. 48.

[64]al-Muḳaddasī, p. 204; 'Abdallaṭīf, *Relation*, p. 311; Dozy, *Supplément*, 2:741.

Although the potato was as yet unknown during this period, similar *tubers* were eaten in the Levant. In Egypt, it was primarily the colocasia which played the role of our potatoes. 'Abdallaṭīf observed that it was a heavy food, difficult to digest and heavy on the stomach, although it strengthened one and filled the stomach when used moderately. But according to what we are told by an Arab physician of the mid-eleventh century, colocasias and chick peas were the chief foods of the inhabitants of Lower Egypt. The colocasia was eaten in Syria, but to a lesser degree.[65] 'Abdallaṭīf also mentioned other vegetables which were popular in Egypt: the *bamia*, which was cooked with meat, and the *melukhiya*, whose consumption was, in his opinion, bad for the stomach.[66]

While Egypt had abundant supplies of wheat and various sorts of vegetables, Iraq and Syria produced a great number of fruits. The Sawwād had always been known for its dates, but in that period there were date palms beyond the 'Āna-Takrīt line, which today forms the limit of its zone of cultivation.[67] Upper Mesopotamia was rich in pomegranates, almonds, *summāq*,* and other fruits, which it exported.[68] But either the production of Upper Mesopotamia was insufficient or its fruits were less esteemed, for horticultural products were also imported into Iraq from Syria.[69] Indeed, Syria was famed for the excellent quality of its apples, pomegranates, plums, figs, sycamore figs, and apricots.[70] Various breeds of apples were available in Syria, the one most esteemed being the *fathī*, and there were twenty-one varieties of apricots.[71] Until the end of the Middle Ages, travelers who visited Syria praised the region's wealth in various species of fruits.[72] On the other hand, Egypt—although it produced a great number of dates, especially in the Saʿīd (Upper Egypt),

---

[65]al-Muḳaddasī, p. 203 ff; 'Abdallaṭīf, *Relation*, p. 23; al-Maḳrīzī, *Khiṭaṭ*, trans. U. Bouriant (Paris, 1900), 1:44; al-Dimashḳī, *Nukhbat ad-dahr*, p. 207; see Mez, *Die Renaissance des Islâms*, p. 406.

[66]'Abdallaṭīf, *Relation*, p. 16.

[67]Mez, *Die Renaissance des Islâms*, p. 409; and Ibn Ḥauḳal, *Opus geographicum*, p. 221.

*Translator's note: Rhus coraria; the highly acid seeds of this plant could be dried, ground, and served with thyme as a condiment.

[68]Ibn Ḥauḳal, *Opus geographicum*, pp. 220, 227; al-Muḳaddasī, pp. 136, 145.

[69]Ibn al-Faḳīh, *Compendium Libris Kitab al-Baldân*, ed. de Goeje (Leyden, 1885), p. 117; al-Thaʿālibī, *Laṭāʾif al-maʿārif*, ed. Pieter de Jong (Leyden, 1867), p. 95, copied by an-Nuwayrī, *Nihāyab, al-arab fī funūn al-adab* (1964–65), 1:344.

[70]Ibn Ḥauḳal, *Opus geographicum*, p. 172; al-Muḳaddasī, pp. 172, 174, 176, 180, 181.

[71]See H. Zayyat, "Le livre de cuisine" ("Les pommes de Damas" [in Arabic]), pp. 29 ff; and ibid. ("Les abricots de Damas"), pp. 365 ff.

[72]Burcardus de Monte Sion, in *Reyssbuch*, fol. 456 a, 464 b; von Breitenbach, in *Reyssbuch*, fol. 65 b; Schefer (ed.), *Voyage de Jean Thenaud*, pp. 86, 93, 114; Varthema, *Les voyages de Ludovico de Varthema*, trans. J. Balarin de Raconis, ed. C. Schefer (Paris, 1888), p. 15.

bananas,[73] and sycamore figs[74] in its oases[75]—was always obliged to import fruit. 'Abdallaṭif pointed out that Egyptian dates were much less sweet than the Iraqi ones,[76] and that the sycamore figs, which were appreciated for their sweetness, were bad for the stomach (he cited Galen).[77] The chief exports from Syria were cherries, pears, and apples.[78] A novelty in the fruit orchards of the Near East during the period of the caliphs was the introduction of several citrus fruits—citrons, limes, and oranges. Although they were already known in the court of the Abbasides in the mid-ninth century,[79] al-Mas'ūdī wrote, a century later, that oranges and citrons were introduced at Oman, then into southern Iraq, and finally into Syria and Egypt after the year 300 of the Hegira, that is, in 912.[80] But since citrus fruits are mentioned in connection with Egypt before the end of the ninth century, we must conclude that al-Mas'ūdī was only referring to certain varieties.[81] According to Ibn Ḥauḳal, citrons were grown in Upper Mesopotamia;[82] and according to al-Muḳaddasī, lemons were cultivated in the province of Baṣra,[83] and citrons and oranges in Palestine.[84] However, it seems that citrus groves developed rather slowly in the Near East, for the geographers writing at the end of the tenth century felt obliged to explain to their readers the nature of these fruits.[85] Later, in Egypt, various species of citrus fruits were cultivated, such as the pomaceous lemon (which was not bitter), the so-called "winter" lemon, and the "runner" lime.[86] Indeed, 'Abdallaṭif observed that in his day there were a great number of acid fruits in Egypt which he had never seen in Iraq. He mentioned the large lemon, the sweet lemon, the lime which they called "composite" and of which there were several varieties, and finally the "sealed" variety, which was a very dark red, brighter than the skin of

[73]Symon Semeonis, *Itineraria*, p. 35; Guglielmus of Boldensele, "Hodoeporicon ad Terram Sanctam," p. 112; Poggibonsi, *Libro d'oltramare*, 2:188, 191.

[74]Poggibonsi, *Libro d'oltramare*, 2:188, 190; Sigoli, *Viaggio*, p. 88.

[75]Ibn Ḥauḳal, *Opus geographicum*, pp. 144, 147; al-Muḳaddasī, pp. 195, 197; see Müller-Wodarg, "Die Landwirtschaft Aegyptens," pp. 60 ff; Poggibonsi, *Libro d'oltramare*, 2:188; Frescobaldi, *Viaggio*, p. 86; Sigoli, *Viaggio*, p. 88; Schefer (ed.), *Voyage de Jean Thenaud*, p. 33, and "Voyage de Domenico Trevisan" in the same work, p. 210.

[76]'Abdallaṭif, *Relation*, p. 32.

[77]Ibid., p. 19.

[78]See Mez, *Die Renaissance des Islâms*, p. 408; and see "Voyage de Domenico Trevisan," p. 210.

[79]See the sources cited by Mez, *Die Renaissance des Islâms*, p. 407.

[80]al-Mas'ūdī, *Murūdj adh-dhahab*, ed. Dāghir (1965–66), 2:438 ff.; and see al-Makrīzī, *Khiṭaṭ*, 1:28.

[81]Müller-Wodarg, "Die Landwirtschaft Aegyptens," pp. 73–74.

[82]Ibn Ḥauḳal, *Opus geographicum*, p. 220.

[83]al-Muḳaddasī, p. 7.

[84]Ibid., p. 181; see also Miquel's trans., p. 220, n. 27.

[85]Ibn Ḥauḳal, *Opus geographicum*, p. 320; and al-Muḳaddasī, p. 482.

[86]See the sources cited by Mez, *Die Renaissance des Islâms*, p. 407.

an orange.[87] European travelers going through the Eastern countries during the later period also referred frequently to various citrus fruits cultivated in Egypt—the citron, the lemon, and the orange. In Syria citrus groves also flourished at the time of the Crusades and in the reign of the Mamelukes. Several passages in travel books, in which mention is made of the various species of citrus fruits, confirm this.[88]

On the basis of evidence we have cited from various sources, we might conclude that the objective possibilities—that is to say the variety of food supplies—ought to have increased under the caliphs.[89] But the resulting changes in nutrition only affected the upper levels of society. Their table became more cosmopolitan. The menu of the rich upper classes, of dignitaries, and of feudal lords changed; that of the artisans changed much less; and the food of the working class did not change at all, although it became more copious in the late period. The diet of the peasantry is unknown to us.

When discussing the nutritional possibilities of the various levels of Levantine society in the Middle Ages, we cannot, however, be content merely to establish the items available for purchase. It is clear that we must also take into consideration the eating habits, that is, the particular tastes which to a large degree determined the choice of foods, for there is no doubt that these preferences also had important consequences for public health.

Through the works of geographers and other Arab authors of the Middle Ages we can immediately perceive a marked taste shown by Levantines for three categories of dishes: those which were sweet, those which were salty, and meats which were spiced or served with fruits.

In Upper Mesopotamia, the city of Sarūdj was known for its syrups and preserves made with raisins;[90] and in Syria, the pastries of Balbec were made with a great deal of sugar, starch, and orange blossoms.[91] Another Syrian pastry was introduced into Europe through the principalities ruled by the Crusaders. We are referring to "gingerbread" (*khubz al-*

---

[87]'Abdallaṭīf, *Relation*, p. 31.

[88]Poggibonsi, *Libro d'oltramare*, 2:188; Frescobaldi, *Viaggio*, p. 107; Sigoli, *Viaggio*, p. 88; Harff, *Pilgrimage*, p. 94; and *Voyage de Jean Thenaud*, p. 113. On citrus fruit in Syria, see Nāṣir-ī Khosrau, *Sefer nameh*, p. 40; Jacopo da Verona, *Liber peregrinationis*, p. 134; and "Ein niederrheinischer Bericht," p. 82.

[89]A. Mazahéri believes that coffee spread throughout the Near East at the time of the Ayyubites, and tea throughout Persia in the thirteenth century; see *La vie quotidienne des musulmans au Moyen Age, X^e au XIIIe siècle* (Paris, 1951), pp. 92–93. Since the manuscript cited by the author was inaccessible to us, we must be satisfied with reproducing his opinion.

[90]Ibn Ḥauḳal, *Opus geographicum*, p. 230.

[91]al-Muḳaddasī, p. 181; see also Dozy, *Supplément*, 2:515; and Rodinson, "Recherches," p. 140, n. 4.

abāzīr), which took the form of cookies—called *"langues de chats"*—covered with white sugar. In France, the city of Dijon became famous for this pastry. In Syria, bakers would cover them with ground almonds.[92] There was also a fondness for very sweet jams; al-Mukaddasī mentioned the *kubbait*, a sort of jam made with carob.[93] 'Abdallatīf told how there was such a variety of sweets in Egypt that in order to describe them in detail he would have been obliged to devote an entire book to them. Among the sweetened dishes then in vogue in Egypt, he mentioned the *heriseh* of pistachios, made of one part boiled and chopped chicken skins and two parts rose syrup, to which ground pistachios were added. He also spoke of sugared, steamed dishes, such as boiled hens placed in syrup, on top of which ground hazelnuts or purslane seeds were sprinkled until they coagulated. The Baghdad physician who left us this recipe did not fail to stress that such dishes were fattening.[94] In his *Egyptian Topography*, al-Makrīzī gave a detailed description of the banquets celebrating the end of the fast of Ramadān, to which the Fatimid rulers invited representatives of the various classes. In addition to the great quantities of meats of all sorts we also find mention there of "constructions of sweets" which were offered to the public.[95] The same author cited the physician Ibn Ridwān (d. 1061), who said that the inhabitants of Upper Egypt fed upon dates and sweets made with sugar cane and exported them to Fostat and elsewhere.[96]

As far as the taste for salty foods is concerned, we can cite a passage in the work of al-Mukaddasī, to which we have already referred so frequently, in which he mentions *ḥālūm*, a sort of salted cheese, as a typical Egyptian food.[97] We must also refer to a precept given to *bons vivants* by Abu 't-Ṭayyib Muḥammad b. Aḥmad al-Washshā (d. 936); he advised them not to eat too much salt.[98]

Meats very heavily seasoned with various spices and fruit seeds, pistachios, and walnuts, over which musk or rose water was poured, are representative of the dishes described by Arab writers and especially those in the cookbooks assembled by various authors during the period of the Crusades. 'Abdallatīf referred to *"raghīf aṣ-ṣīniyya,"* or "platter cake." It was made of two layers of pastry of finest flour between which was placed a whole roast lamb stuffed with shredded meat fried in sesame-seed oil,

[92]H. Zayyat, "Le livre de cuisine" ("Le pain d'épices" [in Arabic]), pp. 380 ff.
[93]al-Mukaddasī, pp. 183–84.
[94]'Abdallatīf, *Relation*, pp. 312–13.
[95]al-Makrīzī, *Khiṭaṭ*, 1:387.
[96]Ibid., 1:44; see also Sibṭ Ibn al-Djauzī, *Mir'āt az-zamān*, pp. 5, 264.
[97]al-Mukaddasī, p. 204; see also Dozy, *Supplément*, 1:318.
[98]Abu 't-Ṭayyib Muḥammad b. Aḥmad al-Washshā, *Kitāb al-Muwashshā*, d. Brünnow (Leyden, 1886), p. 130.

the meat of chickens and small birds, pistachios, and various aromatic and fiery spices such as pepper, ginger, cinnamon, cumin, cardamom, and others. The whole was sprinkled with rose water and garnished with little vases (of pastry), some filled with meats and others with sugar or sweets.[99] The *Kitāb al-Wuṣla ila 'l-ḥabīb fī waṣf aṭ-ṭayyibāt wa 't-ṭib*, written in the first half of the thirteenth century, contains numerous recipes for meats cooked with dates and pistachios,[100] and chickens cooked with pistachios and almonds.[101] In addition, in the cookbook written by Djamāl ad-dīn Yūsūf b. Ḥasan ibn 'Abdalhādī at the end of the fifteenth century, we find recipes for a meat dish with apples, plums, walnuts, dates, *summāq*, etc.[102] We would be wrong to suppose that only persons from the upper levels of society ate such dishes. at-Tanūkhī told a story which portrayed a simple itinerant cook selling his mutton with almonds in the streets of Baghdad.[103]

* * *

Given these dietary possibilities and these preferences, what could the various salaried classes buy? First, let us try to examine the nutritional situation of workers earning a minimum salary.

Since such a worker in tenth-century Iraq probably earned a monthly salary of 1.5 dinars[104] and since a Baghdadian *raṭl* of bread cost about 0.0066 dinar,[105] we can calculate that to feed a family of five persons he would have to spend almost 1.0 dinar for two kilograms of bread daily. The sum remaining would have been 0.5 dinar. If we calculate the expenses for lodging, clothing, etc., we will see that this amount would be barely sufficient to pay for his other needs. We must therefore conclude that such a worker was obliged to choose cheap food of poor quality. Various passages in the works of Arab authors confirm this supposition.

From these texts it appears that in Iraq the poor did not eat white bread, but other sorts of bread. Mention is made of "*khushkār*," or coarse bread,[106] and in the marshy provinces of the Sawwād, of rice bread. A miser offered the latter to his guests.[107] The well-known author Ibn

---

[99]Abdallaṭīf, *Relation*, p. 313.
[100]Rodinson, "Recherches," pp. 138 ff.
[101]Ibid., pp. 132 ff.
[102]Zayyat, "Le livre de cuisine," pp. 371 ff.
[103]at-Tanūkhī, *Table-Talk*, pt. 1, p. 59.
[104]See our article "I salari nel medio Oriente durante l'epoca medioevale," *Rivista Storica Italiana* 78 (1966):339.
[105]See our book *Histoire des prix et des salaires dans l'Orient médiéval* (Paris, 1969), pp. 47–50.
[106]Al-Djāḥiẓ, *Kitāb al-Bukhalā*, ed. van Vloten (Leyden, 1900), pp. 101 ff.
[107]Ibid., p. 129.

Kutaiba (d. 889) told of a young man who had traveled from Medina to Basra—which was, according to him, the paradise for starving people. For there such a man could feed himself for two dirhams a month by eating rice bread and dishes of salted fish.[108] This little story dates from the ninth century. But in the travel account of the famous Ibn Battūta, who traveled throughout Asia in the second quarter of the fourteenth century, we find from the description of his visit to Wāsit that the menu of the poor had not changed in Iraq for five centuries. The Maghrebian traveler lodged in that city at the home of some sufis who in the evening ate rice bread, fish, *laban* (sour milk), and dates.[109]

The texts which we have cited indicate that the poor ate chiefly fish instead of meat, that is, mutton, the preferred meat, which was too costly for them. al-Djāhiz quoted a certain Abū Dhaknān, who said that he had not ceased eating meat from the moment he became rich. Each Friday this man, who was very miserly, would buy beef (which was cheaper than mutton), onions, an eggplant, a gourd, and some carrots.[110] From this story we can infer that the poor could not afford quality meat. Another passage from the same book deals with a miser who refrained from eating meat, being satisfied with a *djuwāfa* (a species of fish) costing one habba.[111] Beef, which was less esteemed and cheaper than mutton, was considered the food of the poor. This is indicated in a story told by at-Tanūkhī which dates from tenth-century Baghdad. We find that beef and a dessert of dates sufficed for beggars.[112] However, we believe it would be prudent not to draw too rapid a conclusion on the basis of this text. It is more than doubtful that the poor ate beef regularly. Let us cite on this same subject another passage in al-Djāhiz's book, which we have already mentioned on several occasions. He said that the butchers at Basra slaughtered more than usual on Fridays, and as a result there were a great number of animal heads left over on Saturday, "because the poor people and the shopkeepers and artisans are not inclined to eat a head on Saturday when shortly before, on Friday, they have eaten meat; and also because most of them still have some leftovers."[113] The poor probably had to be satisfied at times with camel meat.[114] In any case, most of the time

[108]Ibn Kutaiba, *Kitāb 'Uyūn al-akhbār*, 1:221.
[109]Ibn Battūta, *Rihla*, trans. H. A. R. Gibb (Cairo, 1928), 1:114; 2:273. The rice bread which the rich occasionally ate was apparently an entirely different sort, see H. Zayyat, "Le pain de riz" (in Arabic), *al-Machrique* 35 (1937):377 ff.
[110]al-Djāhiz, *Kitāb al-Bukhalā*, p. 131.
[111]Ibid., p. 130.
[112]at-Tanūkhī, *Table-Talk*, pt. 1, p. 66.
[113]al-Djāhiz, *Kitāb al-Bukhalā*, p. 121.
[114]E. W. Lane, *Arabian Society in the Middle Ages* (London, 1883), p. 141.

their food did not include meat. In a text contained in a book by al-Djāhiz, someone wondered what one should give a porter to eat. The reply was that such a man would eat 'aṣīda (a sort of thick porridge made of flour mixed with a little boiling water, with butter and honey added), a rice-based dish (aruzza), and one of bistandūd (a meat paste covered with flour).[115] In the markets of Baghdad, great quantities of chick-pea soup were sold, while well-to-do people only ate such a soup during the two or three months of the year when there was no fruit.[116]

The chief foods of the poor in Iraq were, therefore, coarse bread or rice bread and vegetables, sometimes fish or undesirable cuts of meat, and dates. Dates, pears, peaches, figs, pomegranates, and watermelons were also considered products which only the poor would eat.[117]

Thus, the nutritional situation of workers in Iraq was deplorable for many centuries; that of their Syrian counterparts was also very wretched over a long period, though to a lesser degree. During the late period, their situation changed completely. The information available to us on this subject for the time of the Crusades does not permit us to make even approximate calculations. But sufficient data is available for the late period.

Let us calculate the budget for a family of five—assuming that the father had a minimum salary—on the basis of the average price of 0.012 dinar for the Damascene raṭl of bread in the fourteenth century and 0.015 ashrafī during the fifteenth century, and the average price of 0.125 dinar for a raṭl of mutton in the fourteenth century and 0.09 ashrafī in the fifteenth century.[118] We reach the following approximations:

	MONTHLY SALARIES	BREAD RATIONS	MEAT RATIONS	OTHER EXPENSES
14th century	1.5 din.	60 kg–0.42 din.	12 kg–0.8 din.	0.28 din.[119]
15th century	3 ashr.	90 kg–0.72 ashr.	30 kg–1.5 ashr.	0.78 ashr.

[115]al-Djāhiz, Kitāb al-Bukhalā, p. 67; and on "bistandūd" see in al-Djāhiz' Kitāb, van Vloten's "Notes," p. xii; and the translation by C. Pellat (Paris, 1951), p. 314.

[116]at-Tanūkhī, Table-Talk, pt. 1, p. 71.

[117]Abu 't-Ṭayyib Muhammad b. Ahmad al-Washshā, Kitāb al-Muwashshā, p. 131.

[118]See our study, "L'évolution des prix," pp. 17, 26 ff; and our Histoire des prix et salaires, pp. 400, 402.

[119]N. A. Ziadeh has made a different calculation for the budget of such a family during that era in his book, Urban Life in Syria under the Early Mamluks (Beyrut, 1953), p. 101. This scholar supposes that a family of five would have spent for food 1.5 dinars per month—0.5 dinar for 37 kilograms of bread, and 0.3 dinar for 5.55 kilograms of meat. The sum allocated for the purchase of bread is, in our opinion, too high, for the indicated amount would cost only half that much; and, moreover, Ziadeh's calculations allowed 0.35 dinar for the purchase of sugar, a food which was not eaten by a family with a minimum income.

The enormous improvement of the situation for workers earning a
minimum salary which occurred after the Black Death can in part be
explained by the decrease in the prices of the principal food commodities
in Syria. This was a phenomenon peculiar to that country, whose
economy declined as a result of the devastation caused by invasions and
internal wars and as a result of the policies of the Mameluke sultans, who
diverted the important Indian trade toward Egypt.

In a working-class family of this sort, the consumption of the quantities calculated above would have supplied each individual[120] with the
following daily nutrients:

	CALORIES	PROTEINS (grams)	CARBO-HYDRATES (grams)	FATS (grams)
14th century	1,154	45.6	196	20
15th century	1,930	82	294	45.2

The travel accounts of voyagers during the late period contain information which permits us a glimpse into how the lower classes were
nourished.

We know that the poorest people ate bread of inferior quality.
Ludolph of Suchem, a German prelate traveling through the Levant
during the second quarter of the fourteenth century, spoke of the "various
sorts of bread sold at Damascus."[121] From these travel accounts we may
deduce that instead of mutton the poor ate fish, which was cheap.[122] We
also find that they ate horse and camel meat.[123] While discussing the
Bedouins, a traveler writing in the first half of the fourteenth century
commented that they rarely ate meat. They ate it, we must point out,
when they happened to slaughter a sheep, a kid, or a camel.[124] Even
scholars sometimes ate camel meat.[125]

The documentation available to us for a study of the economic
situation of workers in medieval Egypt is much richer. It offers us the
possibility of retracing the nutritional patterns for the various periods and
even for the various levels within the working class.

First, let us attempt to establish what an Egyptian worker could buy
with a minimum salary.

[120]We are using L. Randoin et al., *Tables de composition des aliments* (Paris, 1961).
[121]Ludolph of Suchem, *De itinere Terrae Sanctae*, ed. F. Deycks (Stuttgart, 1851), p. 98.
[122]Sigoli, *Viaggio*, p. 148.
[123]Varthema, *Voyages*, p. 19.
[124]Jacopo da Verona, *Liber peregrinationis*, p. 90.
[125]al-Ghuzūlī, *Maṭāli al-budūr fī manāzil as-surūr* (Cairo, 1299), 2:28.

MONTHLY SALARIES	BREAD RATIONS	MEAT RATIONS	OTHER EXPENSES
11th century 1.2 din.	60 kg–0.5 din.	8 kg–0.368 dib.	0.33 din.
13th century 2 din.	90 kg–0.855 din.	15 kg–0.66 din.	0.485 din.
14th century 1.5 din.	90 kg–0.63 din.	10 kg–0.6 din.	0.27 din.
15th century 3.33 ashr.	90 kg–0.99 ashr.	30 kg–2.1 ashr.	0.24 ashr.

If on the basis of these data we calculate for one individual the daily nutritive value of the two principal food items, we obtain:

	CALORIES	PROTEINS (grams)	CARBO-HYDRATES (grams)	FATS (grams)
11 century	1,087	41	196	14.87
13th century	1,682	65	294	26.2
14th century	1,598	59	292	19.75
15th century	1,930	82	294	45.2

These tables, conjectural though they are, indicate that, until the period following the Black Death, workers with the lowest salary could not buy enough meat to supply the necessary proteins and fats. If the geographer al-Mukaddasī observed that little meat was eaten in Egypt,[126] he was certainly thinking of the menus of peasants and workers. The latter probably had recourse, to a large extent, to other cheaper foods which contain these nutritive elements.

First of all, this meant fish, so rich in protein. Numerous passages from Arab sources and travel accounts, written in various European languages, mention the consumption of fish. Ibn Ḥaukal and al-Mukaddasī praised the salt-water fish which were sold at al-Faramā.[127] Yākūt told of seventy-nine sorts of fish which were caught near Tinnīs.[128] Damietta was also known for its excellent fish. Jacopo da Verona told how the fish were salted before being transported by camel and boat to the whole of Egypt.[129] A German voyager who visited Egypt at this time reported the same thing while mentioning the city of Damietta.[130] The rich did not turn up their noses at these salted fish. Many fish from the Nile were also very

---

[126]al-Mukaddasī, p. 205.
[127]Ibn Ḥaukal, *Opus geographicum*, p. 144; al-Mukaddasī, p. 195.
[128]Yākūt, *Mu'djam al-buldān*, ed. Wüstenfeld (Leipzig, 1866–70), 1:886.
[129]Jacopo da Verona, *Liber peregrinationis*, p. 86.
[130]Ludolph of Suchem, *De itinere Terrae Sanctae*, p. 62.

desirable.[131] Some of them were salted for export to distant points.[132] On the basis of these texts we may conclude that fish served as the chief food for the lower classes of the population, replacing the meat which they could not afford to buy. But there is more. That excellent observer, the physician 'Abdallaṭīf al-Baghdādi, has left us a precious discussion of the components of the food eaten by the lower classes in Saladin's Egypt:[133]

> As for the common people, they most frequently live on ṣir [small fish],[134] on fish paste, on tellina, on cheese, on *naida*, and other dishes of the sort. . . . Some of them eat the field mice which are born in the deserts and low areas when the waters of the Nile recede; they call them the quail of the low areas. In the Saʿīd certain persons eat snakes and the cadavers of donkeys and other domesticated animals. . . . At Damietta many fish are eaten, and they are cooked with the same ingredients which elsewhere are used with meats . . . rice, *summāq*, minced meat, and other such things.[135]

The evidence is clear and leaves no doubt about the diet of the lower levels of the Egyptian population at the time of the Crusades. From the account of this expert on food we can deduce that only a part of the poor population could replace expensive meat with fish. These were the inhabitants of the Mediterranean coasts. Indeed, travelers referred to the fish which served as a food for the mass of the Egyptian population, especially when describing coastal cities.[136] The Christian physician al-Mukhtār b. 'Abdūn Ibn Buṭlān, who journeyed in 1047 from Baghdad to Cairo,[137] told how the inhabitants of the coastal city of Tinnīs ate cheese, fish, and cow's milk.[138] The salt fish sold elsewhere apparently were expensive and could be found only on the tables of the rich. Indeed, we read in an Arab chronicle that in 1339 two hundred urns (*maṭar*) of salt fish were found among the possessions of the disgraced dignitary an-Nashw.[139] Since fish were not always available, people ate horse and donkey meat. In speaking of his visit to Alexandria in 1384, the Florentine traveler Simone Sigoli told how horse, donkey, and camel meat were

---

[131]Symon Semeonis, *Itineraria*, p. 36; Guglielmus of Boldensele, "Hodoeporicon ad Terram Sanctam," p. 111.

[132]Schefer (ed.), *Voyage de Jean Thenaud*, p. 31.

[133]As contrasted with the exquisite dishes which the author had just described.

[134]See S. de Sacy's notes to 'Abdallaṭīf, *Relation*, pp. 278 ff, 321.

[135]'Abdallaṭīf, *Relation*, pp. 314–15.

[136]See Sigoli, *Viaggio*, p. 80.

[137]See Brockelmann, *Geschichte der arabischen literatur*, vol. 1, pt. 2, p. 636.

[138]Quoted by al-Makrīzī, *Khiṭaṭ*, 1:177. The cheese imported from Sicily (see S. D. Goitein, *A Mediterranean Society* [Berkeley, 1967], 1:46) was probably intended, as were other imported foods, for the well-to-do classes.

[139]al-Makrīzī, *Sulūk*, ed. Zaida, 2:482; on "maṭar," see Dozy, *Supplément*, 2:600.

sold there.[140] According to 'Abdallaṭīf, the *naida* eaten by the poor replaced sugar, which, as we can imagine, was beyond their means. It is even doubtful that they could pay for good cheese, which was too expensive.[141]

On the basis of this information supplied by 'Abdallaṭīf—and we must not underestimate its value—one might think that the quantity of meat within the means of the poor, the workers, the peasantry, and others was even more modest. Our charts are probably more accurate concerning the proportion of bread in the diet of the working classes. It was the chief component. This is an undisputable fact. For example, let us recall that the social services of the Jewish community of Fostat—whose memoranda are preserved in the geniza—distributed only wheat and bread to the poor. Each person received four round loaves (weighing one Egyptian *raṭl* or 437.5 grams) per week.[142] A European traveler who spent some time in Egypt at a later date and who was noteworthy for his talent as an observer, told how, when the Egyptian poor ate vegetables, they mixed them with a great quantity of bread and called a dish of this sort *ṭabīkh*.[143] Now, *ṭabīkh* in Arabic means "cooking"; for them it was their most important dish.

Thus, until the late Middle Ages the diet of the lower classes in Egyptian society was low in calories, proteins, and fats, for the ersatz meats, such as horsemeat, contained relatively little. Moreover, they seem to have had a considerable quantity of carbohydrates available to them in the form of dates and figs, which they ate instead of the sugar which was too costly for them. Above all, they ate bread. This imbalanced nutrition was apparently characteristic of their diet.

The changes in caloric and fat intake indicated in our tables shed light on the actual factors involved in the evolution of salaries and, as a result, on the nutritional situation of the lower classes of Levantine society in the Middle Ages. The increase in the quantity of bread and meat eaten, which was made possible by an increase in salaries, came about after those terrible population drains which resulted from the great famine and the plague at the turn of the twelfth century, and especially from the Black Death in the mid-fourteenth century.

Now let us move on and study the nutritional possibilities of another salaried class in medieval Egypt, the specialized workers and artisans. Their situation was completely different. We are talking of master

---

[140]Sigoli, *Viaggio*, p. 80.

[141]For the later period, see our study, "Prix et salaires à l'époque mamelouke," pp. 65–66.

[142]See S. D. Goitein, "The Social Services of the Jewish Community as Reflected in the Cairo Geniza Records," *Jewish Social Studies* 26 (1964): 72 ff.

[143]G. M. Vansleb, *Relazione dello stato presente dell'Egitto* (Paris, 1671), p. 235.

masons, carpenters, and their equals, whose salaries are found in the documents of the geniza dating from the eleventh and thirteenth centuries, in the titles of *wakf*, and in other sources of the late period. They are as follows:

MONTHLY SALARIES	BREAD RATIONS	MEAT RATIONS	OTHER EX-PENSES
11th century 5 din.	90 kg–0.75 din.	30 kg–1.38 din.	2.87 din.
13th century 6 din.	120 kg–1.14 din.	30 kg–1.32 din.	3.54 din.
14th century 3 din.	90 kg–0.63 din.	30 kg–1.8 din.	0.57 din.
15 century 6.66 ashr.	120 kg–1.32 ashr.	30 kg–2.1 ashr.	3.24 ashr.

This table indicates that after the accession of the Fatimids in Egypt, specialized workers could always pay for the food which supplied their families with sufficient amounts of energy-giving substances.

The menu of this segment of the population, which also included small merchants such as shopkeepers, was undoubtedly rather varied. A head of a family belonging to this group could vary the family's menu with poultry. Yet, even such a specialized worker could not afford olive oil, so rich in calories and fats. Indeed, it was very costly, as were mutton and sugar. A Judeo-Arabic document from the Fatimid period contains very significant indications on this subject. We are referring to the accounts of the Jewish community of Fostat, in which we find the sums spent for the entertainment of a very respected guest, probably a learned foreigner. This man, who had fallen ill, received chickens daily and also certain quantities of linseed oil.[144] In order to avoid overestimating the dietary possibilities of this class, we must also consider that a large portion of the food budget was allocated for spices. Let us cite a passage from the famous *Treatise on Famines* by al-Makrīzī. The Arab historian told of a man who earned a monthly salary of three hundred dirhams—which at the end of the fourteenth century was equivalent to twelve dinars—four-fifths of which was spent on food for his family and servants. He said:

> When he wanted to buy something to meet the needs of his family, out of these ten dirhams in coin,[145] he allocated, for example, two dirhams for purchasing three *raṭls* of mutton, two others for spices, and four dirhams to pay for feeding his children, his family, and his servants who he likewise had to support.[146]

---

[144]T.-S. Box J 1[26].

[145]His daily income.

[146]al-Makrīzī, "Le Traité des famines de Maqrīzi," trans. G. Wiet, *Journal of the Economic and Social History of the Orient* 5 (1962):83.

We will notice that, according to al-Makrīzī, the cost of spices used in cooking by a middle-class family was about equal to the amount spent on meat.

* * *

The diet of the well-to-do classes was characterized chiefly by the abundance of meat and sweetened dishes.

An Iraqi letter comparing the diet of the poor with that of the rich said that the latter alone ate lambs and almond dishes.[147] In the streets of large cities, the rich were offered roasted and boiled meat. European travelers recounted how itinerant cooks would sell such dishes.[148] Cookbooks contain the recipes for meat dishes of mutton or chicken. The *Kitāb al-Wuṣla ila 'l-ḥabīb*, written in the thirteenth century, contains seventy-four recipes for dishes containing chicken.[149] But let us once again cite al-Djāḥiz. This Iraqi author of the ninth century pointed out that the diet of the rich consisted chiefly of fattened chickens, fresh fruit imported from the mountains (Upper Mesopotamia), and dried fruits.[150] Fattened chickens from the province of Kaskar, in addition to kid, were highly appreciated throughout Iraq.[151] Indeed, the consumption of chickens distinguished the menu of the rich from the menu of the poor. For chickens were costly everywhere, even in Egypt, where they were hatched artificially. In Egypt during the first half of the fourteenth century, a good quality chicken cost two or three dirhams. A worker with a mimimum salary could therefore buy, with his entire monthly pay, twelve hens. But, after the great change in the economic situation of workers after the Black Death and the crisis in the early fifteenth century, such a worker could acquire more than twenty chickens with his monthly wages.[152] Let us mention that, according to a German traveler visiting Egypt at the end of the fifteenth century, itinerant cooks sold boiled chickens in the streets.[153] However, the rich were not satisfied with domesticated chickens; they also were fond of wild game, which was a common characteristic of the menu of the rich throughout the medieval Levant, although the ability to obtain such game was not universally equal. al-Djāḥiz mentioned partridges as a

---

[147]at-Tanūkhī, *Table-Talk*, pt. 1, p. 66.
[148]Frescobaldi, *Viaggio*, pp. 98 ff.
[149]See Rodinson, "Recherches," pp. 132 ff.
[150]al-Djāḥiz, *Kitāb al-Bukhalā*, p. 67.
[151]Ibn Kutaiba, *Kitāb 'Uyun al-akhbār*, 3:252.
[152]See our study, "L'évolution des prix," p. 19.
[153]Harff, *Pilgrimage*, p. 109.

dish for the rich;[154] they and other poultry were abundant in Syria[155] as well as in Egypt.[156]

By reading accounts by Arab authors about the meals of the caliphs and the feasts of other princes, especially the Egyptian rulers in the later period, we can picture the style of living and the luxurious eating habits of the higher levels of Levantine society.

Zayyat tells us that the caliph al-Mutawakkil, visiting the monastery of Ṣalība at Damascus, ate mutton prepared by his private cook.[157] Mutton was therefore the preferred meat, even for sovereigns. Let us also cite the account of one of the annual feasts given by al-Malik al-Muzaffar Kökbüri, prince of Irbil (1190–1232), on the occasion of the feast of Maulid. He prepared 100 baskets of sour dishes,[158] 5,000 roast sheep,[159] 10,000 chickens, 100,000 earthenware dishes (of other recipes), and 30,000 platters of sweets.[160] When Emir Ḳausūn married the daughter of the Egyptian sultan al-Malik an-Nāṣir Muḥammad in the year 1327, they slaughtered 5,000 sheep, 100 steers, 50 horses, and, if we are to believe the Arab chronicler, an innumerable quantity of chickens and geese. For the sweetened dishes, 11,000 loaves of sugar were required.[161] Then, on the occasion of the wedding of Ānūk, son of the same sultan, in the year 1332, more than 20,000 sheep, steers, horses, geese, and chickens were slaughtered, and 18,000 kintārs of sugar were used to prepare the sweetmeats (ḥalwā) and syrups.[162] In addition, let us refer to a passage from a report by the embassy headed by Domenico Trevisano, who was sent in 1512 by the doge of Venice to the sultan in Cairo. Here we learn that the sultan's court consumed 500 poultry a day, not to mention other meats.[163] The knights who made up the armies of the Moslem states also ate mutton, scorning beef. al-Makrīzī told how sultan Baibars ordered in 1262 that mutton be sent to a group of Tatars who had come from Syria to rejoin the Mameluke army.[164]

The food considered suitable for the upper level of society, and worthy of being offered to a distinguished European personnage, appears in the list of presents offered Domenico Trevisano by the governors of Alexan-

---

[154]al-Djāḥiẓ, Kitāb al-Bukhalā, p. 59.
[155]"Ein niederrheinischer Bericht," p. 79.
[156]Ludolph of Suchem, De itinere Terrae Sanctae, p. 61.
[157]Zayyat, "Le livre de cuisine," pp. 24 ff.
[158]"Farash ḳishlamish," see Dozy, Supplément, 2:252 ff; see "faras"; and see Radlov, Wörterbuch der türkischen Dialecte (St. Petersburg, n.d.), vol. 2, col. 837.
[159]"Ra's shawī."
[160]Sibṭ Ibn al-Djauzī, Mir'āt az-zamān, p. 451.
[161]al-Makrīzī, Sulūk, ed. Zaida, 2:288 ("ablūdja" = approximately a kintar of sugar).
[162]Ibid., 2:346.
[163]Schefer (ed.), Voyage de Jean Thenaud, p. 211.
[164]al-Makrīzī, Sulūk, ed. Zaida, 1:474.

dria and Rosetta: sheep, chickens and geese, rice, lemons, oranges, and sugar loaves.[165]

A popular tale dating from the Mameluke period, which has been published and edited by J. Finkel, gives a better idea of the nutrition of the various classes than do the tedious accounts found in chronicles and other sources. We are referring to a text entitled "*Kitāb al-Ḥarb al-ma'shūk baina laḥm aḍ-ḍa'n wa-ḥawāḍir as-sūk* (*The Book of the Pleasant War between the Sheep and the Refreshments of the Market*). King Mutton declares war against King Honey, who reigns over the fish, vegetables, fruits, and dairy products. As Finkel has shown, the two camps represent a class antagonism. The foods of the rich are fighting against those of the poor. Mutton is the food of the rich, and vegetables and fruits that of the poor. The scholar who published this text compared it with another folk tale from a later date, the *Hazz al kuhūf* written by ash-Shirbīnī in the seventeenth century, in which a character exclaims to the Egyptian people: "Why do I see you forgetting yellow rice seasoned with honey and turning away from peppered rice, almond cakes, fattened geese, and roasted chickens?"[166] According to the *Book of the Pleasant War*, and according to ash-Shirbīnī, mutton was therefore the most esteemed food.

But why did the author of the *Book of the Pleasant War* name honey as the king of the poor foods? Finkel believes that it was chosen instead of sugar because the latter is not mentioned in the Koran, or perhaps because it was a Sassanid theme.[167] This is going far afield for an explanation. Is not the choice of honey rather than sugar explained by the costliness of the latter?[168] Finkel deduces from the story that peasants ate only a little meat, but he believes this was out of necessity in a region with a hot climate, where they worked in the open air.[169] Once again we would prefer an economic explanation: the high cost of meat.

Not only was meat virtually reserved for the rich, but they could also drink good *wines*, which were beyond the means of the poor. The consumption of alcoholic beverages, which was forbidden by the religious laws of Islam, is a phenomenon which we must bear in mind when considering the consequences of diet upon the public health and upon the demographic evolution of the medieval Levant.

[165]Schefer (ed.), *Voyage de Jean Thenaud*, pp. 178 ff.
[166]J. Finkel, "King Mutton, a Curious Egyptian Tale from the Mamluk Period," *Zeitschrift für Semitistik und verwandte Gebiete* 8 (1932): 122–48:9 (1933–34):1–18. See also Rodinson, "Recherches," pp. 113 ff; and Brockelmann, *Geschichte der arabischen literatur*, vol. 1, pt. 2, p. 358.
[167]Finkel, "King Mutton," pp. 137 ff.
[168]See our study, "L'évolution des prix," pp. 32–33.
[169]Finkel, "King Mutton," p. 138.

The expansion of Islam, as we know, did not result in the decline of winegrowing in the Eastern countries. On the contrary, the varieties of vines cultivated became diversified and multiplied.[170] Grapes were grown in Iraq and in Upper Mesopotamia,[171] especially in the provinces of Syria and Palestine,[172] but also in Egypt. As far as the Nile region is concerned, it seems that winegrowing did not experience a decline during the period of the caliphs.[173] It goes without saying that grapes were not cultivated solely for table grapes and raisins. Bacchanalian songs—a literary genre used by such Arab poets as the famous Abū Nuwās (d. between 813 and 815)—are sufficient proof of this.

The common people had to be satisfied with the simplest drinks, ersatz brandies. The majority of the peasantry and workers drank a wine made of dates and honey.[174] The inhabitants of a number of coastal cities in Egypt drank "*keshkāb*," a drink made of barley which had been sprouted, dried, and milled, and then fermented with mint, rue, nigella, lemon leaves, and pepper.[175] Some intoxicating drinks harmed the health. They were, for example, blamed for an illness which was common among the women of the city of Tinnīs; during menstruation they would be seized by a sort of epileptic fit. This illness, which Arab physicians called "Tinnīs convulsions" (*al-fawāk at-tinnīsī*), was believed to have been caused by their habitual drinking.[176] We must therefore be cautious when reading about the sobriety of the Moslems[177] in accounts by certain European travelers, for they were foreigners, who were unable to understand the Moslems and who were writing on the basis of hearsay; moreover, other passages from the same travel books contradict such statements.

The upper levels of Levantine society did not abstain from wine. We can see this by leafing through the works of Arab authors who described the manner of living in the various countries of the medieval Levant.

The vizier of the Buyid prince of the mid-tenth century and other dignitaries were accustomed to drink;[178] the notables of Old Cairo would

---

[170]See Mez, *Die Renaissance des Islâms*, p. 406.

[171]Ibn Ḥaukal, *Opus geographicum*, p. 230; al-Muḳaddasī, p. 145.

[172]al-Muḳaddasī, pp. 162, 180, 181; Burcardus de Monte Sion, in *Reyssbuch*, fol. 456 a, 464 a; Ludolph of Suchem, *De itinere Terrae Sanctae*, p. 71; Sigoli, *Viaggio*, p. 148; Bertrandon de la Broquière, *Le Voyage d'Outremer*, ed. C. Schefer (Paris, 1892), p. 64; Schefer (ed.), *Voyage de Jean Thenaud*, p. 93.

[173]See Müller-Wodarg, "Die Landwirtschaft Aegyptens," pp. 48, 52.

[174]Al-Makrīzī, *Khitat*, 1:44.

[175]Nāṣir-i Khosrau, *Sefer nameh*, p. 110; see Dozy, *Supplément*, 2:472.

[176]Nāṣir-i Khosrau, *Sefer nameh*, see p. 114.

[177]"Ein niederrheinischer Bericht," p. 39; Felix Fabri, *Evagatorium*, ed. Hassler (Stuttgart, 1843–49), 3:100.

[178]at-Tanūkhī, *Table-Talk*, pt. 1, pp. 42, 77, 161; al-Tha'ālibī, *Yatīmat ad-dahr* (Damascus, n.d.), 2:8 ff.

become shamelessly drunk, according to al-Mukaddasī.[179] In addition, the caliphs themselves, representatives of the Prophet who had forbidden wine, would drink alcoholic beverages; according to information found in the works of Arab writers, almost no caliph can be considered an exception.[180] We must therefore not be astonished at learning that scholars throughout the Moslem countries did likewise,[181] as did judges, the guardians of the religious laws.[182] Almost all princes were heavy drinkers. The Ortokid Nadjm ad-dīn Ilghāzī, lord of Aleppo and of Māradīn (1108–22), drank so heavily that he was drunk for several days.[183] The valiant Zenkī was assassinated in 1146 after having fallen asleep following a drinking bout.[184] Nāṣir ad-dīn Muḥammad b. Shīrkūh, lord of Ḥimṣ and uncle of Saladin, died in 1185 after having drunk too much on the day of a great Moslem feast ('īd al-aḍḥā).[185] Saladin himself drank in his youth but later abstained from wine.[186] But his sons and his brothers drank.[187] A lord who did not drink was considered extremely virtuous.[188] In short, drunkenness was a widespread vice. Everyone kept wine at home.[189] Even when scarcity was at its peak in Damascus during a siege in 1246, people continued to drink.[190]

Several European travelers referred to drunkenness in the Levantine countries they visited. Symeon Semeonis told how the Moslems never drank in public, but in private, secretly, and in a disgusting fashion.[191] Jacopo da Verona, who traveled widely in the Near East during the same period, described how they drank both privately and publicly.[192] In the

---

[179]al-Mukaddasī, p. 200.

[180]al-Jāḥiẓ, Kitāb at-Tāj, ed. A. Zaki (1914), pp. 151 ff; at-Tanūkhī, Table-Talk, pt. 1, pp. 150, 154 ff, 157, 158, 159 ff; and Mez, Die Renaissance des Islâms, pp. 376–77.

[181]Nāṣir-ī Khosrau, Sefer nameh, p. 3.

[182]See the sources cited by Mez, Die Renaissance des Islâms, p. 377; for the period of the Crusades, see Ibn Kathīr, al-Bidāya wa'n-nihāya, 13:163.

[183]Usāmah, Ousâma Ibn Mounkidh, un émir syrien au premier siècle des croisades (1095–1188), ed. Derenbourg (Paris, 1886), p. 88; Sibṭ Ibn al-Djauzī, Mir' āt az-zamān, p. 32.

[184]Ibn al-Ḳalānisī, History of Damascus, ed. H. F. Amedroz (Beyrut, 1908), p. 284.

[185]Ibn Khallikān, Wafayāt al-a'yān (Cairo, 1299), 2:389; a similar case (an emir who died while drunk) is found in Abū Shāma, Dhail, p. 220.

[186]Abū Shāma, Kitāb ar-Raudatain, (Cairo, 1287), 1:160, 163; Ibn Khallikān, Wafayāt al-a'yān, 2:381.

[187]Sibṭ Ibn al-Djauzī, Mir' at az-zamān, pp. 230, 307; Abū Shāma, Kitāb, 2:229.

[188]Ibn al-Ḳalānisī, History of Damascus, p. 198; Abū Shāma, Dhail, p. 229.

[189]Usāmah, Ousâma Ibn Mounkidh, p. 108.

[190]Ibn Kathīr, al-Bidāya wa' n-nihāya, 13:167.

[191]Symeon Semeonis, Itineraria, p. 32: "Vinum quod est ibi carissimum, quia Saraceni perfecti numquam vinum bibunt, nec casu publice, sed private et in absconso etiam usque ad nauseam, cujus rei testes sumus."

[192]Jacopo da Verona, Liber peregrinationis, p. 104: "et tamen Saraceni bibunt vinum publice et occulte, et in hoc male servunt legem suam."

travel diary of a French ambassador sent to the Sultan in 1512, we read that Moslems "drink unrestrainedly as much as they can."[193]

The chief drinkers were the Jews and the Christians, for whom the sale of wine and the keeping of taverns was a good business.[194] In Iraq, the city of Sūra, in which the Jews constituted a large portion of the population, was known for its good wine.[195] Likewise, the Christian city of al-Ḥīra attracted drinkers, including the caliphs.[196] Monasteries were famous for their good wines, and the Moslems, beginning with the Umayyad caliphs, were very fond of spending time there. This phenomenon was common to every Levantine country.[197] But Moslems also kept taverns.[198]

The Islamic authorities often took steps to suppress taverns and to forbid the sale of wine by Christians and Jews. The prohibition promulgated by Caliph al-Ḥākim was not the first of such edicts.[199] Earlier, in 786–87, the governor of Egypt, 'Alī b. Sulaimān al-'Abbāsī[200] and, in 932–34, the Abbasid caliph al-Kāhir had taken identical steps,[201] as did the rulers of the late period on several occasions. Under the rule of the Fatimids, they were content merely to close taverns on the eve of the holy month of Radjab.[202] But the pious Nūrad-dīn (1146–73) and the Ayyubites, who displayed great zeal for Islamic orthodoxy, multiplied the prohibitions and ordered their police chiefs to prevent at any cost the sale of alcoholic beverages and to pour out upon the earth the wine which was found in the possession of Jews and Christians. On this subject we could cite numerous passages from the chronicles of the period. However, after some time these prohibitions were repealed in order to collect taxes on the sale of alcoholic beverages. al-Malik al-Mu'aẓẓam, son of al-Malik al-'Ādil, did this, citing the need to finance the holy war.[203] The revocation of measures taken by Nūrad-dīn was spectacular. If we can believe the Arab chroniclers, the herald who proclaimed the repeal at Mosul carried a goblet in his hand.[204] On several occasions the Mameluke sultans

[193]Schefer (ed.), *Voyage de Jean Thenaud*, p. 47.

[194]Ibn Kathīr, *al-Bidāya wa' n-nihāya*, 14:301; see Fabri, *Evagatorium*, 3:21.

[195]Yāḳūt, *Mu'djam al-buldān*, 3:184–85.

[196]al-'Umarī, *Masālik al-abṣār* (Cairo, 1924), 1:321–22, 389 ff.

[197]ash-Shābushtī, *Kitāb ad-Diyārāt*, pp. 18, 19, 21, 27, 102, 107. See also H. Zayyat's articles on the various monasteries in Syria and Egypt, *al-Machrique* 35 (1937):23; 36:47, 50; and especially a chapter entitled "Le vin chrétien," in his work, "Les couvents chrétiens en terre d'Islam" (in Arabic), *al-Machrique* 36:322 ff; and pp. 328 ff, 330 ff. See also his article, "Kitāb ad-Diyārāt d'al-'Umarī," *al-Machrique* 42:296.

[198]See al-Maḳrīzī, *Sulūk*, ed. Zaida, 2:492.

[199]Nāṣir-ī Khosrau, *Sefer nahmeh*, p. 130.

[200]al-Kindī, *The Governors and Judges of Egypt* [*Kitāb al-Wulāt*], ed. Guest (1912), p. 131; al-Maḳrīzī, *Khiṭat*, 1:308.

[201]Ibn Taghrībirdī, *an-Nudjūm az-zāhira*, ed. Juynboll (Leyden, 1851–55), 2:254.

[202]al-Maḳrīzī, *Khiṭat*, 1:491.

[203]Sibṭ Ibn al-Djauzī, *Mir' āt az-zamān*, p. 392.

[204]Ibid., p. 205; Abū Shāma, *Kitāb*, 2:232; Ibn Kathīr, *al-Bidāya wa' n-nihāya*, 12:285.

promulgated prohibitions against drinking wine and took measures to prevent their subjects from disobeying them.[205]

The military men were especially heavy drinkers. Arab chroniclers referred to drinking bouts in the army camps of the Fatimids,[206] in those of the army of the Zengite princes of Mosul,[207] and in the armies of the Ayyubid princes in Syria[208] and elsewhere.[209]

The guidebooks of European travelers contain curious tales of orgies by the Mamelukes, those foreign soldiers who made up the ruling class in Egypt and Syria in the late period; able to pay for costly wines, they did what was necessary to obtain them.

The German Dominican Felix Fabri mentioned that the Mamelukes would come to visit the pilgrims with whom he was traveling in order to drink wine.[210] The guidebook of the German traveler Arnold von Harff, who came to Egypt at the end of the fifteenth century, contains an account of his encounter with two Mamelukes of German origin who invited him into their homes to drink wine secretly. They also accompanied him to the homes of native Jews and Christians with the same end in mind.[211] In another passage of his travel account, Arnold von Harff observed that the Moslems did not drink wine, although many did so secretly with the Mamelukes and the Jews. "Since taverns cannot be kept openly, on penalty of death, the Mamelukes secretly import great quantities from Crete in little barrels, covered with linen clothing."[212] Finally, in the travel account of Jean Thenaud, to which we have already referred several times, we read that the governor of Jerusalem liked monks "because when he wishes to drink wine they give it to him."[213]

A passage from an Arab chronicle indicates that even Mameluke women drank.[214]

* * *

[205]Abū Shāma, *Dhail*, p. 150; Ibn Kathīr, *al-Bidāya wa' n-nihāya*, 13:115; 14:317; al-Makrīzī, *Sulūk*, ed. Zaida, 1:578, 595; 2:52, 211, 250; Adh-Dhahabī, *Duwal al-islām* (Haidarabad, 1337), 2:132; and ʻAbdallāh b. Asʻad al-Yāfiʻī, *Mir'at az-zamān wa-ʻibrat al-yakzān* (Haidarabad, 1337–39), 4:167. See also the sources cited in our *Histoire des Juifs en Egypte et en Syrie sous la domination des Mamlouks* (in Hebrew), 2:67, 71.

[206]Ibn al-Kalānisī, *History of Damascus*, p. 54.

[207]Sibṭ Ibn al-Djauzī, *Mir'āt az-zamān*, p. 211.

[208]Kamāl ad-dīn, *Histoire d'Alep*, trans. Blochet, *Revue de l'Orient latin*, 4:217; and Ibn Kathīr, *al-Bidāya wa'n-nihāya*, 13:164.

[209]Abū Shāma, *Kitāb*, 2:38.

[210]Fabri, *Evagatorium*, 3:35.

[211]Harff, *Pilgrimage*, p. 102.

[212]Ibid., pp. 118 ff.

[213]Schefer (ed.), *Voyage de Jean Thenaud*, p. 86.

[214]al-Djazarī, *La chronique de Damas d'al Jazari, années 689–698*, trans. Sauvaget (Paris, 1949), p. 48.

In order to make a better evaluation of the nutritional possibilities of
the various classes of the Levantine population in the Middle Ages, it
would be very useful to attempt a comparison with the situation of similar
classes in the West. We can only use samplings, relying on disparate
information; and the results will be presented as mere conjecture.

There is one dominant characteristic of medieval nutrition: this is the
disappearance of pork from the diet of the majority of Levantines. In this
connection the expansion of Islam changed customs which had existed
for millennia. Archaeological research has shown that since the prehistoric period the pig had been a major element of the diet of the peoples of
the eastern Mediterranean. Pork was also eaten in the Aegean Islands,
though to a lesser degree than mutton.[215] In ancient Babylonia very little
pork was eaten,[216] and it seems that in Egypt it was also in disfavor during
certain periods.[217] But the Greeks and Romans were especially fond of
pork[218] and imposed their taste upon the peoples subjected to their
influence. Because Islamization progressed slowly—in Egypt, for example, Christians were not reduced to their current percentage of the
population until the fourteenth century—this reversal continued over
many centuries. On the other hand, the changes in the diet of the lower
classes, which occurred in the West during the later period of our study,
were more rapid. These changes were even more spectacular since they
resulted not only from an upset of economic conditions, but also from
new agricultural systems. Until the end of the Middle Ages, barley was the
predominant cereal in the regions surrounding the western Mediterranean; and in the Byzantine Empire as well, the workers ate barley
bread.[219] Then, after the Black Death, wheat took its place. An economic
historian who undertook a detailed study of the agrarian conditions in
Languedoc has observed that at the end of the fifteenth century all tithes
were paid in pure wheat. At the end of the fourteenth century one-third
had been paid in wheat, one-third in barley, and one-third in a mixture of
the two grains.[220]

But to claim that a certain sort of bread served as the main food in
Western countries for long periods would be to oversimplify. For

---

[215]K. F. Vickery, *Food in Early Greece*, Illinois Studies in the Social Sciences, vol. 20,
no. 3 (Urbana, 1936), pp. 61, 65.

[216]Meissner, *Babylonien und Assyrien*, 1:416.

[217]Ruffer, *Food in Egypt*, pp. 21–22.

[218]Orth, "Kochkunst," vol. 2, cols. 945–46, 949–50, 958, 962 ff, 971, 975; see also
J. André, *L'alimentation et la cuisine à Rome* (Paris, 1961), pp. 136, 139, 142.

[219]L. Bréhier, *Le monde byzantin* (Paris, 1950), vol. 3, *La civilisation byzantine*, p. 58;
see also P. Koukoulès, βυζαντίνων βιὸς χαί πολιτσμος (Athens, 1952), V, p. 12 ff.

[220]Emmanuel Le Roy Ladurie, *Les paysans du Languedoc* (Paris, 1966), p. 181.

nutrition was characterized there by a great variety of breads. We find references to *"faiti"* or *"de brode"* bread, which were the most common and which were always made with a mixture of grains; *"bourgeois,"* "dutch-oven," and *"bisblanc"* bread (whole-wheat, white bread), which were household breads; *"primor"* bread, made with top-quality flour; servant bread; chapter bread (for canons); etc.[221] The vast majority of the population ate a mixed rye and wheat bread, only the rich being able to afford white bread. Indeed, physicians, influenced by books translated from the Arabic, always recommended white bread,[222] but the majority of people could not buy that sort of bread. A journal of a well-to-do Venetian family, dating from the first half of the fourteenth century, informs us that white bread was only bought in the event of sickness.[223] For the inhabitants of rural Italian regions, white bread was, during this period, a very rare food.[224] In France, a great variety of breads was to be found. For example, we find in the *Journal of a Bourgeois of Paris* that, during a period of inflation, in 1419, the authorities ordered each baker "to make good white bread, bourgeois bread, and bread made with all its bran."[225] At the end of the fifteenth and beginning of the sixteenth century the nobles of the south of France ate "homemade" bread and, when giving a feast, would buy a small quantity of "bakery bread."[226] In England, where barley bread was not eaten as in France, bread baked of "mystelon," a mixture of wheat and rye, was the most common sort. Even the high nobility ate it.[227] By studying the daily expenditures of a noble household, we can see that bread still played a dominant role in the total diet. That can also be seen by thumbing through the *Northumberland Household Book*, which detailed the way of life in the castles of a great English noble of the early sixteenth century.[228] For the role of bread in the diet of the middle classes of medieval Europe, we must cite a calculation made by A. Fanfani on the basis of the account books of the Peruzzi, an important middle-class Florentine family. He has calculated that during

[221]A. Gottschalk, *Histoire de l'alimentation et de la gastronomie depuis la préhistoire jusqu'à nos jours* (Paris, 1948), pp. 289 ff.

[222]See Symphorien Champier, *Rosa Gallica* (Paris, 1518), fols. 34 ff.

[223]G. Luzzatto, "Il costo della vita a Venezia nel Trecento," *Ateneo Veneto* 125 (1934):217.

[224]E. Fiume, "Economia e vita privata dei Fiorentini nelle rilevazioni statistiche di Giovanni Villani," *Archivio Storico Italiano* 111 (1953):212.

[225]*Journal d'un bourgeois de Paris, 1405-1449* (Paris, 1881), p. 122.

[226]Georges de Manteyer, *Le livre-journal tenu par Fazy de Rame en langage embrunais* (Gap, 1932), 1:47.

[227]See *Manners and Household Expenses of England in the Thirteenth and Fifteenth Centuries* (London, 1841), p. xxvi.

[228]G. G. Coulton, *Medieval Panorama* (London, 1961), 1:356.

one year, 1314–15, the Peruzzi spent £580 for eighty-two moggia of grain, and £65 12 s. for thirty-four centinaia of meat.[229]

In order to establish the role played by the chief foods in the diet of various Western countries and to obtain the amount consumed, we must use various sources.

Let us begin with a document from Marseilles dated 1248; it is a contract establishing an apprenticeship, drawn up between Jean St-Maximin and Jean Cordier, moneychanger. The former placed his son, Guillaumet Deodat, as an apprentice with the moneychanger for two years and assumed the obligation to dress his son and, for his nourishment, to supply fourteen émines of good wheat and fifty sous of mixed money.[230] Since the quantity of wheat indicated was for two years, we can work out a daily ration of approximately a kilogram of bread.[231] According to other documents from fourteenth-century Marseilles, the owner of a merchant vessel had to give a sailor thirty-six ounces of bread a day,[232] which equals 760 grams. Moreover, it has been established that a middle-class family in the French province of Béarn in the 1580s ate a kilogram of bread per person per day.[233] According to the indications of a contemporary chronicler, a smaller amount of bread was calculated for the daily consumption of Florentines in the mid-fourteenth century, that is, about two pounds or 680 grams.[234] Each member of a middle-class Venetian family of the same period ate about a kilogram of bread a day. Two loaves of ten ounces each were provided as the daily ration for prisoners in the city of Perugia in the years 1312–14. This ration was therefore about 563 grams.[235] Information available about the bread rations for soldiers in various European countries agrees with the texts

[229]A. Fanfani, "Note sull'economia domestica dei Peruzzi e dei loro compagni," *Rivista Internazionale di Scienze Sociali*, series 3, a. 43 (1935), p. 95 (subsequently in Carlo M. Cipolla, *Storia dell'economia italiana* [Turin, 1959], 1:368). The work of a Polish historian brought slightly different results. The portion of the budget which peasants and servants in Poland had to spend in the mid-sixteenth century in order to buy bread and meat was less; see A. Wyczański, "The Social Structure of Nutrition, a Case," *Acta Poloniae Historica* 18 (1968):72, table 4. Meat was probably cheaper and, moreover, a great portion of the income was spent on beer.
[230]L. Blancard, *Documents inédits sur le commerce de Marseille au Moyen Age* (Marseille, 1884–85), 2:155.
[231]Calculating that the "émine" equalled 38.5 liters, and assuming that wheat in that day made approximately the same amount of bread.
[232]R. Pernoud, *Histoire du commerce de Marseille*, 1:261.
[233]Le Roy Ladurie, *Les paysans du Languedoc*, p. 269. The 1.15 kilograms calculated as the daily rations for a worker in Narbonne (560 liters of wheat per year, p. 267) represent a maximum quantity, that is to say the amount for a family, should the worker be married.
[234]Fiume, "Economia e vita privata dei Fiorentini," p. 208.
[235]Luzzatto, "Il costo della vita a Venezia," p. 217; G. Mira, "Il fabbisogno di cereali in Perugia nei secoli XIII–XIV," *Studi in onore di Armando Sapori* (Milan, 1957), 1:509.

already cited. When Marino Sanuto Torsello wrote of his plans for a new crusade, in the first decade of the fourteenth century, he proposed that each man be given one to one and a half pounds of biscuit per day.[236] Since this Venetian author was computing in the "heavy" pounds of his city, this would make 715 grams. The rations of the English navy in 1565 were smaller; the daily supply of bread was only 454 grams.[237] In the mid-sixteenth century Polish peasants and persons living in castles ate much more. According to documents from the prefecture of Sieradz, in western Poland, the bread rations of a peasant were 0.94 kilograms per day, and those of a high-ranking civil servant were 1.24 kilograms.[238] From all this data we can calculate that the middle classes in Western countries ate about a kilogram of bread a day, soldiers and sailors ate 700–750 grams, and persons belonging to the lower classes of the urban population ate even less.[239] In any event, bread, as compared with meat, played a much greater role in the diet than in our day.

Though conditions in this respect were equal in the West and in the East, the quality of the bread eaten in many European countries, as we have seen, was inferior. In many Western countries even city dwellers whose pay was higher than the minimum salary continued to eat barley bread. F. Braudel has shown that white bread only won out in Central Europe between 1750 and 1850. Until that period it was a rarity.[240] Although barley bread supplies as many calories as wheat bread, it is doughy and indigestible.

As for the consumption of meat in the Christian countries, we can see that the lower classes ate very little. Neither in Byzantium[241] nor in Western Europe could the poor pay for the meat rations which would have supplied them with the amounts of protein and fats necessary for their health. On the basis of the facts supplied by the chronicler Villani, it has been possible to calculate the amount of meat eaten in Florence (all

---

[236]*Liber secretorum fidelium crucis*, in Bongars, *Gesta Dei per Francos* (Hanover, 1611), pt. 2, p. 64. This text was studied by F. C. Lane, "Salaires et régimes alimentaires des marins au début du XIVe siècle," *Annales: E.S.C.*, 1963, pp. 133 ff.

[237]C. S. L. Davies, "Les rations alimentaires de l'armée et de la marine anglaises au XVIe siècle," *Annales: E.S.C.*, 1963, pp. 139 ff (based on M. Oppenheim, *A History of the Administration of the Royal Navy, 1509-1660* [Hamden, Conn., 1961], p. 140).

[238]Wyczański, "The Social Structure of Nutrition," p. 67.

[239]We should like to point out that in Ancient Egypt soldiers and royal messengers already received approximately 4 pounds of bread daily; see Breasted, *Ancient Records of Egypt* (New York, 1962), 2, no. 207; 3, no. 208.

[240]Braudel, *Civilisation matérielle et capitalisme*, 1:105–6.

[241]G. Walter, *La vie quotidienne à Byzance au siècle des Comnènes (1081-1180)* (Paris, 1966), p. 181. The same observation has been made on the basis of the available information about the diet of the Ancient Near East, see Meissner, *Babylonien und Assyrien* pp. 413, 416; and A. Bertholet, *Histoire de la civilisation d'Israël* (Paris, 1929), pp. 202–3.

categories, with the exception of poultry) in the first half of the fourteenth century: 37.8 kilograms a year, or 103 grams a day.[242] In another merchant city, Sienna, the consumption of this food item was approximately the same: 40 kilograms.[243] But in a small city such as Volterra in 1334–35, it was only 11 kilograms per person per year.[244] The Venetian Marino Sanuto planned to give future crusaders 1.9/30 ounces of salt pork per day, that is to say only 52 grams. In the French province of Languedoc at the end of the fifteenth century, agricultural workers could buy with their "*compagnage*" 39.5 kilograms of mutton,[245] which is 108 grams a day. This quantity was calculated for a worker: if need be, he would have to share it with his wife and children. Now, we must not forget that the situation of workers was better, much better, at that time than before the Black Death. A century later a worker in Languedoc earned only 18.2 kilograms of meat. Yet it is true that the French soldiers of the same period received 77 kilograms, or 219 grams, a day,[246] and that the sailors of the English navy even got 518 grams a day.[247] Moreover, Spanish sailors in 1599 received 3,884 calories a day from foods composed of 84.46 percent biscuit and 6.99 percent dried beans and chick peas. The chemical composition of this diet would be 12.58 percent protein, 21.76 percent fats, and 65.66 percent carbohydrates.[248] Although the proportions of carbohydrates and proteins were similar to that of Egyptian workers earning a minimum salary before the Black Death, the caloric intake was twice or even three times greater and the quantity of fats was also much higher. Bread rations always remained very moderate. In England the diet of the poor classes, especially of the peasantry, included only small amounts of meat. English nobles gave their serfs working on the *corvée* herrings, beer, and bread made of barley, wheat, and oats. The peasants ate meat only when the lord gave a feast or on other very rare occasions.[249] That changed, however, during the period following the Black Death. We can also see that the domestic servants of nobles benefitted from a better diet, especially in regard to meat. The quantities of meat eaten by workers and artisans in English cities was clearly greater than that of the peasantry, and was very varied; they ate

[242]Fiume, "Economia e vita privata dei Fiorentini," p. 221.
[243]C. Falletti-Fossati, *Costumi senesi nella seconda metà del secolo XIV* (Siena, 1881), pp. 14, 23, 24.
[244]Fiume, "Economia et vita privata dei Fiorentini," p. 223.
[245]Le Roy Ladurie, *Les paysans du Languedoc*, p. 265.
[246]Ibid., p. 267.
[247]C. S. L. Davies, "Les rations alimentaires," pp. 139 ff.
[248]V. F. Spooner, "Régimes alimentaires d'autrefois," *Annales: E.S.C.*, 1962, pp. 93-94.
[249]J. C. Drummond and A. Wilbraham, *The Englishman's Food, A History of Five Centuries of English Diet* (London, 1939), p. 51.

mutton, veal, pork, various sorts of poultry, etc.[250] The amount of meat eaten in western Polish villages in the district of Sieradz, in the mid-sixteenth century, varied between 38 and 68 grams a day, while persons living in the castles received 284 grams. To these rations we must add ham, from 26 to 80 grams on the table of a high-ranking civil servant.[251]

The rations of meat eaten by the middle class of Italian cities also included beef, poultry, and other sorts of meat.[252] Judging by the indications supplied by Villani, the chronicler, much more pork than mutton was eaten in Florence. And the amounts of beef (and veal) eaten there were more sizable than the amounts of mutton and kid.[253] In short, beef was by no means despised as it was in the Arab Levant. We can make the same deduction when studying the *Ménagier de Paris*. There we find numerous recipes for beef (and salted beef) and veal, as well as mutton and venison.[254] The *Journal of a Bourgeois of Paris* shows that the inhabitants of the French capital ate various sorts of meat: beef, veal, mutton, and pork.[255] In the *Ménagier de Paris* we also find precious estimates of the animals slaughtered each week in Paris. The author wrote that each week 3,080 sheep, 514 steers, 306 calves, and 600 pigs were sold.[256] Indications found in fifteenth-century texts corroborate these indications concerning the proportions of the various sorts of meat eaten in Paris.[257] Even the meats eaten at the table of a princely house such as that of Eleanor, countess of Leicester (in 1265), were extremely varied. They included beef, mutton, veal, pork, venison, and chicken.[258]

Two characteristics of Western diet in the Middle Ages are the scarcity of proteins as far as the food of the lower classes is concerned, and a greater variety in the principal foods of the comfortable classes. The same fact, that is, the varied composition of meat, was observed in a study of the foods eaten in castles and villages of western Poland in the mid-sixteenth century.[259]

By making a few more observations about the other foods eaten, we will be able to complement the statistical tables concerning the consumption of bread and meat.

---

[250] Ibid., pp. 56, 59 ff.
[251] A. Wyczański, "The Social Structure of Nutrition," p. 70.
[252] Luzzatto, "Il costo della vita a Venezia," pp. 218, 223.
[253] Fiume, "Economia e vita privata dei Fiorentini," p. 221.
[254] *Le Ménagier de Paris* (Paris, 1846), 2:130 ff, 133, 177, 185 ff.
[255] Ibid., pp. 83, 86, 120, 124, 131, 135, 138, 149.
[256] Ibid., p. 84; see p. 80.
[257] Gottschalk, *Histoire de l'alimentation*, p. 299.
[258] *Manners and Household Expenses of England*, p. xlvi.
[259] Wyczański, "The Social Structure of Nutrition," p. 69.

Sugar long remained very expensive in southern Europe. Imported either from Sicily or Spain, its price was very high in Italy and in Provence.[260] Only the rich could buy this item. Indeed, it was chiefly used in medicines. For many homes olive oil was replaced by other sorts of oil, for example walnut oil and hempseed oil.[261]

The diet of the lower classes lacked certain foods. But since, in most European countries—until the period following the Black Death—meat was cheaper than in the East, there is perhaps reason to modify the results of our sample, which makes no claims of reaching a true comparison. Indeed, it is highly probable that in the Levant a greater proportion of the budget of the urban working class was allocated for bread than we have supposed. The consumption of great quantities of bread, which is indicated by several sources dealing with southern and western Europe, corroborates this hypothesis.[262] Before the great change brought about by the Black Death, it is possible that workers and peasants in the West ate more meat than their Eastern counterparts. Whatever the case may be, the diet of the lower classes in the Levantine world was extremely precarious until the period following the Black Death. On the basis of the calculations of Marino Sanuto Torsello, F. C. Lane has shown what one well-fed category of workers received in Italy after the Black Death. He established that sailors participating in the Crusade planned by Marino Sanuto must have received 3,915 calories a day and 114.4 grams of protein.[263] Moreover, Marino Sanuto himself said that he was basing his calculations upon the rations distributed at that time on board Venetian vessels. In order to indicate the nutritive value of the foods which the majority of Levantines could buy in the Middle Ages, we will compare them with the detailed research carried out by A. Wyczański on the diet of the inhabitants of the fiefs in one region of western Poland in the mid-sixteenth century. In 1542, persons apparently living as simple peasants in the district of Sieradz ate 4,276 calories a day, while the inhabitants of castles ate 4,363 and civil servants received 5,794.[264]

We are including for the sake of comparison a small table indicating the daily consumption in several regions of the world in 1954–57.[265]

[260]E. Rossi and F. M. Arcari, "I prezzi a Genova dal XII al XV secolo," *Vita economica Italiana*, series 3, year 8 (1933), p. 76; E. Baratier, *Histoire du commerce de Marseille*, 2:439, 541; see also our studies, "L'évolution des prix," p. 32, and "Le coût de la vie dans l'Egypte médiévale," *Journal of the Economic and Social History of the Orient* 3 (1960):459–60.

[261]*Journal d'un bourgeois de Paris*, pp. 122, 342.

[262]On the eve of the modern period, the workers of Central Europe spent approximately half their income on bread. See Braudel, *Civilisation matérielle et capitalisme*, 1:99 (bread rations of Parisians, and graph C).

[263]Lane, "Salaires et régimes alimentaires," p. 137.

[264]Wyczański, "The Social Structure of Nutrition," p. 66.

[265]Based on the F.A.O., *Disponibilités alimentaires, Séries chronologiques*, 1960.

	CALORIES	PROTEIN (grams)	FAT (grams)
Italy	2,550	79.9	66
France	2,890	95.3	103
United States	3,150	94.0	142
India	1,880	50.0	25

From this data we can deduce that until the end of the Middle Ages the quantity of protein and fats supplied to a Levantine worker with a minimum salary are comparable to the bread and meat rations of the Indians, inhabitants of an indisputably underdeveloped country. Although we must add to this a certain quantity of nutrients supplied by other foods (beans, etc.). there is no doubt that a great portion of the lower-class population in the Levant was undernourished. In like manner, the number of calories supplied by the diet of European workers and peasants did not exceed 2,000 until the nineteenth century.[266]

In any event, the most marked characteristic of the diet of these classes, and of similar classes in the West, was the imbalance between proteins and carbohydrates. This must have had a prejudicial influence on public health and must have contributed to a greater susceptibility to illness, especially during epidemics. Though both were undernourished, it would appear that the situation of the lower classes in Levantine society differed from that of similar classes in the West in two ways. First, in seeking demographic consequences, we must also take psychological factors into account. Now, the lower classes in the West were struggling against their adversaries, were demanding their rights. Where there is a struggle, there is hope. In the Levant, the superiority of the feudal military system was overwhelming, the middle class was weak and unorganized, and the oppression of the lower classes was complete. Second, there was a difference in climate. The lack of protein and the physiological vulnerability of the poor was much more dangerous in the hot countries of the Levant where epidemics spread more rapidly.

When the nutritive value of the goods which workers could buy increased after the Black Death, only a very limited number of workers appears to have profited, and successive epidemics prevented the increase of the population. As a result there is no contradiction between the improvement of the diet of workers and progressive depopulation. Another argument might also be made against our calculations. Since the workers had to spend such a large part of their income to buy bread and only a little remained for expenses other than food, how could they pay for rent and clothes? Now, the archives of the Jewish community of

[266]Braudel, *Civilisation matérielle et capitalisme*, 1:97.

Fostat include lists of the rent paid by the houses held in mortmain during the Crusades. These lists indicate that the rent on these houses was very low.[267] Workers were also probably very poorly clothed.

These thoughts are not based solely on a study of various medieval sources. There were at this time in the Near East perspicacious scholars who were sharp observers and who summarized in their works observations they had made over many years. The impressions of European travelers confirm these observations.

'Abdallaṭīf al-Baghdādī said that Egyptian children were thin, misshapen, and stunted.[268] He also referred to putrid and lymphatic illnesses which abounded among the inhabitants of the Nile region.[269] Lionardo Frescobaldi observed that the Egyptians were very faint-hearted.[270] To this we shall add a few observations made by travelers at later dates. Volney said that the wretched and rachitic appearance of the Egyptian children of Cairo should be attributed to the bad food. "Nowhere else do little creatures present such a distressing exterior. They perish in incredible numbers, and this city, more than any other capital, can boast of the deadly property of gobbling up the population."[271] A physician visiting Egypt with the [Napoleonic] Army of the Orient observed:

The most unhealthy group is the children, from the moment of their birth until the age of seven or eight; they are weak creatures, poorly developed, and almost always ill; their bellies are swollen, their faces thin and shrunken, the color of their skin over the entire body is yellowish, their limbs are underdeveloped; in a word, one might say that they are all doomed to a premature death; a great number die within that period of time.[272]

Another French physician who came to Egypt in the same period believed that smallpox and *"le carreau"* [*tabes mesenterica*, or chronic abdominal tuberculosis] carried off up to half the children before their fourteenth year.[273] Indeed, the *Necrological Table for Cairo* drawn up by the French indicates that in one year at the end of the eighteenth century children accounted for 11,824 of the total 21,012 deaths.[274]

[267]See our study, *Histoire des prix et des salaires*, pp. 193 ff.
[268]'Abdallaṭīf, *Relation*, p. 5.
[269]Ibid., p. 4.
[270]Frescobaldi, *Viaggio*, p. 96.
[271]C. F. Volney, *Voyage en Syrie et en Égypte pendant les années 1783, 1784, et 1785* (Paris, 1787), 1:223.
[272]"Notes pur servir à la topographie physique et médicale d'Alexandrie rédigées par le citoyen Salze," in R. Desgenettes, *Histoire médicale de l'armée d'Orient* (Paris, 1802), pt. 2, pp. 124 ff; see p. 20 on Menuf and p. 72 on Old Cairo.
[273]*Mémoire sur les fièvres pestilentielles et insidieuses du Levant*, p. 40; see de Sacy's notes to 'Abdallaṭīf, *Relation*, p. 9.
[274]*Mémoires sur l'Égypte* (Paris, year XI), 4:xxxvi.

Since the diet of the lower classes in Eastern countries did not change over many centuries, it would be helpful to use a study made by an Egyptian scholar concerning the diet of peasants and workers in present-day Egypt. He observes that bread, boiled beans,[275] *mesh* (a sort of very salty cheese), and *ṭūrshī* (a dish of various vegetables which are also salted) are the staples of the diet. They eat little meat, chiefly organs, feet, and by-products. They also eat old cheeses and cheap fish. These foods are very low in protein, or else the protein they contain is of inferior quality, as is the case with beans, which form the chief food of the peasants. They eat only durra bread.[276]

The accounts of Arab chroniclers and of travelers from various lands indicate that the observations of scholars of later periods are valid for the Middle Ages. Arab historians referring to plagues in the early Middle Ages and the period of the Crusades did not provide many details.[277] Chroniclers of the later period were more specific. They told how epidemics abounded, especially among children and foreigners who were not yet immune.[278] The number of victims of the epidemics and endemic illnesses was very high at the time of the Crusades and in the late Middle Ages.

Depopulation resulted from malnutrition. Several European voyagers journeying through the Levant during the later period of our study realized this. In addition to the inadequate diet, they also observed the psychological factors which played such a major role.

Walther of Guglingen told how the city of Alexandria was destroyed and desolated. Every day more houses fell into ruin, so that only half the city was inhabitable.[279] Arnold von Harff also referred to the many ruined houses in Alexandria.[280] But it was the Venetian, Domenico Trevisano, who provided the most eloquent testimony. Like other Europeans he chiefly talked of Alexandria, the first Eastern city with which Europeans generally became familiar:

---

[275]"Fūl mudammas," see Dozy, *Supplément*, 1:461.

[276]Ḥasan 'Abdassalām, *al-Aghdiya ash-sha'biy'a*, Silsilat Iḳra, no. 64 (Cairo, 1948), pp. 8, 63, 69, 72 ff.

[277]See the study by A. von Kremer, *Ueber die grossen Seuchen des Orients nach arabischen Quellen*, Sitzungberichte der philosophisch-historischen Klasse, Akademie der Wissenschaften, Berlin, vol. 96 (Vienna, 1880).

[278]Ibid., p. 67; see also D. Neustadt (Ayyalon), "The Plague and its Effects upon the Mamluk Army," *Journal of the Royal Asiatic Society of Great Britain and Ireland*, 1946, pp. 67 ff.

[279]Walther of Guglingen, *Fratris Pauli Waltheri Guglingensis Itinerarium in Terram Sanctam*, ed. M. Sollweck (Tübingen, 1892), p. 241.

[280]Harff, *Pilgrimage*, p. 93.

Nine-tenths are in ruins. Never has such decadence been seen. Such annihilation has as a cause the violence and extortions of the sovereigns, who tyrannize and rob their subjects to the point of forcing them to abandon their country and their homes; the houses lose their inhabitants and, in a short time, they collapse.[281]

As for Cairo, he observed that in two suburbs there were many places uninhabited and encumbered with ruins. "It is believed," he said, "that the population totals a million and a half souls, but there are not half that many, and the majority is composed of riff-raff and wretches."[282]

Just as malnutrition had unfortunate effects upon the demographic development of the lower classes of society, the manner in which the upper classes lived resulted in their decadence and eventual disappearance. For it is not only a question of food. It seems that foreign military personnel preserved their way of life unchanged; they dressed as they had in the northern countries, ate as they had on the steppes of Russia and Central Asia, and drank as one can in a cold climate. The Arab scholar Mustafa Zaida accurately pointed out that the consumption of horse meat at the court of the sultans in the fourteenth century indicates that the Mamelukes had kept their dietary habits of southern Russia, whence most of them came.[283] The German geographer W. Niemeyer quotes the journal of a traveler who observed, during a visit to Egypt in the late eighteenth century, that the Mameluke women, most of whom were also from Circassia and Georgia, kept their children shut up in the house, dressed them too warmly, and gave them food which was inappropriate for the Egyptian climate. Niemeyer credits this way of life for the reduced family size of the Mamelukes in this late period.[284] But there are grounds for making similar hypotheses for the classic Mameluke period, during the century following the Crusades. These rough warriors probably ate too much, especially too much meat. But there is no doubt that it was chiefly their drinking, documented by the European travel accounts we have cited, which played a determining role in the extinction of their caste. For, in the hot Egyptian climate, and in that of Syria, this behavior amounted to a veritable suicide on the part of the ruling class.

[281]Schefer (ed.), *Voyage de Jean Thenaud*, p. 173.
[282]Ibid., pp. 207 ff.
[283]Notes to his edition of the *Sulūk*, 2:288.
[284]W. Niemeyer, *Aegypten zur Zeit der Mameluken* (Berlin, 1936), p. 117.

6
Famine Amenorrhoea (Seventeenth-Twentieth Centuries)

Emmanuel Le Roy Ladurie

A s early as 1946, while studying the famines under Louis XIV, Jean Meuvret[1] discovered that the predictably high death rate was accompanied by a very drastic reduction in births. He was the first to offer a subtle diagnosis of this phenomenon and to point the way to a causal explanation; yet he stopped short of proposing it as a certainty. Going through the parish registers, and especially the records of baptism, Meuvret decided to argue, no longer in terms of births, but in terms of conceptions. To arrive at this basic information, he moved back all the dates of baptism by nine months, as would be logical, and was thus able to follow, month by month, the trend of the conceptions themselves. Immediately and forcefully a truth that had only been suspected came to light: At the very moment when grain prices peaked and when deaths from starvation and epidemics became more numerous, the number of conceptions also plunged. The diagram literally showed "the phenomenon as it was happening." The relationship between famine and sterility, which the gynecologists of two world wars had rightly or wrongly discerned, could be seen, through a clever graph, in the midst of a seventeenth-century food crisis. It now remained to explain how it

Annales: E.S.C., Nov.-Dec. 1969, pp. 1589-1601. Translated by Elborg Forster.
[1]J. Meuvret, "Les crises de subsistance et la démographie de la France d'Ancien Régime," Population, 1946, pp. 643-50. See also D. S. Thomas, Social and Economic Aspects of Swedish Population Movements, 1750-1933 (New York, 1941).

came about. Why was it that married, normally fertile women suddenly became barren during the worst weeks or months of hunger?

Eight years later, Pierre Goubert[2] also asked questions of this kind; he was studying, in the documents of the Beauvaisis, the enormous dearth of 1693–94, characterizing it as a horrendous massacre. Goubert noted that the number of births dropped (down 62 percent in six of the parishes) when the cycle of prices and deaths was at its peak. Invoking a text of Genesis, he originally explained this mysterious shutdown of the wombs as birth control by catastrophe.

Meanwhile, a number of competing explanations were proposed by other scholars. Joseph Ruwet, who also studied the famine of 1693–94 at Liège, found there, as he had expected, a terrific drop in conceptions.[3] Without ruling out the hypothesis of straightforward, voluntary limitation of births, he also proposed that the following factors caused a temporary halt in the birth rate in times of crisis: sexual abstinence due to ascetic foresight or lack of desire, a temporary reduction in the number of marriages, and finally, the likelihood of an increase in premature, spontaneous abortions, brought about by the poor health of pregnant women beset by hunger, infections, and epidemics. In this context, Ruwet also pointed out that the events of 1694 might have been similar to those occurring in the Netherlands during the famine of 1944–45. During these two years more than half of the fertile women in the Dutch cities were struck by temporary amenorrhoea (cessation of menstruation, attended by sterility). If this was true for 1944, Ruwet declared, was it not also true, *mutatis mutandis*, for 1693 or 1661?

This argument, his own research, and the progress of historical demography finally caused Goubert in 1960 to revise his initial position. The research of Louis Henry, especially, had shown that birth control was practiced much less among the lower classes of the seventeenth and eighteenth century than historians had assumed.[4] In 1960, Goubert therefore rejected in one fell swoop his former interpretation that contraception and will power were responsible for the drop in the birth

---

[2]P. Goubert, "Une richesse historique: les registres paroissiaux," *Annales: E.S.C.*, 1954, p. 92.

[3]J. Ruwet, "Crises démographiques: problèmes économiques ou crises morales, le pays de Liège sous l'Ancien Régime," *Population*, 1954, pp. 451–76.

[4]Etienne Gautier and Louis Henry, "La population de Crulai, paroisse normande," *Travaux et documents de l'I.N.E.D.* (Paris, 1958). In the large and small towns, however, the "dread secrets" of contraception became known in the eighteenth century, expecially after 1750. See in particular the studies by A. Chamoux and C. Dauphin on Châtillon-sur-Seine (*Annales: E.S.C.*, 1969, pp. 662–84); by M. Lachiver on Meulan (E.P.H.E., 1969); by El Kordi on Bayeux; by the students of P. Goubert on Argenteuil; and, of course, the demonstration by Louis Henry, "Anciennes familles genèvoises. Etude démographique," *Travaux et documents de l'I.N.E.D.* (Paris, 1956).

rate in periods of famine. Possibly overstating his thinking slightly, he wrote: "The more one comes to know the peasants of the Beauvaisis of the seventeenth century, as well as some others, the less one sees them capable of practicing very often the most elementary birth control, even in times of crisis."[5] Having taken this position, it follows logically that the author of the *Beauvaisis* henceforth gives first priority, among the possible explanations, to famine amenorrhoea as an important (though not exclusive) cause of temporary sterility. In this context he recalls that in 1778 Moheau spoke, as if it were understood, of the "failure of reproduction, which suffering and exhausted creatures cannot achieve."[6]

Finally, the same historian judiciously mentions the matter of documentary evidence: "We can only hope," he writes, "that some old memoir by a physician will tell us . . . about the phenomena of amenorrhoea in times of famine."[7]

The problems thus brought to the attention of researchers almost ten years ago have not, since then, received any striking or coherent response or solution. Without venturing onto the technical terrain of medical history[8] for which I do not feel qualified, being a historian interested in regressive history,* I would simply like to make an indirect contribution to the understanding of food crises in the past by reopening the dossier of famine amenorrhoea. And, indeed, this dossier is much more substantial than the few allusions, by now well known, to the above events of the Dutch famine would lead us to believe.

By way of a conclusion, I shall endeavor to widen the discussion, and I might also try to answer the precise question asked by Pierre Goubert concerning possible testimony by physicians of the seventeenth and eighteenth centuries.

The first systematic observations concerning the so-called famine or war amenorrhoea (*Kriegsamenorrhoe*)[9] were made by a Polish physician.

[5] Pierre Goubert, *Beauvais et le Beauvaisis* (Paris, 1960), pp. 49–50.
[6] Moheau, *Recherches et considérations sur la population de France* (1778), quoted by Goubert, *Beauvais et le Beauvaisis*, p. 50.
[7] Ibid.
[8] For the medical information, the reader is referred to A. Netter, *Comment soigner les aménorrhées* (Paris, 1955), p. 61; and to the work by the same author in collaboration with P. Lumbrose, *Aménorrhées, dysménorrhées*, Le Précis du Practicien (Paris: Baillière, 1962), p. 58 and passim. Here denutrition amenorrhoea is defined as one of the various *secondary* amenorrhoeas. See also the recent article, "Les aménorrhées non ménopausiques," in *Les Assises de Medecine*, vol. 23, year 26, no. 2 (May 1968), especially p. 102.
Translator's note: "Regressive history" draws inferences from the present for the past.
[9] J. v. Jaworski, "Mangelhafte Ernährung als Ursache von Sexualstörungen bei Frauen," *Wiener Klinische Wochenschrift*, Aug. 1916, no. 24, pp. 1068 ff. It should be noted that even in peacetime (1898), mention was still made of the negative influence of bad harvests and high grain prices on the number of births in the poor, backward regions of Polish Galicia, even though such a correlation, which had characterized the cereal situation of the Old

In August 1916, J. von Jaworski, gynecologist at Saint Roch's hospital in Warsaw, discovered among very poor patients who came to his clinic an unusual frequency of cases of amenorrhoea (cessation of menstruation), accompanied, except in a few cases, by temporary sterility.[10] He believed he could explain these facts by the increasingly serious food shortage in the central European countries owing to the war. In 1916 the proletariat of Warsaw ate so poorly that many women and girls, close to starvation, were at the same time suffering from an unusual failure to menstruate. Hence the name of starvation amenorrhoea, which is sometimes used to characterize these phenomena.

This being a new discovery, Jaworski reported the one hundred initial cases of amenorrhoea he had diagnosed in the *Wiener Klinische Wochenschrift*. Very quickly, analagous occurrences were reported from almost everywhere. German physicians were consulted by many young women who were either frightened or delighted because they imagined they were pregnant.[11] Upon examination they were amazed to learn that they were only amenorrhoeic. In Vienna, the "epidemic" diagnosed in the welfare clinics began in October 1916. In Hamburg the first cases were reported on October 2; in Freiburg, in November. All the large cities of the German Empire—Berlin, Cologne, Kiel, etc.—were affected. Only the region of Tübingen seems to have been spared. The phenomenon reached its peak in the spring of 1917 in March and April.[12] These cases of amenorrhoea were generally of rather short duration: two or three months, sometimes six months. In certain particularly fragile women (like the inmates of a clinic for epileptics in Berlin, whose food was strictly rationed) menstruation stopped for much longer, that is, for two years on the average. Various symptoms, among them, of course, sterility, accompanied these episodes.

From the very beginning the gynecologists, led by Jaworski, blamed poor nutrition for this phenomenon. In Hamburg, Spaeth noted that the great wave of menstrual disturbances came immediately after the begin-

---

Regime, had disappeared in the developed regions of Europe. ("In Galicia, after the very bad harvest of 1897, the number of marriages declined by 3,506, while the number of births declined by 45,438," according to Buzek, "Der Einfluss der Ernten, resp. der Getreidepreise auf die Bevölkerungsbewegung in Galicien, 1878–1898," *Statistische Monatsschrift*, 1901, quoted by Julius Wolf, *Der Geburtenrückgang* [Jena: G. Fischer, 1912], pp. 124–25.)

[10]For these phenomena, for the accompanying biological syndrome, and for the few exceptional cases, see "Les aménorrhées non ménopausiques," pp. 101–2.

[11]A. Giesecke, "Zur Kriegsamenorrhöe," *Zentralblatt für Gynäkologie*, 1917, no. 2, pp. 865–73; and E. Czerwenka, "Über Kriegsamenorrhöe," *Zentralblatt für Gynäkologie* 2 (1917): 1162–65.

[12]Ibid. See also F. Spaeth, "Zur Frage der Kriegsamenorrhöe," *Zentralblatt für Gynäkologie* 2, (1917): 664–68; and C. Kurtz, "Alimentäre Amenorrhöe," *Monatsschrift für Geburtshilfe und Gynäkologie*, 1920, pp. 367–78.

ning of meat rationing and the steep rise in the price of all foodstuffs. "Eggs cannot be found. . . . potatoes are replaced with rutabagas." The women were upset by this denutrition. "No physician who has eyes to see will deny it." Elsewhere the lack of bread, flour, fat, or meat was designated as the cause. Besides, the women suffering from this strange affliction were usually cured by removing its cause, that is, by giving them, if at all possible, a more nutritious diet. "Fortunately for the future of the Fatherland, everything returns to normal as soon as the food is improved," wrote Giesecke, one of the physicians who wished to see a rise in the birth rate and prescribed milk, eggs, and fresh vegetables for his patients. In Schleswig-Holstein, 1917 brought a cruel shortage of lard, bread, eggs, flour, and gruel, and these dietary deficiencies were held responsible for very frequent cases of amenorrhoea. For Berlin, quantitative evaluations are available. In the Berlin clinic mentioned above we can compare precise data concerning food intake and amenorrhoea. Between 1914 and 1918 there were 142 female inmates between the ages of sixteen and forty-four, and 129 of them (i.e., 90.8 percent, an overwhelming proportion) were stricken with amenorrhoea, most of them after 1916. These phenomena appeared in the wake of the drastic reduction in the quantity of food served at that institution. Recall that meat rationing was instituted in Berlin on Easter day of 1916; in October, milk was rationed, and at the same time potatoes were replaced by turnips and rutabagas, which were also used for making bread and jam. Following these restrictions, the incidence of amenorrhoea broke all records in this clinic in the last trimester of 1916 and the first trimester of 1917. In this instance, the shortage can be very neatly translated into figures.[13] According to the books of the institution, the nonworking patients who were fed at the clinic consumed an average of 2,955 calories per day in August 1914 and only 1,961 calories in December 1916. Over the same period their intake of fats had fallen by 62.2 percent.

The dietary causes of amenorrhoea, postulated by the German physicians of the time, were corroborated by sociological facts. Among the Viennese patients of the physician Czerwenka (1917), for example, two distinct groups emerged.[14] On the one hand, there were the lower class welfare clients who suffered from amenorrhoea and, on the other, the better-nourished, private patients who were spared this "accident." In Königsberg in the same year, Dr. Hilferding ascertained similar facts.[15] In

---

[13]Kurtz, "Alimentäre Amenorrhöe," pp. 371–72.

[14]Czerwenka, "Über Kriegsamenorrhöe." Czerwenka emphasizes the lack of carbohydrates; this trait is also present in the French shortages of the seventeenth century.

[15]Hilferding, "Zur Statistik der Amenorrhöe," *Wiener Klinische Wochenschrift*, 1917, no. 27, according to the review in *Zentralblatt für Gynäkologie*, no. 50 (1917): 1139, col. 2.

a hospital clinic which treated several thousand welfare clients every year, the number of women suffering from amenorrhoea rose from 0.55 percent of the total number of female patients in 1912 to 14 percent in 1917. By contrast, only 5 percent of Hilferding's more affluent private patients (ten out of two hundred) were in the same situation. Finally, in Hamburg,[16] there was a similar contrast, also in 1917, between one physician's private patients, who did not report a single case of amenorrhoea, and the young women insured by the public *Krankenkassen*—factory workers, waitresses, seamstresses—who were undernourished and often no longer menstruated.

The most detailed research was undertaken by Teebken[17] at Kiel. He presented 375 cases for the period 1916–19. Thirty-three percent of the amenorrhoeic women were factory workers and housemaids, 7.5 percent were "employees" (postal clerks, sales girls, and sewing maids), and the rest of them were primarily housewives, married to workers and artisans. While 68 percent of the female patients of the polyclinic studied by Teebken were city-dwellers, the group of amenorrhoeic women was 84 percent urban and only 16 percent rural. Obviously, the poor living conditions of a city where food was scarce had something to do with this. Chronologically the first cases of amenorrhoea appeared in August 1916, after the bread ration was cut and at the very moment when meat rationing was instituted. There was an increased incidence of cases during the autumn of 1916, when the individual rations fell to 1,558 calories (48 grams of protein, 27 grams of fat, 274 grams of carbohydrate). Their incidence was highest in the winter of 1916–17, when rutabagas completely replaced potatoes and "jam." By the autumn of 1917 the rations increased somewhat—large amounts of potatoes were distributed, and the number of cases of amenorrhoea declined. In short, during the harvest year 1916–17 Kiel experienced a moderate food crisis, comparable to a relatively benign shortage of the Ancien Régime—one of those shortages whose effects in the seventeenth century we would be able to measure much more precisely if the observations of physicians were available.

In Lille,[18] a French town in German-occupied territory (which happens to be the classic region of historical demographic studies), the situation in 1914–18 seems to have been much more serious. The physician Boucher interviewed two hundred hospitalized women and found that seventy-nine who had been normal before the war were suffering from amenor-

[16]Spaeth, "Kriegsamenorrhöe,"
[17]G. Teebken, "Amenorrhöe in der Kriegs-und Nachkriegszeit, ein Rückblick 10 Jahre nach dem Kriege," *Zentralblatt für Gynäkologie* 52 (1928): 2966–78.
[18]M. Boucher, "L'aménorrhée de guerre dans les régions envahies" (Dissertation, Faculty of Medicine, University of Lille; Lille: Imprimerie centrale du Nord, 1920), especially p. 24.

rhoea, lasting in fifty-seven cases for more than six months. Half of these cases occurred during the last year of the war, "the year of the most severe restrictions."[19] Without denying the influence of psychological factors, Boucher pointed, above all, to the "profound denutrition,"[20] citing the drastic curtailment of food rations, which was worse than in Germany, noting that of some twenty amenorrhoeic women who kept track of their weight during the war, twelve gave him "precise figures of weight loss of ten kilograms or more."[21]

In Germany, meanwhile, the situation had improved even during the last year of the war (1918). There was a drop in the number of cases of amenorrhoea. Did food in Germany become more substantial once the shortage of the winter 1916–17—since known as the rutabaga winter[22]—was over? This is possible, but it is not likely that the harvest of 1917 brought any real abundance. Is it correct to think, with Selye[23] and other authors, that after the initial shock of the restriction (1916) the human body gradually adapted to dearth? I certainly do not know, nor would I care to offer an explanation, *ne sutor ultra crepidam.* But for the historian, simply from a bibliographical point of view, certain facts are evident. Beginning with that year (1918), discussions of amenorrhoea, which for a time had been so lively in German medical literature, calmed down.[24] By 1920, the food situation had become more or less normal, and the German women "statistically" no longer had problems of this kind. Henceforth, relevant observations were made in Russia during the historic years (1917–21). In Petrograd, where the restrictions on bread and fats were very heavy, Leo von Lingen saw the first examples of abnormal amenorrhoea in his practice in 1916, as did physicians every-

[19]Ibid., p. 51.

[20]Ibid., p. 28.

[21]The median weight of these twelve persons dropped from 65 kilograms to 49.5 kilograms (ibid., p. 29).

[22]T. Heynemann, "Die Nachkriegsamenorrhöe," *Klinische Wochenschrift,* March 26, 1948, pp. 129–32.

[23]H. Selye, *Stress, The Physiology and Pathology of Exposure to Stress* (Montreal, 1950), pp. 366–67.

[24]In addition to the articles already cited, see also: Schilling, "Kriegsamenorrhöe," *Zentralblatt für innere Medizin,* 1917, no. 31 (reviewed in *Zentralblatt für Gynäkologie,* 1918, no. 2, p. 712); Graefe, "Uber Kriegsamenorrhöe," *Münchener Medizinische Wochenschrift,* 1917, no. 32 (reviewed in *Zentralblatt für Gynäkologie,* no. 50, 1917, 2nd issue, p. 1140. In 1916, a major debate was engaged between, on the one hand, A. Hamm of Strasbourg ("Geburtshilflich-gynäkologische Kriegsfragen," *Zentralblatt für Gynäkologie* 1 [1918]: 82), who believed that psychological trauma was the most important factor in the onset of amenorrhoea and, on the other hand, those who defended the thesis that malnutrition was the primary cause. (The views of the latter were expressed in the already cited articles by Graefe and Spaeth; in Dietrich and Pok, *Zentralblatt für Gynäkologie,* 1917, nos. 6 and 20; and in Schweitzer, *Münchener Medizinische Wochenschrift,* 1917, no. 17.)

where.[25] Over the next few years he observed 320 cases, most of which emerged in the winter of 1918–19, when the young, lower-class women of Petrograd suffered and worked very hard under unbelievable conditions of hunger and cold. Von Lingen eventually emigrated, so his observations did not continue. But a Soviet physician, W. Stefko, was there during the hunger years (1920–21). Following procedures which were undertaken for various other reasons but gave him material for a histological study of the ovary, he found that 120 women affected by food shortage and amenorrhoea had suffered a more or less complete "breakdown" of the physiological processes necessary for ovulation.[26]

World War II is "rich," alas, in similar data, and the dossier of amenorrhoea again took on considerable proportions in the tragic ten years between 1936 (Spanish Civil War) and 1946 (last food shortages).

This time, the data came from a wider area than Austro-German Europe; they were available all over Europe, including France, where food restrictions were more painful in 1940–44 than during the war of 1914–18. During World War I the physicians of the Allied[27] countries had known "war amenorrhoea" only through their impersonal reading of the gynecological reviews of Germany and Austria. Teebken's[28] exhaustive reviews of the literature, written in 1928, cite only one article published in the medical literature of England, France, and the United States for the war and postwar years. It appeared in *The Lancet* in 1918[29] and turns out to be no more than a brief, anonymous note of little value.

Twenty or twenty-five years later, the situation had changed in the major Western countries.[30] In Spain, in Madrid and Barcelona, cases of amenorrhoea were frequent in 1936–38, and their number was to decrease only after the Civil War.[31] In France, the medical profession was alerted

[25]L. von Lingen, "Kriegsamenorrhöe in Petersburg," *Zentralblatt für Gynäkologie*, Sept. 1921, no. 45, pp. 1247–48.

[26]W. H. Stefko, in *Virchows Archiv*, 1924, no. 252, p. 385, cited by Heynemann, "Die Nachkriegsamenorrhöe," pp. 130 and 132.

[27]The case of the occupied territories is, of course, different (Boucher, *Aménorrhée de guerre*).

[28]See note 17, above.

[29]"Amenorrhoea in Wartime . . . ," *The Lancet*, 1918, p. 712.

[30]This time, the bibliography of the subject for France is extensive. See especially *Questions gynécologiques d'actualité*, vol. 3 (1943), a collective volume; also G. Laroche and E. Bompard, "Les aménorrhées de guerre," *Paris médical*, Aug. 30, 1943, pp. 217–19; the same authors with J. Tremolières, "Les aménorrhées de guerre," *Revue française de gynécologie et obstétrique*, Mar. 1943, pp. 65 ff; G. Cotte in *Lyon médical* 169 (Mar. 28, 1943): 263 (Cotte stresses psychological factors); M. Sendrail and J. Laserre, in *Revue de pathologie comparée et d'hygiène générale* 48 (Jan.-Feb. 1948): 63–75 (important bibliography). The information in the following paragraphs is taken from these articles, except when stated otherwise.

[31]E. Oliver-Pascual, in *Clinica y laboratorio*, Nov. 1941, cited by Sendrail and Laserre, *Revue de pathologie comparée*.

to the problem by 1940 and especially 1942. In June 1942, at the moment of a "difficult preharvest period" (food stocks confiscated by the occupier; new harvest not yet in), the Obstetrical Society of Paris expressed its alarm at the growing incidence of amenorrhoea. It was pointed out that the marks of puberty (first menstruation) appeared later in Parisian school girls. In the lower-class suburbs, girls began to menstruate at thirteen and a half or fourteen rather than at twelve and a half as they had in 1937. Many women, suffering from overwork, nervous disorders, and dietary deficiencies, no longer menstruated. All things considered, it appears that the year 1942 marked the high point of the incidence of amenorrhoea in France during World War II (just as 1917 had been its high point in Germany during World War I). After 1942, the food supply in France remained low; nonetheless, either because of possible inurement[32] or for some other reason, the number of cases of amenorrhoea reached a plateau or even declined. The phenomenon was so widespread, to return to 1942, that Laurent Quémeré, a young physician in the Department of Finistère, wrote a thesis about it and defended it in Paris in November of the same year.[33] Unfortunately, Quémeré limited himself to compiling certain findings already observed by the German authors and by Boucher in 1914–18; his cases of amenorrhoea were one war behind the times. It was only in the following year that a few figures became available; they were plausible but approximate and—as even their authors admitted—too general to be entirely trustworthy. According to Guy-Laroche, Bompard, and Tremolières, 4 to 7 percent of the French women of childbearing age were affected by "war amenorrhoea" during these last years of the Occupation. In one large factory the percentage reached 12.6 percent of the female work force. The first of these figures (4–7 percent) is close to the undisputed figure advanced by Teebken[34] (5.11 percent) for Kiel in 1917.

Whatever the exact percentages, the geographical distribution is noteworthy. The undernourished south of France[35] appears to have been stricken particularly severely, notably Toulouse, Bordeaux, Montpellier. But for an especially clear and tragic "regional" example, we must go outside of France. In 1944–45 the northwest of the Netherlands experienced, in the midst of our own twentieth century, a distress matching that of the worst famines in medieval or early modern times.

On September 19, 1944, a general transportation strike, called at the behest of the Dutch government-in-exile in London, began in the area of

[32]Laroche, Bompard, and Tremolières, "Les aménorrhées de guerre."
[33]F. L. Quémeré, "Les aménorrhées de guerre" (thesis, Paris, 1942).
[34]This figure, to be sure, means 5.11 percent of the patients treated at a particular clinic.
[35]Theses by S. Vidal, 1945 (Toulouse) and Castan-Pollin (Montpellier), according to Sendrail and Lassere, *Revue de pathologie comparée.*

Amsterdam, Rotterdam, and The Hague.[36] The liberation seemed at
hand. Not so. It was to come only in May 1945. But the strikers stood
their ground and the railroads remained paralyzed. As a reprisal measure,
the Germans blocked the roads and canals. The cities received very little
or no food, and the result was a winter of starvation. In The Hague more
than one hundred persons died of starvation every week between January
and May of 1945, and even more died in Rotterdam. The official rations
for pregnant women, who were relatively well off, dropped to 1,144
calories per day. At the beginning of 1945 everything plunged to the
lowest levels at the same time, whether it was the intake of proteins, fats,
or carbohydrates. Hence the incidence of amenorrhoea reached enormous, historical proportions, such as had been unknown in the Germany
of 1917 and the France of 1942, where the shortage was really tragic only
for the poorest minority. But in the Dutch cities of that last winter of Nazi
occupation, practically all women were suffering from hunger. The result
was that only 30 percent continued to menstruate normally. The number
of conceptions, as revealed by the births nine months later, fell to a third
of its normal level. Amenorrhoea and its accompanying sterility are
obviously one of the causes—but not the only one!—of this temporary
drop in the birth rate. At Utrecht, another author independently reached
analogous conclusions. Taking all the other factors into consideration,
the winter of starvation in that city caused amenorrhoea in 33 percent of
the women of childbearing age.[37]

These appalling statistics, hitherto unknown in medical literature, are
still mild by comparison with the data revealed by the inmates of
deportation camps immediately after the war. At the camp of Theresienstadt, 54 percent of the 10,000 female prisoners ceased to menstruate after
one, two, or three months of detention. After eighteen or twenty months
at the camp, the great majority of the survivors of that "54 percent"
started to menstruate again. It was not that the living conditions at
Theresienstadt had improved; but somehow a process of adaptation had
taken place. The organisms of these women had involuntarily become
"accustomed" to the intolerable.[38] Many similar facts have been reported,
notably at Auschwitz.[39]

[36]On this point, the most important and very remarkable articles are those by C. A.
Smith, "Effects of Maternal Undernutrition upon the Newborn Infant in Holland
(1944–1945)," *The Journal of Pediatrics* 30 (Mar. 1947); and "The Effect of Wartime
Starvation in Holland upon Pregnancy," *American Journal of Obstetrics and Gynecology*,
Apr. 1947, pp. 599–608.
[37]J. A. Stroink, "Kriegsamenorrhöe," *Gynaecologia* 123 (1947): 160–65.
[38]Selye, *Stress*, pp. 366–67.
[39]A. Binet, "Les aménorrhées chez les deportées," *Gynécologie et obstétrique* 44, nos.
1–2–3; Binet, "1944," *Gynécologie et obstétrique*, 1945, p. 417. (See also, L. S. Copelman,
"L'aménorrhée des déportées," *Revue de pathologie comparée et d'hygiène générale*, year 48

In 1944–45 Hungarian physicians[40] also reported some extraordinary percentages which may be in part exaggerated:

	Amenorrhoeic Women
Women living at Budapest during the siege of the city (1944–45)	50–60%
Women deported by the Germans	99%

Here is what A. Netter, who devoted two books to the question of amenorrhoea, states in this connection:

Any state of denutrition, and especially protein deficiency, can lead to amenorrhoea. This fact has been established over and over again during the last war, particularly in deported women. When these women returned from deportation, and when the consequences of hunger were overcome, the only remaining cause for amenorrhoea was the memory of the atrocious psychological conditions of deportation. . . .[41]

Aside from the severe food shortages, which were very evident in the death camps, psychological or psychosomatic factors thus played an important role in the onset and the duration of amenorrhoea. Famine, after all, is an encompassing phenomenon which brings about denutrition, but also causes debilitating anxiety. These psychosomatic factors[42] are well documented in the publications of American physicians who, during World War II, were prisoners in Japanese camps together with a large number of American-born women. In Manila, at the Santo Thomas camp, 14.8 percent of the female inmates had ceased to menstruate. But this happened before there were any food shortages. It usually began with the bombardment of the city and the first day of internment. The cause was simply anxiety and shock.[43] Similarly, 60.6 percent of the women

---

[1948] pp. 102–7 also pp. 386–391), who concludes his detailed study with the following reflection: "The proportion of cases of amenorrhoea is directly related to the intensity of hunger . . . in these camps. The resumption of ovarian activity took place as soon as sufficient food became available."

[40]K. Horvath, C. Selle, and R. Weisz, "Beiträge zur Pathologie . . . der kriegsbedingten Amenorrhöe," *Gynaecologia* 125 (1948): 368–74. The observations of these authors concerning the resumption of ovarian activity after famine are more cautious than those of Copelman, "L'aménorrhée des déportées."

[41]Netter and Lumbrose, *Aménorrhées, dysménorrhées*, pp. 59 ff; and Netter, *Comment soigner*, p. 61.

[42]In this connection, see also the already cited (note 8, above) collection of articles of the *Assises de médecine*, 1968, pp. 102–3.

[43]F. Whitacre and B. Barber, "War Amenorrhea: A Clinical and Laboratory Study," *Journal of the American Medical Association* 124, no. 7 (Feb. 12, 1944):399–403.

held at Camp Stanley in Hong Kong (1942) were striken with amenorrhoea. Very often, the condition developed as soon as restrictions were
imposed and was due only to the psychological shock caused by imprison-
ment. As for the diet itself, it was quite insufficient at Camp Stanley to be
sure, but it was not different from that on which Chinese women had
subsisted long before the war without having developed amenorrhoea.
But as Dr. Annie Sydenham, who gathered and published these data,
notes, the low level of the daily ration in absolute figures is less significant
than the sudden deterioration of food "in quality as well as in quantity."[44]

Even in the United States, where food restrictions in 1941–45 were
insignificant or nonexistent, an increase in the incidence of amenorrhoea
was noted during World War II. In the hospitals of Dallas, Texas,
menstrual disorders of this type affected only 82 of the 9,141 who sought
help there during the "prewar" year of 1940. But in 1945, after four years
of nervous tension accumulated because of the war, the disturbances in
question affected 368 of the 2,398 women who visited these hospitals.[45]
Statistically evaluated,[46] the difference between 1940 and 1945 would be
significant. It can be said that these American women, perturbed by the
last year of the war, were not suffering from denutrition. But they were
the wives, daughters, or fiancées of combat troops. For this reason, they
were anxious. This must have contributed substantially, among other
factors, to their condition.

In any case, according to the specialists, "war amenorrhoea" must be
the result of multiple stress on the female organism. Anxiety and
restrictions, dietary shortages and psychological frustration form an
inextricable complex of causes.[47] The formation of such a complex does
not, of course, necessarily require the traumatizing background of a
world war. Peacetime as well can bring hunger or disabling anxiety. This
fact, which is highly significant for the study of famines in earlier times,

[44]A. Sydenham, "Amenorrhoea at Stanley Camp, Hong-Kong, during Internment,"
British Medical Journal 2 (Aug. 1946): 159.

[45]J. S. Sweeney et al., "An Observation on Menstrual Misbehavior," *The Journal of
Clinical Endocrinology* 7 (1947): 659 ff.

[46]Ibid., p. 660.

[47]In this connection, it is useful to recall the definitions of Alfred Netter: "Amenorrhoea
is a symptom, like fever or weight loss. . . . It is never a disease, only a symptom, a
disturbing sign of a lesion or of a functional disorder affecting the complex mechanism
involved in bringing about the menstrual cycle. . . . Amenorrhoea is often but a *cry of
suffering*, physical suffering due to infectious or debilitating disease, mental suffering due to
sudden emotion. . . . The investigation must consider the patient as a somatic, social and
psychological entity. . . . Amenorrhoea is not always caused by lesions of the uterus, the
ovaries or the pituitary gland, it can be connected with a variety of causes which affect other
organs and other functions. . . . Amenorrhoea can be the 'witness of organic suffering' or
'the witness of psychological suffering,' sudden emotion, conflict situation, nervous exhaustion" (Netter, *Comment soigner*, pp. 5, 6, and passim; see also Netter and Lumbrose,
Aménorrhée, dysménorhée, pp. 7, 59, and passim.

has been proven in a number of instances.[48] In 1948, for example,
Theodor Heyneman, in his resumé of innumerable observations made in
the Hamburg University hospitals, was able to speak of *Nachkriegsamen-
orrhoe*, postwar amenorrhoea. This expression would make us smile if the
problem were not so real. Very briefly, Hitler Germany was fairly well
protected from food shortages, thanks to what it confiscated from
conquered nations, and thus did not experience the most serious privation
with its attendant amenorrhoea until the beginning of 1945. Paradoxi-
cally, it was only in 1945–46, in other words, mostly after the war, that the
most serious restrictions in the quantity of food, calories, and proteins
had their greatest impact on German women; to which we must, of
course, add the psychological factors attendant upon total defeat. In any
event, the number of cases of amenorrhoea in Heynemann's polyclinic
rose from 16 (0.8 percent of his patients) in 1938 to 396 (8.7 percent of his
patients) in 1946. The percentage of similar cases had varied between 2.1
and 3.5 percent of his patients in the years 1939–44. They had risen to 7.6
percent between May and December 1945, subsequently reaching a peak,
as we have seen, in 1946, and finally decreasing after 1947 as the situation
became more normal.

*   *   *

In 1947, precisely as the world was coming out of the tragedy, two
American scholars, Strecker and Emlen, decided to study this difficult
problem of the relationship between famine and sterility experimentally
in a mammal close to man. Their method consisted in bringing about a
food crisis, famine or shortage, in a population of mice. To anyone
interested in social history beyond the anthropocentric limits,[49] this
comparative episode (despite its shocking aspects from a humane point of
view) is unfortunately relevant, for the food crisis is indeed a painful
occurrence in the demography of Western societies of the past. An
increased death rate, a reduction in the number of marriages, and a more
than proportional decline in the number of births, or rather conceptions,
appear together with almost mechanical regularity. It is therefore important to know just what is happening in such a case to animals in their
own habitat or in the laboratory.

Strecker and Emlen conducted their crucial experiments with the help
of mice live-trapped in the city of Madison, Wisconsin.[50] They placed

[48]Heynemann, "Die Nachkriegsamenorrhöe."
[49]C. Lévi-Strauss, *La pensée sauvage* (Paris, 1962), p. 326.
[50]R. L. Strecker and T. T. Emlen, "Regulatory Mechanisms in House-Mouse populations: The Effect of Limited Food Supply," *Ecology*, 1953, pp. 375 ff. See also B. Ball,
"Caloric Restriction and Fertility," *American Journal of Physiology* 150 (1947): 511 ff.

these little creatures into the empty, carefully mouse-proofed buildings of an empty army barracks in Wisconsin. They fed them wheat, ground corn, meat scraps, salt, and cod liver oil. They also counted and weighed them at regular intervals.

The food crisis was simply brought about by "laissez-faire." While the population of mice in the barracks was constantly increasing, the total amount of food distributed remained stable at a fixed daily level. In the beginning the daily ration was more than ample. As a result of demographic multiplication it eventually reached the point where it became insufficient. The shortage had begun.

The first effects took the form of an increase in infant mortality, even though the nestlings born before the famine did well. They did not die. But of thirteen mice (in three litters) born immediately after the onset of the shortage, twelve died within five weeks of birth. Strecker and Emlen were unable to determine the exact cause of these deaths. Did the food situation affect the lactation or the maternal care of the mothers? This is possible, but not certain. For all of these infant deaths occurred after weaning. They may have resulted simply from competition for food and the fact that the very weak young mice were pushed away from the feeding places by more vigorous adults. In this case, the young were condemned to death by starvation; in a certain sense, this was infanticide.

Another very important finding was the limited fertility of the mice in times of food shortage. The sexual appetite of the subjects of the experiment diminished when they had to fast, while their unappeased appetite for food became exacerbated. This reduction in reproductive activity is quantifiable. The two authors observed *in vivo* or autopsied a large number of mice. In those that had been fasting they found none, or very few, of the habitual signs of reproductive activity: pregnancy, perforate vagina, etc. As for this last criterion, the percentage of females exhibiting it fell from 70 percent among well-fed subjects to 17 percent among those that had been fasting.

After the beginning of the shortage, the two American researchers described a number of symptoms in the males as well which stemmed from a decrease in the sexual functions, such as a reduction in the size of the sperm vesicles, etc. On the basis of a whole series of signs arrived at by comparing the findings of dissections of fasting and nonfasting males, it appeared that the percentage of sexually active males fell from 100 percent to 80 percent as soon as food deprivation developed. This drop is obviously less pronounced than the corresponding percentages among the females, which fell from 70 percent to 17 percent, as we have seen.

The experiment is decisive. It does away with the popular notion that animals, not knowing how to limit their numerical growth, are hopelessly condemned to physiological misery and death as soon as they are faced with a severe food shortage. In the case studied here, at least, this is not the case; for mortality is confined to the very young. Moreover, an unconscious but very effective "policy" bringing about a decline in conceptions comes into play. By the interaction of certain physiological mechanisms, this policy prevents the normal multiplication of the mice, which would be disastrous in times of food shortage. There is no doubt that the adults become "chaste." But they do not die. Better yet, they do not even lose weight. By severely limiting their numbers, they somehow manage to maintain their ration of food. Using a pedagogical, inexact, and goal-oriented figure of speech, one might say that these mice are born practitioners of Malthusianism and that their organism prefers, if necessary, "virtue" to "misery." In more scientific terms, it is permissible to apply to them what A. Netter wrote concerning secondary amenorrhoea brought on by denutrition or some other cause seriously affecting a woman's general health. "It would be a mistake," Netter notes, "to treat the amenorrhoea in this case, for it undoubtedly constitutes a defense reaction. It is as if the organism were suspending the reproductive function since it is a *luxury* by comparison with the survival function."[51]

* * *

At the end of this essentially bibliographical investigation, one conclusion seems obvious: The scientific observation of animals close to man and especially the scientific record of the bitter and repeated experience of two world wars clearly show that there is a correlation between acute famine and temporary sterility. It is not for me to explain the physiological nature of this correlation, but there can be no question that the process does exist. Clearly, famine amenorrhoea is *one* of the factors responsible for the pronounced drop in conceptions[52] during the worst periods of food crises described by the historian of the seventeenth and eighteenth centuries.

Finally, I must try to respond to the question asked by Pierre Goubert: "We can only hope that some old memoir by a physician . . . will tell us about the phenomena of amenorrhoea in times of famine."[53] An investigation—incomplete, to be sure—of the relevant works of the seventeenth and eighteenth centuries has not been very fruitful. The *Emmenology* (science of menstruation) of the English physician Freind (d. 1728) did

[51]Netter, *Aménorrhée, dysménorrhée*, p. 59.

[52]One of these factors is, of course, abstinence, and perhaps certain attempts to limit fertility as well. The problem now is to determine the relative importance of all these various factors in the decline of conceptions during periods of acute food shortages.

[53]See above, the beginning of the present article.

not yield anything. Freind felt sorry for the unfortunate condition of women and also pointed out that in his day girls reached puberty at the age of fourteen. But that is all he has to say about the phenomena in which we are interested. By contrast, the philosopher and materialist physician La Mettrie, in his commentary on Boerhave, is more explicit, yet not totally relevant to our subject. He does not establish a direct relationship between famine and amenorrhoea, but he notes that *atrophy*, which he defines by symptoms of malnutrition—"excessive thinness," consumption, marasmus—is accompanied by the cessation of menstruation. "Women suffering from atrophy," he writes, "usually menstruate scantily or infrequently."[54] Would it be an exaggeration to follow La Mettrie's implicit reasoning to its conclusion and to state that the number of these atrophied and, hence, amenorrheic women rose considerably in times of famine?

Whether this interpretation is correct or not, the conclusions formulated by V. C. Wynne-Edwards in an excellent book[55] are definitely based on facts. It is true that man (just like the animals) is equipped with mechanisms which can drastically curtail births in cases of distress and severe food shortages. Voluntary contraception is not absolutely indispensable for reaching this objective. In women, just as in female rats or mice, potential automatic reactions are always ready to come into play. If necessary, they will suspend the "luxury" function of reproduction; they are like an unconscious power humanity has over its own destiny. These reactions have been exposed in Europe, during the famines of the seventeenth century, and two centuries later, during the world wars of our own time. And the latter can give us the measure of the former. In both cases, denutrition amenorrhoea is truly the "cry of silent suffering"[56] of millions of undernourished and traumatized women.[57]

[54]H. Boerhave, *Institutions de médecine, avec un commentaire de M. de La Mettrie, docteur en médecine* (Paris), trans. of vol. 1 (1743 ed.), p. 231, and vol. 6 (1747 ed.), pp. 108 ff. Moreover, there are pertinent texts on delayed puberty, a phenomenon that was especially prevalent in the poorest regions. See for example (in data given to me by J.-P. Peter) some passages concerning Bressuire and Brittany: "The girls in this area are very prone to paleness and rarely menstruate before the ages of eighteen, nineteen, and twenty" (Archives Départementales des Deux-Sèvres, C 14, Subdélégation de Bressuire, "Topographie de la ville et de la subdélégation de Bressuire" by Berthelot, doctor of medicine, July 1786). And again: "Those persons of female sex who do not work in the fields begin to menstruate between the ages of eleven and fourteen; those who are so employed begin between the ages of fourteen and nineteen" (Académie de Médecine, Archives S.R.M., Carton 179, Baudry, doctor of medicine, "Topographie de Vieillevigne, Bretagne," Oct. 1787).

[55]*Animal Dispersion in Relation to Social Behavior* (London, 1962), particularly chap. 21.

[56]Netter, *Comment soigner.*

[57]I should like to thank Jean-Pierre Peter, Antoinette Chamoux, and Dr. Michel Bitker for their kind help with bibliographic and medical information.

7
The Biological Index of the Buying Power of Money

Zbigniew Zabinski

The buying power of money is subject to constant fluctuation. Efforts have long been made to find an index which would make it possible to follow these fluctuations precisely. So far, however, these efforts have amounted to only one of three things: either a comparison of the nominal value of the currency studied with the nominal value of another currency which is taken as the basis of comparison; the use of certain foodstuffs, such as cereals or cattle, to express the value of the currency; or else the establishment of comparative price indices on the basis of certain goods and services. Now that we have very rich statistical material at our disposal, the indices of price fluctuations, in other words, of the buying power of money, are characterized by great structural complexity, but also by their fairly precise nature. However, these modern indices have one major drawback. It is quite impossible to compare them to one another, because the basis for calculating them varies not only from country to country, but also from one period of time to the next, even within a relatively short time span. This means that the figures available to us are comparable only to a limited extent, and that they express the variations in prices, wages, etc., only in terms of percentages. And matters become even more critical if we are dealing with a study in economic history. The more effective these modern techniques of investigation are for studying the present, the less suitable they are for studying the past.

Annales: E.S.C., July–Aug. 1968, pp. 808–18. Translated by Elborg Forster.

Having been collected, in principle, to determine price fluctuations over relatively short periods of time, the statistical indices that have been used hitherto were arrived at on the basis of only one series of indicators, representing a fairly wide spectrum of foodstuffs. Moreover, the price indicators available for the past are always of a rather fragmentary nature, not only as to continuity, but also as to content. For the documents we must use give us no more than the orders placed by individuals or groups, various private or public bills, contracts, etc., referring to the period under study. While these documents contain a great deal of valuable information which enables us to make comparisons, they are unfortunately not related to each other and, therefore, cannot serve as a basis for precise, systematic evaluations. This is not really surprising. In the past, no one was interested in systematic statistical studies, and the data which have come down to us are not an organized body of information, but rather a mass of scattered fragments. For any economic study of the past, we are therefore obliged to make exclusive—and I mean exclusive—use of the descriptions furnished by the texts.

However, we should not become discouraged, but continue to use historical material to reconstruct the social relations of the past. We should not lose sight of the example of the archaeologists who, on the basis of tiny fragments, reconstruct whole objects, reconstitute the uses to which they were put, and with the help of such findings even try to deduce the patterns of life in the social system they are investigating. No one is shocked by the fact that archaeology builds its case on simple vestiges. The same attitude must prevail when we historians are trying to study the past more closely from an economic point of view, since we too can only use fragments, even very small fragments, which have come down to us.

Since we cannot apply the statistical indices of our own time, we must try to adopt another index, one that is sufficiently flexible to be used even under the least favorable circumstances. Such an index should be both precise enough and supple enough to evaluate various situations which could subsequently be developed further.

At first sight, it might not seem feasible to evaluate the buying power of a currency in historical times, since the available data are insufficient to establish an index that can serve as a tool. Moreover, it is a fact that the choice of an adequate index to translate the fluctuation of the buying power of money is always a difficult problem. And yet, such an index exists within us. It is none other than the simple biological need for food, which is essential to our metabolism and necessary for sustaining both the life of the human organism and any work it is called upon to perform. In fact, man can do without almost anything, but without food he will starve to death. We can therefore conclude that the need for food is the first and fundamental condition for his existence. The great majority of people earn their food by their work. They are therefore entitled to a wage which will enable them, first and foremost, to satisfy their biological need for food and, also, to a surplus for feeding their families, buying clothes, shelter, entertainment, and so forth. The greater the difference between the subsistence minimum and the surplus, the greater an individual's prosperity.

The daily intake of food should thus assure the individual of the calories needed for maintaining his metabolism. This need is not always the same and varies widely from case to case (between a minimum of 700 calories and a maximum of 9,000 calories per day). However, we will use an average figure of 3,000 calories per day, which represents the average needed by an adult performing a moderate amount of physical work.

We must also take into consideration that man absolutely needs a certain variety in the food he consumes. The daily intake of food should consist of proteins, fats, and carbohydrates, but also of water, trace elements, and vitamins. But the fundamental role is played by the first three items, which should be consumed in the following average quantities:

75 g. of protein X 4 calories	300 calories
100 g of fat X 9 calories	900 calories
450 g of carbohydrates X 4 calories	1,800 calories
	3,000 calories

The composition of this ration does not have to be absolutely fixed, and certain variations are permissible, particularly the substitution of carbohydrates for fats, since carbohydrates are cheaper. However, the complete elimination of fats would result in a so-called "bare" diet, which would be literally difficult to swallow for an individual who would have to live on it for any length of time. While such a diet would provide the quantity of calories needed by the organism, the person eating it would dislike it so much that the normal process of nutrition would be jeopardized. Under such circumstances the life of the individual would become so miserable that we would have to consider it below the minimum standard.

In establishing the daily diet, we must choose its elements in such a way that they will add up to a total as close as possible to the composition mentioned above. We must also keep in mind that we are speaking exclusively of elements that can be digested. To take only one example, starches and cellulose are both carbohydrates; but the latter has no nutritional value for man. Similarly, all fats cannot be digested by the human organism.

The question might be raised as to how man went about determining the quantity and the composition of the food he needed in times when the modern science of nutrition was unknown. The answer is that the organism itself took care of that, because it somehow demands what it needs.

I must point out that my research is not based on real workers' budgets. I am not interested in what people actually ate at a given period, but in what they should have eaten, given the resources of their time, in order to be properly nourished. My investigation will therefore be concerned with standards of nutrition rather than with consumption itself. In this manner, famines and natural disasters, while unquestionably playing a decisive role in the nutritional situation of their time, since they led to steep price rises for the basic foodstuffs, have nonetheless not had any influence on the biological minimum standard of man's nutritional needs, which is in no way affected by events of that kind.

My deductions in this study are based on the principle that basic foodstuffs of equal nutritional value always cost the same. No one will pay more than he has to for wheat if he can buy rye for less money. Whenever one product is temporarily unavailable, it can be replaced to a certain extent by substitutes. It is therefore sufficient to know the prices of a few basic products to know the cost of the calories contained in the basic daily ration. Needless to say, moreover, I am only concerned here with the basic standard of nutrition, that is, with the minimum necessary to sustain life, rather than with the satisfaction of desires for luxury.

To decide what the actual composition of a diet was in a concrete case, we must make use of the statistical data at our disposal. And, of course, this task will be the easier the more numerous the data are. Also, the particular economy of the country under study must be taken into consideration. Thus, we may have to substitute fish for meat, rice for rye, oil for butter, and so forth. In addition, the actual quantities of calories in the daily diet should sometimes be adjusted in view of the latitude in which a country is located. For example, the standard of 3,000 calories might be lowered for tropical countries and raised for arctic regions. But all of this is a different matter.

Calculated in this manner, on the basis of 3,000 calories coming from the various products yielding the life-sustaining ration of 75 grams of proteins, 100 grams of fats, and 450 grams of carbohydrates, the cost of these 3,000 calories would not be expressed correctly if we neglected to take the following factors into account: (1) the cost of the trace elements and vitamins, (2) the cost implied in the neccessity of bringing a minimum of variety to the human diet, and (3) the cost of the preparation of the foodstuffs and of a moderate amount of seasoning.

In my calculations I have accounted for the value of these three factors by adding an additional 20 percent (more or less arbitrarily arrived at) to the cost of the basic factors of nutrition (proteins, fats, carbohydrates). I have called the index calculated in this manner a *trophē* (from the Greek, meaning food). It can be considered to be the index of the cost of the daily food ration.

As for the usefulness of the *trophē*, I should particularly like to emphasize its flexibility. This index will in fact enable us to compare the basic cost of food at different periods, in different countries, and under different conditions of life. The common denominator is always the standard of the daily minimum requirement, and we can subsequently fill in this minimum with a whole variety of products. It is, of course, unfortunate that this index will not tell us anything about the value of goods other than food nor about the value of services, both of which play an important role in human life. Furthermore, this index is much less precise than modern indices, which are calculated on the basis of a greater variety of goods. On the other hand, its very simplicity makes it easy to use in practice and also permits us to make comparisons easily visualized by everyone.

Nonetheless, it must be understood that a simplified index, like any other index, cannot contradict the basic trends in price and wage fluctuations. Consequently, it is impossible for the variations in our index to run counter to the price indices, since the general variation of all the indices must be about the same.

I shall demonstrate the use of the *trophē* with the example of research findings concerning the buying power of money in Poland before the Partition. While insufficient for an exact statistical study, the available relevant data have already been used for detailed studies. In this connection the work of Professor Bujak on the price fluctuations at Crakow, Warsaw, Danzig, Lvov, and Lublin is particularly noteworthy. The information assembled by him and other scholars is organized in tables, where prices are given in the currency of the time, accompanied by their equivalents in gold and silver. Unfortunately, these details concerning prices at a given time, even when carefully asscmbled, leave many gaps, which can be seen in the tables as so many empty columns. What is worse, in many cases the prices indicated by the authors are of doubtful exactitude, since they differ appreciably from prices indicated for other goods or other periods. This, of course, is not the fault of the authors; the reason is that the statistical material is incomplete and often includes data

Table 1. Simplified Daily Ration (*Trophē*) in Poland, 1500–1800

PRODUCTS	QUANTITIES	CARBOHYDRATES	FATS	PROTEINS
Wheat	450 g.	228.6	3.0	24.3
	(= 800 g. flour)			
Peeled barley	300 g.	219.6	5.1	23.1
Beef	250 g.	–	70.0	37.5
Eggs	2	1.1	13.8	15.0
Total grams		449.3	91.9	99.9
Total calories	3,023.9	1,797.2	827.1	319.6

of an accidental or exceptional nature. The same gaps and the same problems can be found in the excellent book by E. J. Hamilton, *War and Prices in Spain* (Cambridge, Mass., 1947).

On the basis of these materials I have calculated the *trophai* and, by means of the *trophai*, the buying power of money as well as the level of wages for Poland from the fourteenth to the eighteenth century and for Spain during the sixteenth and seventeenth centuries.

The tables presented here will illustrate the various steps of this operation.

Table 1 presents a simplified diet, the equivalent of the standard daily ration in Poland, such as I was able to calculate it on the basis of the available data. Whenever the data are more plentiful, it is of course preferable to show a more varied diet; the evaluation would then be more precise. But the historian is often obliged to work with very incomplete data, which is not the best of conditions.

Taking the daily food ration as my basis, I calculated the value of the *trophē* and translated its price into grams of pure silver (see table 2). As

Table 2. Value of the Daily Ration in Poland, in Grams of Silver

PERIOD	430 G. WHEAT	300 G. PEELED BARLEY	250 G. OF BEEF	2 EGGS	TOTAL	20% ADDED	*TROPHĒ*
1391–1400	0.076	(0.040)	0.140	0.119	0.375	0.075	0.450
1441–1450	–	–	–	–	–	–	(0.300)
1491–1500	0.034	0.030	0.112	(0.063)	0.239	0.048	0.287
1541–1550	0.119	0.041	0.150	0.080	0.390	0.078	0.468
1591–1600	0.176	0.114	0.294	0.225	0.809	0.162	0.971
1641–1650	0.209	0.235	0.443	0.180	1.067	0.213	1.280
1691–1700	0.204	0.357	0.184	0.100	0.845	0.169	1.014
1741–1750	0.150	0.330	(0.340)	0.112	0.932	0.187	1.119
1791–1795	0.222	0.555	(0.340)	0.195	1.312	0.262	1.574

Note: The figures in parentheses are interpolations.

Table 3. Value of the Currency in Poland

PERIOD	NAME OF COIN	WEIGHT OF METAL IN COIN	VALUE OF COIN EXPRESSED IN *TROPHAI*	NAME OF COIN	SILVER WEIGHT OF COIN	VALUE OF COIN EXPRESSED IN *TROPHAI*
1391–1400	Denar	0.0675	0.15	Kwartnik	0.279	0.62
1441–1450	–	0.0475	(0.16)	–	–	–
1491–1500	–	0.0462	0.16	Demi	–	–
1541–1550	–	0.036	0.13	Groschen	0.77	1.65
1591–1600	Groschen	0.69	0.67	Talar	24.31	25.0
1641–1650	–	0.20	0.23	–	24.31	19.0
1691–1700	Six Groschen	1.26	1.24	–	24.31	24.0
1741–1750	–	1.26	1.13	–	24.31	19.30
1791–1795	Zloty	2.8	1.78	–	24.41	14.25

Note: The figures in parentheses are interpolations.

the metallic weight of every coin is known, it is easy to calculate the value of each of them in *trophai*. One might even omit the operation of expressing its value in terms of silver, for the *trophē* can very well be calculated directly in the currency of the time. Expressing the *trophē* in terms of silver does, however, have the advantage of showing the fluctuations in prices in relation to the value of the metal. The value expressed in silver is more constant than the value expressed in terms of currency (see Table 3).

At the present time, one *trophē* is approximately the equivalent of 5½ shillings. Thus, if we see in Table 3 that in 1750 the Polish dollar (talar) was the equivalent of 19.3 *trophai*, this means that its buying power was the same as that of 5 £ 3 s—expressed in terms of the basic food ration, since a man engaged in moderately strenuous physical work could live on this sum for 19.3 days. An analogous calculation for the Spanish dollar (8 reales) at the same period yields a value of 12.1 *trophai*, that is, 3 £ 3 s 4 d. The difference in buying power for an equal amount of silver in the two countries is easily explained by the rarity of precious metals in Poland at that time and the resulting lower prices in foodstuffs, which were consequently exported in great quantities.

But we can go even further in our deductions. For here we have a common denominator which permits us to compare the scale of wages in these two countries. Wages were higher in Spain than in Poland, since in 1750 an unskilled Spanish agricultural laborer earned 2.5 *trophai* per day, while his Polish counterpart earned only 1.5 *trophai*. The higher wages of masons and carpenters can be explained by their more strenuous work; since they worked harder, they needed more food, namely about 5,000

Table 4. Daily Wages in Poland

PERIOD	UNSKILLED WORKER		MASON		CARPENTER	
	WAGE IN G. OF SILVER	WAGE IN *TROPHAI*	WAGE IN G. OF SILVER	WAGE IN *TROPHAI*	WAGE IN G. OF SILVER	WAGE IN *TROPHAI*
1591–1600	2.36	2.90	4.90	6.02	3.60	4.42
1641–1650	2.64	2.35	4.75	4.22	3.70	3.38
1691–1700	1.72	1.78	3.90	4.05	2.51	2.60
1741–1750	1.60	1.52	3.50	3.33	2.40	2.37
1791–1795	1.95	1.28	3.26	2.14	3.02	1.97

calories per day. We can also observe a lowering of the wages in both countries in the course of the seventeenth and eighteenth centuries.

Tables 8 and 9 give another example for the application of this method of evaluation, this time referring to Ancient Greece and Rome.

At the time of Diocletian, 1.0 *trophē*, which we calculate on the basis of his edict concerning prices of 301 was the equivalent of 19.33 dinares. At that time, an agricultural laborer earned 25 dinares per day, or 1.29 *trophai*. A stone cutter, engaged in heavy labor, was paid 50 dinares per day, or 2.58 *trophai*. Thus, the wages of these workers were clearly insufficient for maintaining a family.

Conditions were slightly better in Greece in the fourth century B.C., when 1.0 *trophē* (calculated on the basis of very fragmentary data) was the equivalent of 0.4 drachma. At that time, an agricultural laborer earned 1.0 drachma per day, or 2.5 *trophai*. One drachma was therefore equal to 13s 8d if we base our calculation on the value of the basic foodstuffs.

Table 5. Simplified Daily Ration (*Trophē*) in Spain, 1651–1800

FOODSTUFFS	QUANTITIES	CARBO-HYDRATES	FATS	PROTEINS
Bread	500 g.	252.0	6.5	42.5
Beef	100 g.	–	28.0	15.0
Wheat	286 g (= 200 g. flour)	152.4	2.0	16.2
Apples	250 g.	26.2	–	0.7
Grapes	100 g.	18.5	–	1.0
Olive oil	65 g.	–	65.0	–
Total grams		449.1	101.5	75.4
Total calories	3,011.5	1,796.4	913.5	301.6

Table 6. Value of the Daily Ration in Spain, in Maravedis

PERIOD	500 G. BREAD	100 G. BEEF	286 G. WHEAT	250 G. APPLES	100 G. GRAPES	65 G. OLIVE OIL	TOTAL	20% ADDED	*TROPHĒ*
1651	8.1	9.1	2.5	12.2	2.6	6.2	40.7	8.1	48.8
1700	(8.1)	7.0	2.6	10.9	2.6	6.8	38.0	7.6	45.6
1750	(12.2)	6.1	4.0	14.7	3.4	7.0	47.4	9.5	56.9
1795	12.7	14.5	8.3	24.2	5.5	9.5	74.8	15.0	89.0

Note: The figures in parentheses are interpolations.

Table 7. Daily Wages in Spain

PERIOD	TROPHĒ IN MARAVEDIS	EQUIVALENT OF THE VELLON, MARAVEDIS, OR G. OF SILVER	TROPHĒ IN G. OF SILVER	WAGES IN MARAVEDIS			WAGES IN TROPHAI		
				UNSKILLED WORKER	MASON	CARPENTER	UNSKILLED WORKER	MASON	CARPENTER
1651	48.8	0.06142	3.0	–	–	–	–	–	–
1700	45.6	0.04997	2.28	–	–	–	–	–	–
1750	56.7	0.03631	2.05	140.3	272.0	272.0	2.5	4.8	4.8
1795	89.8	0.03524	3.15	170.0	280.5	252.9	1.9	3.1	2.8

Table 8. Evaluation of the *Trophē* on the Basis of Diocletian's Edict of 301

FOODSTUFFS	QUANTITIES	CARBO-HYDRATES	FATS	PROTEINS	PRICE IN DINARES
Rye	430 g. (= 300 g. flour)	215.6	6.6	35.4	1.49
Wheat	357 g. (= 250 g. flour)	190.6	2.5	20.2	2.0
Fruit	250 g.	26.2	–	0.7	1.25
Beef	100 g.	–	28.0	15.0	2.44
Olive oil	40 g.	–	40.0	–	3.0
Milk	1/3 l.	14.7	12.0	11.0	4.93
Egg	1	0.5	6.9	7.0	1.0
Total grams		447.5	96.0	89.3	
Total calories	3,011.2	1,790.0	864.0	357.2	
Total dinares					16.11
20% added					3.22
Trophē					19.33

In studying the wages earned in the past we must keep in mind that workers were paid both in money and in kind. In studies of this type this practice should be demonstrated by detailed descriptions complementing the numerical evaluation of the wages. And even in cases where part of the wage was paid in kind, it is still possible to evaluate this portion by calculating on the basis of the *trophē*. Such a calculation will provide a much more meaningful idea of that part of the wages as well. However, a detailed treatment of all the problems connected with the determination of the level of wages would go beyond the limits of the present article.

I should like to add that it was not my aim to provide calculations for specific wage levels in the past, but rather to outline a method showing

Table 9. Evaluation of the *Trophē* in Greece, Fourth Century B.C.

FOODSTUFFS	QUANTITIES	CARBO-HYDRATES	FATS	PROTEINS	PRICE IN DRACHMAE
Wheat	860 g. (⁻ 600 g. flour)	467.2	6.0	48.5	0.114
Beef	300 g.	–	84.0	45.0	0.192
Total grams		467.2	90.0	93.5	–
Total calories	3,052.8	1,868.8	810.0	374.0	–
Total drachmae					0.336
20% added					0.067
Trophē					0.403

how this can be achieved. Despite its lack of precision, this method can also be used to compare present-day wages in different countries whenever a more precise evaluation is not feasible, either because concrete information is unavailable or because the ways of life of the populations in question are not comparable.

Whenever a great variety of data is available, the method of evaluation by means of the *trophē* can be improved by using what I will call the *megatrophē*. The *megatrophē* would be, briefly, any multiple of the *trophē—decatrophē, hectotrophē, kilotrophē*. The use of these multiples would make it possible to do the following:

1. Include a greater number of foodstuffs in our calculations.

2. Determine the proper weight of these foodstuffs. By using the multiples of the *trophē*, we can show the actual quantities consumed, which we can then reduce, if need be, to the standard of 75 g. + 100 g. + 450 g. postulated at the outset. The *megatrophē* can always be reduced to the *trophē* by dividing it by the same number used as a multiplier to arrive at the megatrophē (10, 100, 1000).

Calculated in this manner, the *trophē* would, obviously, be more precise and more interesting, but it must be admitted that the procedure of calculating the *trophē* by way of the *megatrophē* is not always easy, so that it will probably not be used to any great extent in the practice of historical research.

8
Blazing a Trail to a History of Customary Law By Means of Geographic Hematology

Michèle Bordeaux

Geographic hematology is a new science based on human ecology and the genetic characteristics of populations.[1] Reading a treatise on geographic hematology,[2] a science of synthesis, gives one some surprising perspectives in anthropology, biology, human geography, and social futurology. In our case this multidisciplinary study has been successful on the highest levels of scientific collaboration. This new view of the world, taken as a whole, is a magnetic subject for the historian.

By moving backward in time to find the sole genetic blood group of populations, we are able to see the path they have taken. Publications on this subject, rare before World War II,[3] are today multiplying.[4] Articles

Annales: E.S.C., Nov.–Dec. 1969, pp. 1275–86. Translated by Patricia M. Ranum.

[1] Human ecology is the science which studies the conditions in the milieu in which men live or have lived, "milieu" being interpreted in its broadest sense.

[2] J. Bernard and J. Ruffié, *Hématologie géographique* (Paris, 1966), vol. 1.

[3] The stress upon the link between serological traits and racial traits was put forward by the end of World War I by L. and H. Hirzfeld, especially in their article, "Essai d'application sérologique aux problèmes des races," *Anthropologie*, 1918, no. 29.

[4] We shall cite here only a few general publications, giving a more detailed listing for the various French regions in note 15. (For a complete bibliography on the subject, see Bernard and Ruffié, *Hématologie géographique*, at the end of each chapter.)

P. Bosch-Gimpera, "La prehistoria de los Iberos y la etnologia vasca," *Revue internationale des Etudes basques*, 1925, p. 492; B. Glass and C. C. Li, "The Dynamics of Racial

such as that by J. Ruffié—which retraces the history of the collaboration between anthropologists[5] and biologists and defines very precisely the characteristics of a race—are beginning to appear in the daily press,[6] an indication of the maturity and success of this field of inquiry. Ruffié gives an ethnic group a reality which is other than cultural and religious: a biological reality which is adaptive as well as genetic and which leads us to a less arbitrary consideration of the notion of race. The political ramifications of such studies cannot be avoided. All human populations have the same biological value, and racism, which claimed to isolate the so-called superior races, is contrary to scientific data. Thus, "to speak of the Jewish race is biological nonsense." There is no Jewish blood group.[7] Such a method of politicohistorical study cannot be ignored by the historian, and it ought not remain unused.

The importance of the new data thus offered, either for verifying hypotheses which have already been drawn up or for approaching problems which had long been shelved for lack of scientific methods of study, was perceived by P. Ourliac when he entrusted me with making the first test of these new possibilities in a history of customary law.

I am summarizing the results of this first attempt; I will begin by explaining the unusual nature of the proof before interpreting its meaning and impact.

Intermixture: An Analysis Based on the American Negro," *American Journal of Human Genetics* 5 (1935):1–20; J. Haldane, "The Blood Group Frequencies of European Peoples and Racial Origins," *Human Biology* 7 (1940):457–80; H. Vallois, "La répartition anthropologique des groupes sanguins en France et plus particulièrement dans le Sud-Ouest," *Bulletin et mémoires de la Société d'anthropologie de Paris*, 9th series, 5 (1944):53–80; H. Vallois, "L'anthropologie en France durant la guerre," *Man* 18 (1947); C. Boyo, *Génétique et races humaines*, trans. Bourlière and Sutter (Paris, 1952); J. Ruffié, "Hémotypologie et évolution diversifiante des groupes humains," *Comptes rendus hebdomadaires des scéances de l'Académie des sciences* 262 (1966):657; J. Ruffié, *Les groupes sanguins chez l'homme. Étude sérologique et génétique* (Paris, 1953); and M. Lahovary, *Les peuples européens. Leur passé ethnologique et leur parenté réciproque d'après les dernières recherches sanguines et anthropologiques* (Neuchâtel, 1946).

[5]H. Vallois, medical doctor and anthropologist, is working in this field; in addition to the works cited in note 4, see "Les groupes sanguins de part et d'autre des Pyrénées," *Primer Congreso Internacional del Instituto de Estudios Pirenaicos* (Saragossa, 1951), no. 56; along with P. Marquer, "La distribution des groupes sanguins A, B, O en France," *Comptes rendus hebdomadaires des scéances de l'Académie des sciences*, 1964, p. 258.

[6]J. Ruffié, "Les races humaines et la biologie moderne," *Le Monde*, Sept. 30, 1967, p. 11.

[7]The Jews developed from two racial branches: the Anatolian brachycephalics and the southern-oriental dolichocephalics. They present genetic frequencies—be they Ashkenazi or Sephardi—which are comparable to those of the populations in which they lived during the Diaspora.

The Nature of the Sero-
Anthropological Proof

Each human race is characterized serologically by a combination of hereditary systems[8] which form a perceptible type within the same mixed population.[9] Among these hereditary systems, certain are carried by red blood corpuscles, which are commonly called "blood types." To date we know of a dozen different systems.[10] The first system discovered—the ABO system[11]—is the one whose geographical distribution is best known and whose means of transmission is universally agreed to be hereditary. We are therefore dealing with scientific certainties: the serological characteristics of a race are transmitted according to hereditary mechanisms. They are permanent in time. They are far superior to all the morphological data on which anthropology has long been based.[12] The latter, subjected to influences by the environment—by the physical, biological,

---

[8]On the one hand, it is a question of erythrocytic systems carried on the red cells and of platelet and leukocyte systems, and, on the other hand, of enzymatic systems or enzymatic deficiencies and of serologic systems (plasma protein molecules as determined immunologically or electrophoretically).

[9]F. Bernstein, "Ergebnisse einer biostatistischen zusammenfassenden Betrachtung über die erblichen Blutstrukturen des Menschen," *Klinische Wochenschrift* 3 (1924):1495; R. Huron and J. Ruffié, *Les méthodes en génétique générale et en génétique humaine* (Paris, 1959).

[10]Systems ABO, rhesus, Lewis, MNSs, Kell, Duffy, etc.

[11]Let us recall for the reader that there are natural substances or agglutinogens (A for example) carried by the red blood cells, whose specific property is agglutination by corresponding antibodies or agglutinins (α for example). Under normal physiological circumstances the phenomenon does not occur, for each individual has agglutinogens and agglutinins of a different type, which are therefore incapable of reciprocal agglutination (A and β for example). On the other hand, under certain artifical conditions (transfusion, blood-grouping) agglutination, whether desired or not, may occur. These are the accidents resulting from transfusions which led Landsteiner to undertake his research before 1900.

Group	Agglutinogens	Agglutinins;
A	A	β
B	B	α
O	–	$\alpha\beta$
AB	AB	–

[12]H. Vallois writes: "From the point of view of general anthropology . . . we must then ask ourselves whether, in interpreting the racial peopling of various parts of the world, we ought not to employ a sort of hierarchy for the traits used: some, such as those of a serological nature, strictly independent from any events occurring in the milieu, indicate ancient kinships, the original distribution of groups; others, such as those involving the shape of the head and coloring, certainly more unstable, indicate secondary differences which shaped the races as we see them today."

and social "climates"—supply important but secondary information. Indeed, if there is a contradiction between serological data and morphological data, the serological data must be accepted; we must, in the words of H. Vallois, recognize the existence of a "hierarchy of characteristics." The sero-anthropological characteristic is the most independent and the simplest criterion for the genetic investigation of a population.

It is the most independent criterion, for the blood group is not linked to any other hereditary trait and is therefore transmitted *alone*. It is the simplest criterion, for it is a *short* chain of chemical reactions which separates out the characteristic of the chromosomal gene, as contrasted with the morphological characteristics resulting from a long chain of reactions which are vulnerable to external influences.

This indisputable data is put to work through statistical techniques. Only by computing the frequency with which certain genetic characteristics occur can a protohistorical analysis of contemporary populations be made.

Beginning with a certain number of subjects, one establishes, for a very specifically defined geographical region, the distribution of the ABO system in terms of absolute frequencies for each of the groups, then in terms of approximate and corrected relative frequencies. Using x^2 as a test, we can judge the significance or the nonsignificance of the difference, when results are compared sample by sample, or region by region. Finally, in order to find the initial elements in a heterogenous population, we can use Bernstein's method[13]—though we must immediately point out its limitations in the case of very heterogenous populations. The Bentley-Glass method, more dynamic in the sense that it takes into account the number of generations which have passed since the two original races began to mingle, is rarely usable. Indeed, it presupposes the existence of two parent populations and at least approximate knowledge of the historical setting which gave birth to this blending of races.

---

[13]A diagram is drawn using as coordinates the values of p (the frequency of gene A) and the values of q (the frequency of gene B), for each of the samples taken within a specific geographical area.

One then demonstrates that, when a race M results from two original races R_1 and R_2, the three points M, R_1, and R_2 are found on a same line (M occupying the intermediary position between R_1 and R_2); that the reciprocal importance of the elements constituting R_1 and R_2 is inversely proportional to the distances between MR_1 and MR_2.

The explanation, the criticisms, and the obsolescence of this technique are made perfectly understandable on pp. 41–48 of J. Ruffié's thesis, *Étude séro-anthropologique des populations autochtones du versant nord des Pyrénées* (Toulouse and Paris, 1958). See also note 17 of this article, in which a chart gives the data concerning the genetic frequencies in the Pyrenean valleys; and also the diagram on p. 197.

The main pattern of the distribution of the ABO blood groups in France, on the basis of approximately 40,000 individuals distributed throughout the various departments of the nation, has been established, and the following genetic frequencies have been determined:[14]

> O: 65.8%
> A: 28.6%
> B: 5.4%

Phenotype A is particularly frequent in the east and the Mediterranean south. It is at its lowest near the Atlantic. Phenotype B decreases regularly from northeast to southwest, with a minimum in the Basque country. Phenotype O is at its maximum in the southwest and decreases rather regularly, on the one hand, to the northeast, and on the other hand, toward the Mediterranean south.

A more subtle and detailed analysis of certain regions[15] indicates that the variations in distribution are not always so clear and regular. Such is the case for the northern slopes of the Pyrenees. Through a more detailed analysis of this biogeographical region with its deep valleys, I will show that even the apparent diversity has a meaning.

The Populations of the North Pyrenean Slopes

The criteria for racial characterization will be established on the basis of the ABO system.[16] The Rhesus system is not significant here, for the populations of the northern Pyrenees are largely Rh positive. The other

---

[14]H. Vallois referred to "gradients in blood groups," and drew up a map of these regular variations in "La distribution des groupes sanguins A, B, O en France," p. 2179.

[15]To the publications already cited concerning French sero-anthropology, let us add P. Cazal and R. Graafland, "Les groupes sanguins dans la population montpelliéraine," *Le sang* 21 (1950):623–27; J. Moulinier, "The Rh Factor in Southwestern France," *American Journal of Physical Anthropology* 7 (1949):545–48; and A. Mourant, "The Blood Groups of the Basques," *Nature* 160 (1947):505.

[16]The chief work is Ruffié, *Étude séro-anthropologique des populations autochtones,* whose bibliography includes previous studies. To this add A. Eyquem, "Répartition des groupes sanguins chez les Basques," *Bulletin de l'Académie nationale de médicine* 7–8 (1950):171; which should be followed by the series edited by Hermann, entitled Monographies du Centre Hémotypologie de Toulouse (Paris), which analyzes the components of the different ethnic groups (for example, J. Ruffié and N. Taleb, *Étude hémotypologique des ethnies libanaises* [1965]).

systems sometimes confirm the results obtained through ABO; they are less well known, at least in terms of their geographical distribution.[17]

The original populations of the north Pyrenean valleys were formed by three successive waves of unequal size.[18] Though superimposed, mingled, and diluted, the following three elements can be distinguished:

(1) a dolichocephalic (Basque) paleolithic element with O dominant, A weak, and B extremely rare;[19]

(2) a brachycephalic (proto-Celtic or Alpine) neolithic element, with A dominant, O still very common, and B quite pronounced;[20] and

(3) a Mediterranean element—undoubtedly double—which has more As and Bs than the two preceding groups.[21]

These three elements are distributed as follows. As a whole, the paleolithic element increases from east to west, while the neolithic element

[17]Table of the frequencies observed among north Pyrenean populations (each sampling includes several lots which have been averaged). Based on Ruffié, *Étude séro-anthropologique des populations autochtones*, pp. 41–48.

LOCALIZATION OF SAMPLINGS	RELATIVE FREQUENCIES OF PHENOTYPES				GENIC FREQUENCIES (CORRECTED)		
	A	B	AB	O	p	q	r
Pyrénées-Orientales	51.83	6.42	2.75	38.99	0.330	0.047	0.623
Spanish Catalonia (Miserachs-Rigalt)	46.2	6.8	2.9	44.1	0.287	0.049	0.664
Region of Foix	43.65	6.50	2.80	47	0.267	0.045	0.687
Basin of Salat-Couserans	38.94	7.14	2.54	51.36	0.234	0.048	0.718
Comminges	41.64	7.68	2.47	48.20	0.254	0.053	0.694
Bigorre	36.84	3.83	1.20	58.37	0.211	0.024	0.764
Béarn	40.9	6.26	1.12	52.13	0.236	0.038	0.726
French Basques (Moulinier)	38.4	2.7	1	57.9	0.220	0.015	0.764
Spanish Basques (Mourant)	37.9	4.9	1.9	55.3	0.224	0.035	0.742
Dordogne (Couze). Proto-Celtic Centers	44.79	7.69	3.29	44.23	0.278	0.055	0.665
Sud du Tarn. Proto-Celtic Centers	45.86	5.65	3.20	45.29	0.280	0.037	0.683
Bas Languedoc (Cazals et Graafland)	43.72	9.67	2.77	43.82	0.269	0.065	0.662

[18]For the exact geographical location of the zones cited, see the map included in this article, which at the same time indicates the original elements from which the current populations originated.

[19]The other systems are distributed: Rhesus: chromosome r dominant, R relatively rich. M and H: same frequency.
Kell: 10%.
P: 75% P +.

[20]Other systems: Rhesus: dominance of r, impoverishment of R_2.

[21]The other systems are particularly important to study, for upon them rests the separation of the Mediterranean element into two groups. For the first group, M_1: N > M, p > p, Kell weak— 3 percent. For the second group M > H, p > p, Kell 5 percent.

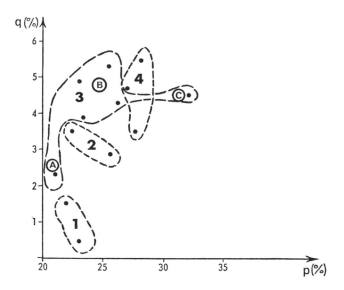

Figure 1. Initial Constituents of the Pyrenean Populations

Source: Based on J. Ruffié, *Etude séro-anthropologique des populations autochtones du versant nord des Pyrénées*, p. 42.

Notes: Cluster 1: French Basques, primitive paleolithic. *Cluster 2:* Spanish Basques. *Cluster 3:* (A) Bigorre, near 1, rich in paleolithic element, (B) Bend to right, superimposed Mediterranean element from the Pyrénées-Orientales, (C) Median zone stretched toward top (increase in importance of neolithic element) and pulled toward right (Mediterranean element), *Cluster 4:* Dordogne and south Tarn region, neolithic proto-Celt.

increases from west to east. It is comparable to the Alpine element, which forms the essential substructure of the population of the Dordogne and of the southern banks of the Tarn River.[22] The Mediterranean element predominates in the east, in the department of the Pyrénées-Orientales, and is clearly evident in Comminges and Béarn, but nowhere else. At the outset we must point out that type M_1, akin to the population of Lower Languedoc, predominates in these two provinces. Type M_2, on the other hand, is the dominant form in the Roussillon.

_____

[22]The Celtic populations of the Dordogne (samplings scattered throughout that department and the regions about Couze and Bergerac) show no significant difference when compared with those south of the Tarn (Lacaune, Labrugière, Dourgne, etc.) Ruffié, *Étude séro-anthropologique des populations autochtones*, pp. 34–35.

From valley to valley, therefore, we can note discontinuities, contradictions. All along the mountain range, these irregularities can be attributed to the biogeographical barriers which hindered lateral migratory movements. "Isolates" were thus created.[23] These endogamic groups are in our day very precious for studying relatively pure populations on which external influences have had little effect.

The assertion that original racial elements can be discerned in the heterogeneity of a contemporary population requires a few nuances. These nuances are necessary, for our aim is not to make people believe that all the obscure origins of social institutions will miraculously be clarified thanks to the panacea called sero-anthropology. There is no doubt that at this time by the word "race" we mean the result of the admingling of racial groups which must originally have been completely pure. Yet it is certain that human groups, which we know historically descended from a single branch, present blood-group patterns which are not at all related. The confrontation of the two methods of approach, even with contradictory results, should permit us to move ahead in solving questions about protohistorical migrations.

The proofs offered by the historian to the anthropologist, through the systematic geographical analysis of genetic frequencies, are not all equally attractive or equally important. We must base our proofs on *stable* systems and realize that the ABO system does not permit us to go back more than four or five thousand years. We must also realize that certain blood factors are not very resistant to infectious illnesses, which, for example, means that plague would be more frequent among those with O-type blood, on the one hand, and smallpox among those with A-type, on the other.[24] A major epidemic similar to that of 1348 might have caused a

---

[23]

REGIONS	PALEOLITHIC ELEMENT	NEOLITHIC ELEMENT	MEDITERRANEAN ELEMENT	
			M_1	M_2
Pyrénées-Orientales				++ M_2 +
Region of Foix		+++		
Basin of Salat-Couserans	++	++		
Comminges	+	++	M_1 +	
Bigorre	+++	+		
Béarn	++	+	M_1 +	
French Basques	++++			
Spanish Basques	++	+		M_2 +

---

[24]According to Humbolt, Bogel, and Pettenkoffer, the existence of heterologous antigens on plague bacilli or smallpox viruses is responsible for the phenomenon, which

massive decrease in the paleolithic element and, to a lesser degree, the Alpine element. The Mediterranean element seems to have been more resistant. As a result, a new proportional distribution of the three blood groups would have occurred during the succeeding generations.

The whole body of these nuances as they affect biology is therefore a source of information for the historian; the exception is as useful as the rule.

Hemotypology and the Geography of Customary Law in the Southwest of France. A Few Clues

We have just described the possibility of analyzing the initial racial components of the native Pyrenean populations. Juridically, in these same valleys we encounter customary laws which were already archaic in the Middle Ages; islets of customary law formed within biological isolates. Indeed, a difference in customary laws or, at least, an evolution in such laws, separates the mountain from the plain.[25]

The family institutions in the deepest valleys follow the very strict principle of the inalienability of possessions, especially of the house and of the agricultural property which is its mainstay. If by chance someone were to sell one of his buildings, the right of lineal redemption would permit the seller's relatives to take the buyer's place. Such is the case in Bigorre (the valley of Luz-Barèges), in Béarn, in Soule, in Lower Navarre, and in the customary regions of Bidache or of Saint-Palais, for example. In the plain, the specific ruling against selling property no longer exists; lineal redemption is merely a possible way by which relatives may retain control of possessions when the family chain has been broken. It is the "*présentation*" of the customary law of Dax, or the "*perparance*" of the customary law of Bayonne—in which the seller holds the initiative.[26] The manifestation of solidarity by the basic human group, either the family or the community in which one lives, has weakened in those customary laws which are more modern, more "open."

Integral primogeniture, that is, primogeniture without distinction of sex, is also a very ancient institution. By the early Middle Ages its

---

might in the end play a considerable role in the distribution of ABO blood groups in certain parts of the world.

[25]See I. Poumarède, "Recherches sur les successions dans le sud-ouest de la France au Moyen Age" (thesis for the faculty of law, Toulouse, 1968).

[26]Ibid., pp. 363–78.

Representation of the Sero-Anthropologic Data for the Northern Pyrenees and the Observance of Lineal Redemption and Integral Primogeniture on the Basis of Sources Available to Date.

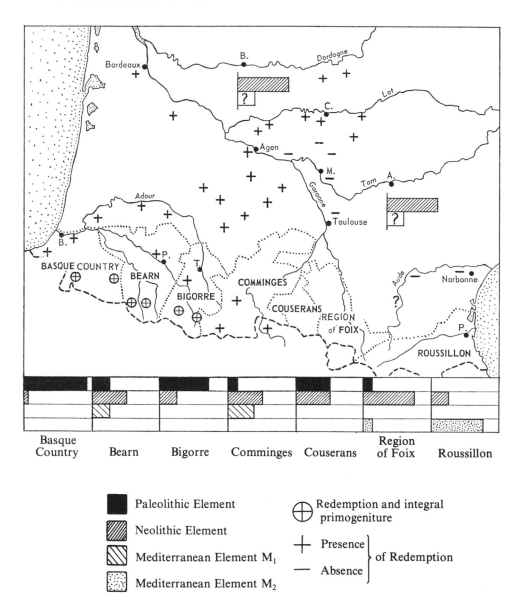

Source: Drawn upon a map from G. Seguy (ed.), *Atlas linguistique et ethnographique de la Gascogne,* 4 vols. (Paris: C.N.R.S., 1964).

observance was limited to the primitive endogamic clusters of the deepest and most isolated Pyrenean valleys. Thus, integral primogeniture was observed in Béarn—in the Ossau, Aspe, and Baretous valleys—and in Bigorre—in the valleys of Barèges-Lavedan—while the more accessible valley of Bagnères had already incorporated the principle of masculinity.[27]

In the Basque country, the contrast between the plain and the mountain is less clear, for in the plain itself strict and often original customary laws concerning inalienability and primogeniture can be discerned.[28] This fact is extremely important, for it conforms to the unusual racial unity of the French Basque provinces. It emphasizes the link between ancient customary laws and the initial constituent race. It leads us back to the heart of the problem: that of the origins of the institutions of customary law.

The antiquity of the practice of lineal redemption in the region of written law[29] has made it impossible for certain authors to agree with the classical hypothesis according to which this redemption originated in the *laudatio parentum*.[30] Nor can we accept a "feudal" explanation for integral primogeniture, when only 1 single noble household can be found in the 486 households of the Aspe Valley, 8 out of 859 in the Ossau Valley, and 2 out of 156 in the Baretous during the fourteenth century! If, as R. Grand suggests, we must untangle the "ethnic, economic, social, and political elements" from which customary laws spring,[31] I believe that we are now in a position to separate out the ethnic element.

In the valleys, an analysis of genetic frequencies indicates that the palcolithic racial element, which had originally settled along the fertile river banks, was pushed back by a neolithic invader toward the less fertile

[27]Ibid., pp. 379–409.

[28]As an aside let us point out the persistence up to the present of certain manifestations of customary law in the Basque country, such as the private tomb attached to the property of the house, the vestige of an ancient family funerary cult (Lesbeyguerie v. Lacuey y Perez, Court of Appeals, Pau, [June 14, 1967]).

[29]P. Ourliac, "Le retrait lignager dans le sud-ouest de la France," *Revue d'histoire du droit*, 1952, pp. 328–55; R. Caillemer, "Le retrait lignager dans le droit provençal," *Studi giuridici C. Fadda* 4 (1906): 15; E. Jarriand, "Histoire de la Novelle 118 dans les pays de droit écrit" (thesis, Paris, 1889), pp. 204 ff. See A. Soubie, "Le retrait lignager dans la Coutume de Bordeaux," *Revue juridique et économique du Sud-Ouest*, série juridique (Bordeaux, 1961), which credits "common primitive traits" with the originalities found in the customary law of Bordeaux and in those of the West (p. 6) and stresses their resistance to Roman influences.

[30]Ourliac, "Le retrait lignager," p. 345: "The antiquity of redemption being accepted, it becomes difficult to make it derive from the *laudatio parentum*." See L. Falleti, "Le retrait lignager en droit coutumier français" (thesis, Paris, 1923), p. 61; and J. de Laplanche, "La réserve coutumière dans l'ancien droit français" (thesis, Paris, 1925), pp. 66–115.

[31]R. Grand, "L'histoire de la Coutume de Paris," *Journal des Savants*, p. 5, 22 (1924): 57–64, quoted by Ourliac, "Le retrait lignager," p. 350.

highlands and toward the sides of the valley. The latter in his turn became solidly implanted in the valley bottoms. He then dominated and succeeded in imposing his own proto-Celtic law, which would remain unknown to us were it not for a few unusual manifestations of it which puzzle us because of their persistence and their localization.

Indeed, serological analysis indicates that no major Germanic invasion had occurred wherever lineal redemption was practiced during the ninth and tenth centures. Such an invasion cannot be seen through statistics or from distribution diagrams. Here and there we can discern a Mediterranean contribution, which on the contrary could only have affected the disappearance of this redemption. If the wave of Germanic invasions had been a powerful one, it would have pushed back to the hills the neolithic components which had settled in the valleys. Without a strong demographic substructure, without a coherent political organization, how could it have exerted a formative influence upon local customary laws?

Therefore, we will side with P. Ourliac in support of a proto-Celtic origin for lineal redemption.[32] And Alpine proto-Celtic law managed to persist where the vehicle-race was solidly established. From the zones studied, we can risk a more general interpretation which would be valid for mixed populations. Finally, and conversely, we might agree that the nonexistence of redemption in such neighboring regions as Roussillon, Toulouse, and Carcassonne corresponds to a retreat of the neolithic race in the face of Mediterranean immigration, a reversal in the balance of power.

Using the Data Concerning the Mediterranean Component

The final important component of the north Pyrenean populations was, as we have seen, undoubtedly a *double* one. This is extremely important. It enables us to understand how the mixed population of Béarn and Comminges was formed and how, despite a considerable proportion of the Mediterranean "race," the customary laws of these provinces in no way resemble those of Roussillon or of the regions south of the Pyrenees, in which the Mediterranean element predominates.

---

[32]See F. Lafferière, *Histoire du droit civil de Rome et du droit français* (Paris, 1846), vol. 2; and F. Jobbé Duval, "Études sur la condition résolutoire en droit romain. L'histoire du retrait lignager et la vente à réméré" (thesis for the faculty of law, Paris, 1874), pp. 82 and 102.

Let us compare the provinces at either end of the chain of mountains: Roussillon and the French Basque country have nothing in common.[33] The Mediterranean component dominates in the former and is absent in the latter; it is the simplest possible situation. There is no lineal redemption in Roussillon, but there is redemption in the Basque country, where the dominant race is not, however, the Alpine one but the dolichocephalic paleolithic one.[34]

In Roussillon as in Cerdagne, the increase of the Mediterranean component coincides with the absence of redemption. The "*retorn*" of Roussillon bears no relation to lineal redemption; it simply indicates, in the case of a sale of tithes, for example, the dispossessed buyer's right for redress by demanding the seller's possessions.[35] Between these two provinces, lineal redemption exists wherever the neolithic Alpine element is present. Thus, two questions immediately come to mind and appear to contradict categorically the proto-Celtic origin of redemption. First, the Basque population is purely paleolithic; yet redemption is practiced there. Second, in Béarn and Comminges, the Mediterranean component is quantitatively important, but redemption is observed there.

In the first instance we can reply that there is no conflict between proto-Celtic and proto-Basque customs in the case of an institution such as redemption. And in a more general fashion, there is no conflict owing to the presence of the same communitary conception of the family—a very ancient form of family solidarity.[36]

In the second case, we must be aware that the Mediterranean component to which we are referring is the M_1 component of Lower Languedoc,

[33]About half the Spanish Basques—a more mixed group—belong to the paleolithic element and the other two quarters represent the neolithic and Mediterranean components. This indicates that there were Mediterranean migratory tracks south of the Pyrenees range. This Mediterranean influence is real, but weak.

[34]It is certain that a study of comparative hemotypology would clarify the "Basque mystery." See the recent study by Estornes Lasa, *Origines de los Vascos* (Saint-Sébastien, 1965). The high frequency of O which chiefly characterizes these Basques is found in "peripheral" populations (Scotland, Ireland, Iceland, South West Africa), and appears in certain valleys which are somewhat closer, such as Bigorre, in which the neolithic influx was less dense. The absence (in the purest groups) of gene B, the rarity of gene E, and the frequency—unique among world populations—of gene d are not to be found anywhere else. A certain kinship through the frequency of d can be established with Ukranian regions; of O, as we have seen, with "peripheral" groups; and in their very low B they resemble the Lapps. The latter, like the Basques, speak a language which belongs to no other Indo-European group.

[35]A. Brutails, *Études sur la condition rurale du Roussillon au Moyen Age* (Paris, 1891), p. 93, n. 2, referred to by Ourliac, "Le retrait lignager," p. 350.

[36]Moreover, special characteristics keep alive an original Basque form of redemption, in particular the special redemption granted to all neighbors in regard to outsiders.

and not the M_2 one of Roussillon. We must take into account the possibility of an ethnic bridge between Provence, the north Pyrenean region, and the northwestern portion of Aquitaine. Unfortunately, we know little about the origin and expansion of these two Mediterranean components. A precise study is now under way concerning the circum-Mediterranean populations and, in particular, those which settled along the northern coast, the principal crossroads of the world in the early days of civilization. It may indicate for us whether the M_2 component forms the backbone of the population in the region around Narbonne, the Narbonnais.

Through this we could find out where the disputed frontiers of this Roman province actually were. Meanwhile, methodologically usable data is available. Instead of going ahead and tracing the region of expansion—of moving ahead with the invader and with the institutions—we shall begin to count backward. We shall analyze the fringes of resistance and the frontier zones of cultural contact,[37] with the aid of three types of information: history, biology, and linguistics.[38]

We possess a first-class methodological tool. The independent activities of these three sciences guarantee the objectivity of the joint proof to be obtained. Starting with the actual structures of the race and the language, we will move on to their history, to their legal manifestations. All too often working from the present back into the past has led the historian into a blind alley.

Numerous possibilities for new research are opening. Many questions are to be asked. We would like to be able to answer each of them. But we must accept a limit, the limit imposed by sero-anthropology itself, a new science whose contributions are, as a result, still very incomplete. We must waste no time in carrying out research of this type, for it will soon be impossible. Human migration from untouched rural areas is becoming increasingly intense. Racial mixtures will in the near future have become inextricable in our industrialized and urbanized countries. In the field of linguistics, few regions have as yet been the subject of a minute and

---

[37]Once again using the Basques as an example, we will see, on the basis of the chart showing the distribution of racial elements (p. 200) that the paleolithic Basque element was spread across neighboring valleys. The exceptions are due to biogeographic barriers (Foix).

[38]It is possible, for Gascony (including the central west region of the northern Pyrenees), to compare linguistic maps (G. Seguy, *Nouvel Atlas linguistique et ethnographique de la Gascogne*, 4 vols. [Paris, 1964]) with those which could be made for the distribution of genic frequencies of blood groups. Though the editing of this series of volumes is not complete, those volumes which have already appeared make no reference to the institution of redemption which would permit us to draw a conclusion on the basis of this specific example.

detailed study such as that made for Gascony. And much remains to be done in the geography of customary law.

And so we shall limit ourselves to a few major trends.[39] The first and most limited one, which would give us the indispensible technical experience, would be to trace the limits of the Narbonnais in relation to its neighbors. At the same time it would be possible to collect common characteristics of limitrophic customary laws in order to separate the original institutions from the neoformations.[40] The second, more ambitious program would be to enlarge the field of research to include "kinships" in French customary laws as they relate to the genetic structure of the population. Then we could proceed beyond our frontiers to the problem of affinities with the old Swedish or Danish laws,[41] on the level of family institutions of a communitarian sort, to the degree that racial similarity can be proved (which is a hypothesis to be verified before any research is carried out). It is undoubtedly by studying very old familial laws and communitarian legal practices concerning marriage and, especially, inheritances that our investigations have the greatest chance of succeeding. This possibility is a very intriguing one, for it leans in the direction of comparative history. However, it cannot be envisaged within the classical framework of individual research. It presupposes a team of researchers capable of analyzing ancient laws in different languages. And finally, even on the level of individual research, such subjects require the use of modern techniques of handling information.

[39]We have made an effort to stress multiple interrogations as we went along.

[40]This study should be as complete as possible. It is a question of searching the legal records of a predetermined region for all the customary institutions going back beyond the thirteenth century, and then of subjecting them to the scouring of biological and linguistic proof (with the nuances referred to in the preceding note).

[41]Rereading Beauchet's old works can only push us in this direction, for we find: "The hereditary right which we encounter in almost all the Indo-Germanic peoples . . ."; and, "Though this regime still functions among certain southern Slavic peoples, it was no longer observed by the German peoples during the period in which their laws were compiled . . . ." (Ludovic Beauchet, "De la propriété familiale dans l'ancien droit suédois," *Nouvelle revue historique de droit français et étranger*, Dec. 1900, p. 604, and Jan. 1901, p. 5).

And could we not put an end to the controversies over the rights of the Menapii? (Meijers, "Le droit ménapien," *Tidjschrift voor rechtgeschiedenis* 17 (1950):5–18. "If, therefore, the right in question is not a right of German conquerors but a right of a subjugated population, it calls to mind those who preceded the Franks in that country" (p. 6).

The Johns Hopkins University Press

This book was composed in Times Roman text and Craw Modern display type by Jones Composition Company, Inc., from a design by Patrick Turner, and printed on 60-lb. Warren 1854 paper. It was printed and bound by Universal Lithographers, Inc.

Library of Congress Cataloging in Publication Data
Main entry under title:

Biology of man in history.

    (Selections from the Annales, économies, sociétés, civilisations; 1975)
    Includes bibliographical references.
    CONTENTS: Patlagean, E. Birth control in the early Byzantine Empire.—Flandrin, J.-L. Contraception, marriage, and sexual relations in the Christian West.—Biraben, J.-N. and Le Goff, J. The plague in the Early Middle Ages. [etc.]
    1. Diseases—History—Addresses, essays, lectures.
2. Population—History—Addresses, essays, lectures.
3. Diet—History—Addresses, essays, lectures.

Library of Congress Cataloging in Publication Data

I. Forster, Robert, 1926–   II. Ranum, Orest A.
III. Annales, économies, sociétés, civilisations.
IV. Series.
R702.B56   362.1'04'2209   74-24382
ISBN 0-8018-1690-4
ISBN 0-8018-1691-2 pbk.